# THE MAKING OF THE NEW ZEALAND PRESS

A Study of the Organizational and
Political Concerns
of New Zealand Newspaper Controllers

1840 - 1880

PATRICK DAY

VICTORIA UNIVERSITY PRESS

VICTORIA UNIVERSITY PRESS
Victoria University of Wellington
P.O. Box 600 Wellington

© Patrick Day 1990
ISBN 0 86473 089 6

This book is copyright. Apart from
any fair dealing for the purpose of private study,
research, criticism or review, as permitted under the
Copyright Act, no part may be reproduced by any
process without the permission of the publishers.

Printed at Victoria University of Wellington

# Contents

1. Introduction ........................................................................ 1

Part One: THE NEW ZEALAND NEWSPAPERS
IN THE YEARS OF CROWN COLONY
GOVERNMENT ................................................................ 9

    New Zealand Newspapers of the
    Crown Colony Government Period ........................................ 10

2. The New Zealand Newspapers of 1840-1844 and
their Relationships with the Crown Colony Government
and the New Zealand Company ................................................ 12

    The Northern Press and the
    Crown Colony Government, 1840-1844 ................................ 12
    The New Zealand Company
    Settlements and the Press, 1840-1844 ................................. 24
    Press Independence ................................................................ 33

3. The New Zealand Newspapers of 1844-1853 and
their Part in the Agitation for Self Government ...................... 35

    Auckland ................................................................................. 35
    Wellington ............................................................................... 38
    Nelson ..................................................................................... 44
    Otago ....................................................................................... 45
    Canterbury .............................................................................. 50
    The Press and Political Representation ................................ 52

4. Newspapers and Journalism in the
Crown Colony Government Period ............................................ 56

    The Multiple Roles of the New Zealand Newspapers ............. 58
    An Illustration ........................................................................ 59
    The Provision of News ............................................................ 60
    Newspapers as Community Advocates .................................. 62
    Newspapers as Class Papers .................................................. 64
        1. The Class Nature of the New Zealand Settlements
            and the Practice of Journalism within them ............... 64
        2. Price ................................................................................. 68

3. The Cost of Establishing and
   Maintaining Newspapers ............................................. 69
   Auckland .................................................................. 69
   Wellington ............................................................... 71
   Nelson ..................................................................... 73
   Otago ....................................................................... 74
   Canterbury .............................................................. 74
4. The Voluntary Nature of Newspaper Work ................... 77
Crown Colony Government Journalism ................................. 80

Part Two: GOVERNMENT AND BUSINESS
—THE PRESS IN THE PROVINCIAL YEARS ........... 85

5. The New Zealand Newspapers in the Early
   Provincial Period ............................................................ 86

   New Zealand Newspapers and the 1853 Elections ............... 87
   Newspapers and Provincialism ........................................... 91
   Auckland ............................................................................ 92
   Taranaki ............................................................................. 95
   Wellington .......................................................................... 96
   Nelson ................................................................................ 99
   Canterbury ....................................................................... 102
   Otago ................................................................................ 105
   The Provincial Press and Political Advocacy ..................... 107

6. The Start of the Daily Press in New Zealand .................... 111

   Julius Vogel and the Daily Press in Otago ......................... 111
   Daily Journalism, Political Advocacy
   and the Press in Otago ....................................................... 115
   Commercial Growth, Political Advocacy
   and the Canterbury Press .................................................. 119
   Newspaper Proprietors as Entrepreneurs ......................... 126
   Political Advocacy and Political Independence ................. 134

7. Politics and Profit: Main Centre
   Daily Newspapers 1860-1879 ........................................... 137

   Auckland .......................................................................... 138
   Dunedin ............................................................................ 146
   Wellington ........................................................................ 155

8. New Zealand Journalism and the Daily Press .......................... 164

    Journalism as a Profession ...................................................... 165
    Timaru Herald ............................................................................ 173
    Newspaper Readership ............................................................. 174
    Political Emancipation and the Press .................................... 175
    Newspaper and Political Advocacy ......................................... 176

Part Three:   THE STATE, THE TELEGRAPH AND
                 THE NEW ZEALAND PRESS ................................. 183

9. Press, Government and the Telegraph to 1870 ........................ 184

    New Zealand Telegraph Construction .................................... 185
    The New Zealand General Telegraph Agency ...................... 189
    Vogel and Government Sponsored Press Agencies .............. 192
    Competitive Press Agencies ..................................................... 198
    Press Cooperation ..................................................................... 200

10. Press, Government and the Telegraph in the 1870s ................ 204

    Press Associations Use of the Telegraph Service ................. 204
    The Telegraph Libel Case ........................................................ 207
    The Holt and McCarthy Agency ............................................. 210
    The New Zealand Times .......................................................... 217
    The New Zealander .................................................................. 220
    The Return to Competitive Press Agencies .......................... 221
    Pressures Towards Amalgamation ........................................ 224
    The Closing of the New Zealander ......................................... 227
    The United Press Association ................................................. 229

11. Conclusion ...................................................................................... 234

    Epilogue ...................................................................................... 242

    Appendix .................................................................................... 244

    Bibliography .............................................................................. 262

To My Parents

William and Brenda Day

# 1. Introduction

In 1840 the first two New Zealand newspapers began publication. They started in small settlements which were, at best, in irregular contact with each other. Yet by 1880 the controllers of New Zealand newspapers had formed the United Press Association, a cohesive national organization. On a daily basis newspapers combined to receive and share both national and international news. Over these four decades newspaper controllers faced up to a variety of organizational problems associated with regular newspaper production in an isolated country. A supply of necessary materials, from paper to treacle, an essential ingredient for the rollers used to ink the bodies of type, had to be regularly available. A competent staff to perform the literary and manual tasks of newspaper production had to be found and kept, and this was no easy task in the underpopulated and largely illiterate settlements. Decisions had to be made as to just what a newspaper was to be in New Zealand where conditions were so different from those the emigrants had previously experienced. And always there was the problem of obtaining news from afar. During these four decades newspaper controllers were not only concerned with such organizational matters but were also deeply involved in the political life of the country. Most newspapers were committed political advocates and many newspaper controllers became important political office-holders. This placed newspapers on the different sides of the various political conflicts of the 1840-1880 years. Newspaper activity was largely conducted in terms of these organizational and political concerns and the often uneasy relationship between them.

The years 1840 to 1880 were years of memorable change in New Zealand society as well as in newspaper publication. The political organization of New Zealand changed from the status of a Crown Colony, through a period of Provincialism, to, finally, centralized Government from Wellington. The changes in communication technology were momentous. Notably they included the connection of the New Zealand settlements by telegraph and the laying of sea cables between the North and South Islands and between New Zealand and Australia. From 1840 to 1880 the New Zealand settlements moved from experiencing isolation, often for months at a time, to world wide communication on a daily basis. The European population of New Zealand increased greatly with corresponding changes in newspaper circulation. The demographic changes, from the point of view of newspaper controllers, were such as to allow a movement from the publication of political journals restricted by circulation to an elite, to the publication of daily newspapers oriented towards a mass readership. This was particularly so for the larger population areas and New Zealand newspapers came to be dominated by the dailies from the main centers.

There is little material on the newspapers of New Zealand, especially those of the nineteenth century. Even basic information such as the number of newspapers that have been published is not available. To enjoy the low newspaper postage rate, newspapers, from an early date had to be registered with the Post Office. But this register, along with all other General Post Office records, was lost in the fire of 1887. From 1868 newspapers were required, under the Printers and Newspapers Registration Act 1868, to register with the Supreme Court. These records are no longer complete. Before their loss Sir Henry Brett and Sir George Fenwick had copied all registrations from the Supreme Court records. But even Brett and Fenwick's copy has been lost. Scholefield had the use of their copy and the most detailed, though by no means complete, information on the number, names and ownership of New Zealand newspapers appears in his history.[1]

The proprietors and employees of the New Zealand newspapers have been largely unconcerned with the collection and preservation of their early records. R.B. O'Neill's experience, on beginning the centennial history of *The Press*, was one I was to repeat:

> I asked then if I could get a file of annual reports — being little in them, he [A.R. Cant, then editor of *The Press* ] replied; and added 'They usually try to keep as much out of them as possible.' Later I went to the manager, Sandy [A.J. Sandom], and made a similar inquiry. 'No', he said, 'nothing of historical interest has been left on file — no documents, no reports, no old registers, or balance sheets.'

O'Neill was later to find that some relevant material could still be located:

> In the last two years I've found the direct approach has succeeded the least - it is necessary to probe through and ferret out stuff when people are not looking.[2]

1  *Newspapers in New Zealand* (1958).
2  O'Neill Manuscripts, Canterbury Museum.

*Introduction*

At least in the case of O'Neill's excellent history, one may applaud the results of such a research technique. But O'Neill was a long term employee of *The Press*. Such a technique is not generally available.

I have used what material is available. Some primary source material does remain. New Zealand also does have some excellent studies of various aspects of the early newspapers. These notably include Patricia Burns doctoral study, *The Foundation of the New Zealand Press, 1839—1850*, G.M. Meiklejohn's *Early Conflicts of Press and Government*, a detailed study of the first Auckland newspaper, R.B O'Neill's centennial history, *The Press 1861—1961: The Story of a Newspaper* and Guy Scholefield's *Newspapers in New Zealand*. As well newspapers and newspaper controllers feature prominently in various fine regional studies such as A.H. McLintock's *History of Otago* and Russell Stone's study of early Auckland, *Makers of Fortune: A Colonial Business Community and its Fall*. My major source of information, however, has been the files of copies of the newspapers themselves. While there are some tantalizing gaps in these collections, and despite the attitude towards records that O'Neill alluded to, New Zealand has in general been well served by those who have collected these newspapers.

This book does not pretend to be a history or an exhaustive study of the early New Zealand newspapers. It is a focused investigation of the political and organizational concerns of the controllers of the early newspapers with particular regard to the way these concerns influenced the nature of New Zealand journalism and led to the institutionalization of the New Zealand press as a cohesive and cooperative grouping. For this purpose most attention is on the major newspapers in the main centres, for it was the controllers of these journals who were most influential in these processes.

I have three main contentions concerning the early New Zealand press. Firstly, New Zealand journalism and the type of newspaper dominant in New Zealand during and beyond the 1840—1880 period can best be understood as the outcome of the political and organizational concerns of the early newspaper controllers. Secondly, the newspapers over the 1840—1880 years were journals supporting a developing upper class in New Zealand. In spite of the movement towards a mass readership, press understanding of the preferred development of New Zealand is best seen in terms of the understandings and divisions within an emerging upper class. Thirdly, in a country dominated in the nineteenth century by regional considerations and affiliations, the press was in the vanguard of the development of a national focus. The early development of a cohesive national organization gave to the member newspapers of the New Zealand press a relative immunity from competition and increased chances of survival. Of the current New Zealand daily newspapers, all but *The Dominion* and the *National Business Review* began publication before 1880.

The organizational concerns of newspaper controllers are examined over four decades of considerable change. Most newspapers began under the control of sole proprietors who worked with the voluntary assistance of partisan activists. By 1880 many newspapers were controlled by limited liability companies. They were profit oriented commercial concerns produced by a professional, salaried staff. The pattern of organizational change over the four decades is that of the emergence of the newspaper as a business enterprise conducted in terms of an economically defined rationality.

Parallel with their organizational concerns, newspaper controllers throughout the four decades were to value their newspapers for the political power they deemed inherent in the press. That the press is of political utility was as undoubted to the nineteenth century newspaper controllers as it is to contemporary observers. The newspaper was valued for its role as a partisan advocate in political conflict. The newspaper was also valued for its ability to promote a particular understanding of the nature of New Zealand society and what that society should become.

These two areas of concern, organizational and political, were in an ambivalent relationship with each other. During the 1840s and 1850s profitability was seldom available for New Zealand newspapers and they were managed principally in terms of political considerations. But in the 1860s and 1870s newspapers became profitable, high circulation dailies and proprietors recognized a need for their newspaper concerns to be arranged on economically sound organizational principles. Conversely, while proprietors were not adverse to their newspapers becoming profitable businesses, they also wished to continue them as political advocates. These desires, organizational and political, impinged on each other. Press development in New Zealand is an outcome of the implementation of these two interests and the modifications each forced on the other.

Throughout these four decades newspapers were to regard themselves as the voices of their communities, but within those communities they

*Introduction*

were to speak consistently only for a minority. European settlers arrived in the New Zealand settlements already with significant differences among them in terms of wealth, status and power. The privileged start some enjoyed did not stop them being joined by others who came to dominance in New Zealand. But movement into this group became increasingly difficult. Within each settlement a small group came to be preeminent in regard to social status, in regard to wealth by virtue of their dominance in the ownership and control of land and commerce, and in regard to their holding of political power. These groups were the first New Zealand social class to develop an inter-regional understanding and it is them that I refer to as an emerging upper class. It was their interests that were best represented by the New Zealand newspapers.

Class is one of the more contentious words in the language. It refers to the economic divisions of a population. Associated with these divisions are differences in political power and social prestige. Individual class position may be, and usually is, determined by the circumstances of one's birth. But unlike concepts such as caste or estate, class position is not immutable and may change during an individual's lifetime. It changes with changes in an individual's economic standing. Class membership thus refers to an individual's position within the broad economic divisions of a population. These divisions are currently regarded as comprising three classes; upper, middle and lower or working. The growth of the middle class is, however, largely a twentieth century phenomenon. A middle class is of less consequence in nineteenth century New Zealand. While class membership refers to an individual's objective economic position it is also often regarded as referring to individuals' conscious acceptance of their membership within such an economic division and to their allegiance to their class. I use the term upper class in both senses of the word class. It refers to those who became economically dominant in New Zealand and who enjoyed the prestige and political power associated with their economic superiority. It also refers to the fact that this group were conscious of themselves as belonging to and owing allegiance to an upper class. I do not wish to suggest that by 1880 New Zealand had an unassailable upper class. Political and social change after 1880 was to indicate that this class position was anything but secure. But I do contend that the early ownership and allegiance of the New Zealand newspapers was greatly influential on the nature and outlook of the twentieth century press.

## The Making of the New Zealand Press

The New Zealand newspapers developed a cohesion over the 1840—1880 period that came from their shared experiences and expectations and, eventually, took expression in the acceptance of a number of self-imposed regulations, the membership rules of the United Press Association. This ensured a co-operative interchange of national news among all newspapers as well as a regular and shared flow of international news. Such a uniform news service was not only the least expensive news supply possible but also meant newspapers had both a national cohesion and a distinctive national character well before analogous processes of nationalization occurred in other aspects of New Zealand life. Such cooperation also offered a protection from competition which made more likely any individual newspaper's long term survival. Considerable difficulties were placed in the way of any new newspapers being established against existing publications. By 1880 the New Zealand newspapers had gained a long term monopoly over news collection and dispersion. Not only would the New Zealand press continue but the particular newspaper concerns operating in 1880 would face competition only among themselves.

This book follows a generally chronological treatment of the topic. Part one deals with the Crown Colony Government period. By 1844, newspapers were acquiring a status independent of both the New Zealand Company and the Crown Colony Government. Newspaper personnel were prominent in the agitation for self-government. Press representation was a major part of the settlers' *de facto* political representation. Newspapers performed wide ranging roles and acted as political advocates for their communities in general. However, they were the consistent voice of only a small section within each of the settlements. The newspapers were class newspapers linked predominantly with those men who were becoming both the major landowning and the dominant commercial groups in New Zealand.

Part two begins with the first years of the Provincial period, which are considered in Chapter 5. Not only were newspaper personnel disproportionately successful in winning elected official positions but newspapers became recognised forces in the political process. A pattern of partisan political advocacy by newspapers developed with individual newspapers being recognised as the advocates for individual politicians.

Chapters 6, 7, and 8 deal with the period of commercial growth of newspapers. The repercussions of daily journalism and of a new group of enterpreneur newspaper proprietors on the political role of the press

*Introduction*

are discussed. A new notion of political independence appeared in New Zealand journalism but this is not to be confused with political neutrality. The various attempts to start daily newspapers are considered as are the new attributes of journalism — the regular provision of news, the extension of the newspaper readership and the rise of professional journalism. Their relationship with the nature of newspaper political activity is examined. While press partisan activity continued, newspaper controllers were developing an ideology which placed the press as an institution distinct from and separate to Government.

Part three, which is Chapters 9 and 10, is concerned with the development by newspapers of a national organization. This took place within the context of a similar national focus being developed by the state. For newspapers the telegraph was the major technological innovation, the development and use of which expedited their national orientation. The telegraph, press agencies and the nature of newspaper cooperation are discussed as is the relationship between press and government. The foundation of the United Press Association is discussed and seen as the administrative expression of the New Zealand press as a distinct institution.

This book is the outcome of research which first appeared as a doctoral dissertation at the University of Waikato. To my doctoral supervisors, Peter Cleave, the co-supervisor, and David Bettison, my chief supervisor, I offer my thanks and gratefully acknowledge their influence and careful assistance. I am also grateful for the assistance offered by John E.P. Thomson, Acting Director of the Stout Research Centre, Victoria University of Wellington, during a pleasant and productive three month period I spent there.

Finally, I wish to sincerely thank Margaret Comer, Lorraine Brown, Gaye Miller and Cathy Moss of the University of Waikato for their patient, careful and cheerful attention to my manuscripts.

PART ONE:

# THE NEW ZEALAND NEWSPAPERS IN THE YEARS OF CROWN COLONY GOVERNMENT

# NEW ZEALAND NEWSPAPERS OF THE CROWN COLONY GOVERNMENT PERIOD

**Bay of Islands**

*The New Zealand Advertiser and Bay of Islands Gazette*  15 June-10 December 1840

*The New Zealand (Government) Gazette*  30 December 1840-15 July 1841

*Bay of Islands Observer*  24 February-27 October 1842

**Auckland**

*The New Zealand Herald and Auckland Gazette*  10 July 1841-6 April 1842

*Auckland Chronicle and New Zealand Colonist*  8 November 1841-13 February 1845?
Suspended:
  December 1841-12 November 1842
  May-August 1843?

*Auckland Standard*  18 February-28 August 1842

*The Auckland Times*  29 August 1842-17 January 1846
Suspended:
  13 April-7 November 1843

*The Daily Southern Cross*  22 April 1843-28 December 1876
  Title Changes
  *The Southern Cross; New Zealand Guardian* (subtitle varies)  22 April 1843-16 May 1862
Suspended:
  26 April 1845-10 July 1847

*The New Zealander*  7 June 1845-May 1866

## Wellington

*The New Zealand Gazette and*
*Wellington Spectator*            21 August 1839-25 September 1844
    Title changes:
    *The New Zealand Gazette*      21 August 1839-15 August 1840
    *The New Zealand Gazette*
    *and Britannia Spectator*       22 August 1840-21 November 1840

*Victoria Times*                      15 September 1841

*New Zealand Colonist and*
*Port Nicholson Advertiser*          2 August 1842-2 August 1843

*New Zealand Spectator and*
*Cook's Straits Guardian*            12 October 1844-5 August 1865

*New Zealand Times*             2 April 1845-22 January 1927
    Title change:
    *The Wellington Independent*    2 April 1845-30 May 1874
                                      Suspended:
                                           2 August-26 November 1845

## Nelson

*The Nelson Examiner and*
*New Zealand Chronicle*             12 March 1842-15 January 1874

## Otago

*Otago News*                          13 December 1848-21 December 1850

*Otago Witness*                     8 February 1851-28 June 1932

## Canterbury

*Christchurch Times*             11 January 1851-29 January 1935
    Title change:
    *Lyttelton Times*               11 January 1851-31 July 1929

## 2. The New Zealand Newspapers of 1840-1844 and their relationships with the Crown Colony Government and the New Zealand Company

The publishing of newspapers in New Zealand begins in 1840 with the first New Zealand printing of the *New Zealand Gazette and Wellington Spectator* and the commencement in Russell of the *New Zealand Advertiser and Bay of Islands Gazette*. For the first four years the dominant influences on the press were to be the Crown Colony Government in the north and the New Zealand Company in Wellington.

My immediate intention is to discuss the relationships between these authorities and the New Zealand newspapers, to point to the influence held by these authorities over the press and to indicate that, by the mid 1840s, the New Zealand newspapers were acquiring a status increasingly free from the power of either the Crown Colony Government or the New Zealand Company. During the period of Crown Colony Government the press became a major component of the settlers' *de facto* political representation. The initial stage of this development was an emerging press independence from both the Crown Colony Government and the New Zealand Company.

Press personnel, particularly in the north but also in Wellington and Nelson, were to find that both authorities were prepared, and often able, to command a press policy counter to the settlers' interests. The lessons learnt in these first four years were to be applied in a new group of newspapers which dominated New Zealand journalism for the following two decades and whose controllers were to aid in co-ordinating and leading the movement for self-government.

### The Northern Press and the Crown Colony Government; 1840-1844

The New Zealand northern press was born under the influence of a government intolerant of criticism and willing to resort to harsh measures to suppress it. This is seen at its starkest in the first paper in the North, the *New Zealand Advertiser and Bay of Islands Gazette*. The paper, first issued on 15 June 1840 was sited in Russell. It would not have begun publication had William Hobson, the Lieutenant-Governor, who had established his administration in Russell, not required a newspaper in which to publish his official decrees. However

## The New Zealand Newspapers of 1840-1844

the paper also represented the interests of the local settlers, and its editor, the Rev. Barzillai Quaife[1], could not forever neglect discussing the major topic of concern to the settlers, the land question. The validity of any purchase of land from the Maori was not recognised by the Government until an official inquiry was held and a government grant issued. The settlers' concerns centered on both this policy and the lack of progress towards the official inquiries. To quote Hocken, "like the proverbial moth, (Quaife) circled nearer and nearer to his doom, and after the issue of his twentyseventh number, on the 10 December, which contained various moderate suggestions for reform he was peremptorily directed to appear before Mr. Shortland, the Colonial Secretary"[2].

At the time New South Wales law was applicable in New Zealand and Hobson's answer to this first act of criticism was to revive a series of antipress laws instituted in 1827 by Governor Darling during the Emancipists - Exclusives debate. In Darling's conflict with the press the editors of both the *Australian* and the *Monitor* had been imprisoned and heavily fined. In New South Wales the laws lay in abeyance under the subsequent Governors, Bourke and Gipps. Their complete revival in New Zealand, under Hobson, was, however, not needed. The first of the Acts, which required a newspaper proprietor and at least two sureties to deposit £300 each with the Supreme Court, was sufficient to ensure the *Advertiser* ceased publication[3].

Settler opinion, as exemplified by the Wellington paper, was outraged.

> It (the New South Wales anti-press law) is arbitrary, oppressive and inapplicable to the state of society in this Colony. It was intended to prevent attempts to weaken the Government of a penal settlement, where the major part of the population might be considered rife for revolt against the constituted authorities, instead of being, as we are in New Zealand, prompt to support Her Majesty's representative, and to maintain the rights of property and social order.... Are we not justified, then, in

---

1  Bibliographical Notes on Quaife and others of the press figures mentioned appear in the appendix.
2  (1901), p. 106.
3  This was the only time the New South Wales Acts were applied to New Zealand. In May 1841 New Zealand became a Crown Colony independent of New South Wales. But, in an indication of contemporary communication speed, the repealing ordinance (repealing the applicability of all New South Wales laws, ordinances etc, to New Zealand) did not come into operation until 25 April 1842. See the *Auckland Standard* of the same date.

characterising this proceeding of the Thames River functionaries as an insult to the good sense and loyal disposition of the Queen's subjects in New Zealand?
(*New Zealand Gazette and Wellington Spectator*, 30 January 1841)

Requiring a journal in which to print official notices, the Government soon began the *New Zealand Government Gazette*, the first number of which contained the following:

> Notice is hereby given that in consequence of the Editors of the *New Zealand Advertiser and Bay of Islands Gazette* having declined publishing any advertisements from Her Majesty's Government, all communications from this Government inserted in the Gazette Extraordinary are to be deemed official.
> (*N.Z. Government Gazette*, 30 December 1840)

This official rationale was a convenient fiction which, Scholefield has noted, offered no explanation as to "why a struggling little paper had the temerity to reject government advertising"[4]. We may dismiss this official rationale as an inaccurate but convenient justification for the suppression of the *Advertiser*. The first issue of the *Gazette* was printed on the Mission Press at Paihia but the next eighteen were issued at Korororeka. In mid 1841 Hobson began his permanent residence at Auckland and, on 7 July 1841, the *New Zealand Government Gazette* was first published there.

After moving to the Waitemata, the Crown Colony Government was to continue its stormy relationship with the press. The first two years of Auckland based Government were to see five newspapers started. All were to run foul of the Government and feel the wrath of Hobson or his successor as administrator, Willoughby Shortland. The position was complicated in the first Auckland paper for nearly all the senior members of the Administration were shareholders in the paper and within a month of the paper's first issue, four of them were on the five member controlling board of trustees[5].

---

4   [1958], p.70.
5   The Government member trustees were Matthew Richmond (Land Claims Commissioner), W. Mason (Superintendent of Public Works), W.C. Symonds (Deputy-Surveyor-General and member of the Legislative Council) and J. Johnson (Colonial Surgeon).

## The New Zealand Newspapers of 1840-1844

This paper was the *New Zealand Herald and Auckland Gazette*. The *Herald* was to last four days short of nine months. The trustees had little business acumen and, in the sudden closure of the paper that was to come, it is necessary to allow for their readiness to be done with a non-profitable concern. However, the immediate reason for the closure of the *Herald* was editorial conflict with the Crown Colony Government.

The paper's proprietors were at pains to indicate that the *Herald* was not a Government paper.

> We feel extremely anxious that no erroneous impressions should prevail in consequence of the Government Gazette being published weekly from our press. It may be consequently imagined that this journal has been established under its auspices. We beg, most unqualifiedly, to deny any such imputation, reiterating our prospectus, that this journal will be conducted entirely upon independent principles.
> (*New Zealand Herald and Auckland Gazette*, 10 July 1841)

It is correct that the trustees did not have editorial control other than in a punitive sense. With Charles Terry, the first editor, the matter was never tested for he resigned almost immediately to attend to his flax business. Under William Corbett, the second editor, the paper was generally supportive of the Government. However, on the all important topic of land policy it was to speak out in opposition. The tactic of using land sales as a revenue raising device was criticised early on.

> It is very problematical whether the extraordinary high price of the late town allotments will not militate against the rapid and ultimate prosperity of this Colony. It may be that the coffers of the Colonial Treasury are deeply replenished, but it is equally true that the majority of the present population of Auckland are proportionately impoverished by such large drain and abstraction of their active capital. Let the Government receive fair, but not immoderate compensation for their right in the soil....
> (*New Zealand Herald and Auckland Gazette*, 31 July 1841)

However, the topic generally received scant attention in the *Herald* until 10 November 1841 when Corbett made a strong attack on the land policy and the delay in coming to a decision on the various land claims. Trustee pressure was brought to bear on Corbett in order to quieten

## The Making of the New Zealand Press

him. It had the reverse effect. The next editorial was, as Meiklejohn phases it, "vibrant with defiance"[6]. It also indicates an editor overestimating the strength of his paper.

> This journal has lately operated remarkably upon public feeling. It has acted upon the public mind with the certainty, the force, the energy of truth. That truth, and force, and energy have been unwelcome to some ... Our's was a young community which here had not before experienced —had had no example of that power of the Press which it has now begun to feel. The public has become conscious that a great change has taken place—one of those changes which from time to time occur in new settlements, and which mark their growth and progress— the public have come aware, as a moral certainty, that the character of this journal was such that it could not fail to stir the slumbering spirit, to arouse the inactive mind .... that it was no longer a mere vehicle of commonplaces—that it did not appear with a mask, to be changed as caprice, or selfishness, or vanity might dictate—that it did not foist upon the public a mere pretense of independence, or flippant surface essays upon unimportant subjects; but that it came forward and evaded not the discussion of any great question affecting the interests of the Colony...
> (*New Zealand Herald and Auckland Gazette*, 13 November 1841)

After a meeting of trustees on 17 November 1941, Corbett was dismissed.

> Resolved, that as repeated complaints have been made to the trustees regarding the style and manner of the leading articles of the *Auckland Herald*, it be deemed expedient to dispense with the services of Mr Corbett at the expiration of three months from the present date, and that a notification of the decision of the trustees be forwarded to that gentleman.[7]

The *Herald*'s criticisms of the Crown Colony Government were coincident with the start of Auckland's second newspaper, the *Auckland Chronicle and New Zealand Colonist*. It was first published on 8 November 1841.

---

6    (1953), p.39.
7    Ibid, p.38.

## The New Zealand Newspapers of 1840-1844

As Crown Colony Government personnel dominated the Auckland Newspaper and General Printing Company, which held the only printing press in Auckland, it is certain that this paper began with Government approval. In the light of subsequent support given by the Government to the *Standard*, it is possible the *Colonist* was deliberately started as a counter to the *Herald*'s criticisms. But before the end of the year it had also run foul of the authorities. It was refused use of the press and forced to suspend publication until November 1842. The details are unavailable because none of the 1841 issues has survived.

Corbett, the fired *Herald* editor, must have left before his three months notice were worked through, for Samuel Martin, the third and final editor, took over the paper in late January 1842. Martin, a scot who had been resident in New South Wales prior to his appointment to the *Herald*, was to become a staunch and active opponent of the Crown Colony Government. He insisted on, and gained as a condition of his appointment, full control of the paper. It is probable that shareholders, concerned at the paper's waning circulation and prestige, insisted that the trustees accept this condition. Immediately Martin took up his position, however, Shortland attempted unsuccessfully to bribe him into supporting the Government's position.[8]

Martin was soon at odds with his employers and, within a month of his becoming editor, the following appeared in the advertising columns.

> Dr S.M.D. Martin begs leave to intimate to the Public, that he is not responsible for any Article that may appear in this days Paper, or in any future number of the *Auckland Herald* until further notice; the Trustees of this paper having sanctioned the conduct of their Printer in refusing to insert his leading articles today, notwithstanding that several of Dr Martin's friends have come forward and offered security (without Dr Martin's sanction and knowledge) that they would be responsible in the event of his publishing any thing libellous.

---

8   "Before I had been a day here, Mr Shortland sent me a message that he wished to see me. His object was to endeavour to make me a convert to his plan (for deciding the land claims). Before I left, he made some hints which disgusted me so much with himself and his ideas of political integrity, that I shall never go near him again. I have no doubt, if I were to accede to his views and terms, that I might become one of the objects of Government patronage; but I trust I shall never require to sell my independence to an ignorant, unprincipled Government." S.M.D. Martin, January 1842, in *New Zealand; in a series of letters*, London, 1845.

> Dr Martin cannot view the circumstances in any other light than as an attempt on the part of some persons connected with the Government to suppress the expression of public opinion through the Press.
> (*New Zealand Herald and Auckland Gazette*, 23 February 1842)

Martin in turn was to write on land claims but he did not confine himself to the long standing Pakeha ground of complaint, the Governmental refusal to recognise the validity of any purchase until an official inquiry had been made and a grant issued. He looked directly at Auckland and attacked the considerable irregularities and apparent official corruption in the allocation of land there. This criticism was intolerable to the Government. Martin was dismissed, the paper closed down and the plant, land and buildings purchased by the Crown Colony Government.

During Martin's period of strife with the Government, the *Auckland Standard* began publication. Its first publication date was 28 February 1842. It is a significant aspect of the Government's management of the press that, prior to using its private control to close down the *Herald*, it first attempted to counter it by starting an opposing paper. While the Government personnel had been able to silence press criticism they had had little success in gaining press support. This problem was overcome with the *Standard*, at least in its early months, by the appointment of William Swainson, the Attorney-General, as its editor. It is difficult to produce a fair assessment of the *Standard* for so few issues survive. What is available suggests that it championed the Government but generally kept to trivial topics. One surviving editorial, for instance, is devoted to criticising the poor attendance at a Ball held by Mrs Hobson.

> Fear of taking cold can be no excuse, for those who stayed away are about the strongest advocates of the salubrity of this climate, and have been heard to state that the utmost amount of wet produces no inconvenience to the body in this country.
> (*Auckland Standard*, 25 July 1842)

It is doubtful if the *Standard* was successful in winning support for the Government. It was certainly regarded with disdain by the other New Zealand papers. A letter on the topic from Auckland, dated 5 April 1842 to the *Gazette* in Wellington was reprinted in the *Nelson Examiner*.

## The New Zealand Newspapers of 1840-1844

> The *Herald* is defunct; but, by some sort of management, under the plea of accommodating the public, the *Standard* will be printed at the Government office. This paper has a nominal editor; but every publication is a patchwork, manufactured by Shortland and Co.
> (*Nelson Examiner and New Zealand Chronicle*, 11 June 1842)

A northern contemporary of the *Standard* also noted:

> A friend has sent us the second number of the *Auckland Standard* with which we have felt as much amused as a serious topic would permit us to be...
> (*Bay of Islands Observer*, 17 March 1842)

However, towards the end of its short existence, the *Standard* was also to discuss the land claimants, and in a manner far from offering unquestioning support for the Government's position.

> ...we have no hesitation in stating, that had the Land Claimants been confirmed in their titles to land on the arrival of his Excellency in the Colony, the consequences would have been the immediate introduction of several thousands of Emigrants both from England and the adjacent Colonies—the discredit thrown upon their titles has not only ruined the old settlers, but has tended much to impede the settlement itself. Another and a no less powerful cause of mischief has been the limited quantity of land put up for sale, as well as the high price at which the land was offered—higher, indeed, at this settlement by three times, than either in Port Nicholson or Nelson.
> (*Auckland Standard*, 4 August 1842)

I have been unable to ascertain whether Swainson edited the paper to the end. It is possible he did not for, as the above quote indicates, it was starting to adopt a more critical stance towards the Government. The paper's contract with John Moore, who operated the Government press, still had a month to run when the paper ceased publication, and it is likely that the Government officials deserted the *Standard* and transferred their journalistic hopes to the next paper in Auckland.

Prior to examining the final Auckland paper of this period there is another Northland paper to consider. It began in the same month as the *Standard*. This newspaper, the *Bay of Islands Observer*, with the

## The Making of the New Zealand Press

Rev. Quaife again editor, became a strong opponent of the Crown Colony Government and soon found itself facing the threat of defamation from the Government for the following:

> ... curious reports are abroad respecting sums deficient in the late Treasurer's accounts. Perhaps the new Treasurer may soon be able to tell us whether there is any connexion between the extreme land-jobbing speculations which have been carried on by certain individuals in high stations and the vast unaccounted-for sums which have been swallowed up somehow or other in the bottomless abyss.
> (*Bay of Islands Observer*, 12 May 1842)

The collapse of the paper after nine months of publication was seen as due, at least indirectly, to protracted Government pressure which led to a weakening of the resolve of many supporters of the paper. The final issue strongly complained:

> ... of the desertion of several shareholders and many subscribers, so remarkably thin-skinned that offence has been taken at the most harmless sallies, and so tenacious of their purses, that, on the first rumour of the establishment being what is called "a losing concern" buttoned up their breeches pockets and refused the necessary supplies.
> (*Bay of Islands Observer*, 27 October 1842)

The paper continued its opposition to the Government to its final issue. It was, for instance, publishing in serial form Samuel Martin's letter to the Secretary of State when its press was finally silenced[9]. Contemporary opinion certainly saw the *Observer* as stopped by the Government. The Wellington *Gazette*, for one, accused the Government of attacking the *Observer* in order

> to stop up the only channel of free discussion within the reach of the northern part of these colonies.
> (*New Zealand Gazette and Wellington Spectator*, 2 November 1842).

---

9   S.M.D. Martin, *New Zealand in 1842; Or the Effects of a Bad Government on a Good Country*. In a letter to the Rt. Hon. Lord Stanley, Principal Secretary of State for the Colonies. Martin wrote this pamphlet, described by McLintock (1958, p.452) as "the first major attack on the Crown Colony system by a forceful writer", after being fired from the editorship of the *Herald*.

## The New Zealand Newspapers of 1840-1844

By this time, however, the northern centre of population and journalistic activity was Auckland. The *Observer* was crushed as much by the lack of a supportive population as by official pressure.

In Auckland the *Standard* was succeeded by Henry Falwasser's *Auckland Times* which, first appearing the day after the *Standard's* final issue, received initial Government acceptance. It was printed on the Government press, but after nine issues, Willoughby Shortland, then Acting-Governor, refused Falwasser use of it. Hocken is unsure whether "any suspicion arose as to Mr Falwasser's ability to pay for the printing or as to the doubtful odour of his articles"[10]. The non-availability of the early issues precludes any definite statement on this point. Both interpretations are possible. The earliest issue still available is No. 7 of 26 September 1842. Its "doubtful odour" is illustrated by an advertisement for Dr Martin's *New Zealand in 1842; or the Effects of a Bad Government on a Good Country*, and also by an editorial critical of Shortland and of the colony in general. This issue, however, also includes the following which casts doubt on the paper's financial viability.

> Before commencing the publication of the *Auckland Times* we canvassed for subscribers, expressedly declaring that we should only publish upon realizing a certain number. After taking two, three or five or our numbers, as the case may be, we now constantly have them referred by partners who originally gave in their names—we are not conscious of any deficiency in the performance of our part of the contract, and of course must hold these gentlemen liable for the fulfilment of theirs .... we have taken care in all cases to possess competent legal proof of the obligation these kind friends continue under—and shall enforce it in every case.
> (*Auckland Times*, 26 September 1842)

Falwasser was not stopped by the unavailability of a press. He gathered a variety of old types and coarse paper and carried on printing his paper by use of a mangle. The results are extraordinary. He kept this up, delivering his weekly barbs *gratis* to his subscribers until the *Southern Cross* was to begin. Falwasser then considered the Auckland press in sufficiently safe hands for him to suspend his paper, thus allowing him to journey to Sydney to obtain suitable plant. The *Auckland Times*

---
10   (1901), p.109.

reappeared seven months later and continued until January 1846 when the final issue appeared a week before Falwasser's death. In all Falwasser produced 159 issues of his paper. He gained a lasting reputation for journalistic courage and imaginative endeavour especially during the period of outright opposition from the Crown Colony Government when he was denied access to a press.

After deserting Falwasser and the *Times*, the hopes of the Government were once again laid on the *Chronicle* which was brought out of suspension to resume publication. The paper was to publish for six months before going into suspension once again, due to the financial difficulties it experienced from competition with the *Southern Cross* when that paper began. During this second round of publication the paper was regarded as very much a tool of the Government.

> ... if gentlemen holding public offices will club together—some with their purses, and others with whatever other influence they possess—to monopolise the press, and destroy the just channel of public intelligence—and if, with all their energy, they can do nothing better than lay such a joint-stock egg as the *Chronicle*, they are fair game for ridicule.
> (*Auckland Times*, 2 February 1843)

A similar criticism was made by the newly appeared *Southern Cross* on the eve of the *Chronicle*'s second suspension.

> For sale or hire, in about a fortnight, a defunct engine used for stifling the fire of the people; rather shaky, having lately stuck fast in the swamp of Queen Street. Has been well greased lately, its head turning with marvellous facility in any direction. Apply at the Chronicle Office.
> (*Southern Cross*, 29 April 1843)

The *Southern Cross* began publication in Auckland in April, 1843. Despite experiencing some difficulties in its early years, this paper represents the start of a stable press in Auckland. The great advantage of the *Southern Cross* was the possession by its proprietors of their own printing press and consequent lack of reliance on continued permission to use the Government press. Ironically, Crown Colony Government personnel provided the funds for the *Southern Cross* press. Samuel Martin, the dismissed editor of the *Herald*, was the inaugural editor of the *Southern Cross*. Martin sued the trustees of the *Herald* for the balance of his contract and, in spite of a counterclaim by the Attorney General for libel, was awarded £641.13.4d. It was this money that paid for the type and press for the *Southern Cross*.

The record of relations up to this point indicates an extreme antagonism between the press and the Crown Colony Government. Of the seven attempted newspapers the *New Zealand Advertiser and Bay of Islands Gazette* had been forced out of existence by official financial demands, the *New Zealand Herald and Auckland Gazette* had been closed down by Government personnel acting in their private capacities, the *Auckland Chronicle and New Zealand Colonist* had been similarly denied access to a press, the *Auckland Times* was officially refused use of the press, the failure of the *Bay of Islands Observer* was at least partly due to official pressure, and the demise of the *Auckland Standard* leaves the likely suspicion that it also succumbed to a withdrawal of official patronage. Only the *New Zealand Gazette* was untouched but this publication acted as a newspaper only while based in the Bay of Islands. In Auckland it had taken on the usual role of a Government Gazette.

This early antagonism between the press and the Crown Colony Government placed them in mutual distrust. Although Governor Grey came to command the support of two newspapers, this distrust continued until the Government's replacement in 1853. Meiklejohn, in describing these "blackest pages in the early history of New Zealand", attributes major responsibility to Willoughby Shortland. In a charge echoed by McLintock he states, "He, more than any other officer of Hobson's administration, squandered the Government's greatest asset - the confidence and goodwill of the people"[11]. This antagonism was not as intense after Shortland's replacement. The repudiation of Shortland by Robert FitzRoy, the second Governor, at first gained him considerable press goodwill but his subsequent actions were soon to lose it. Press confidence in the Government was never to be gained. Indeed, it is difficult to envisage the two institutions being other than antagonistic. For while it is true that Shortland and Hobson by their heavy-handedness exacerbated the problems, the two institutions were always to be divided on their approaches to basic New Zealand issues, and particularly on that of land acquisition. Although, as in the case of the *Herald*, the *Chronicle* and the *Standard*, sometimes financed by the Administration,

---

11  (1953), pp.109-110. McLintock, (1958), p.144.

## The Making of the New Zealand Press

the press was to champion the settlers. Its subscribers were to be settlers; its printers, editors and other personnel were to be settlers; and settler interests were to become press interests. Where settler interests and Crown Colony Government policy were to differ, the press and the Crown Colony Government were to be antagonists.

### The New Zealand Company Settlements and the Press, 1840-1844

The first New Zealand newspaper was issued at Wellington on 18 April 1840 when Samuel Revans, six weeks after arriving on the *Adelaide*, published the first New Zealand edition of the *New Zealand Gazette*. The *Gazette*'s issue of 18 April was, however, its second. The first, which gave information for emigrants and a history of the New Zealand Company, had been published in London on 21 August 1839 and, with a slightly extended second edition, was reprinted on 6 September.

The *Gazette* had been started under the initiative of Edward Gibbon Wakefield, who had chosen Revans to be its founder. Revans, the major figure in the life of the paper, is referred to by Scholefield as the "ostensible owner"[12]. The common assumption was that the New Zealand Company was the backer of the paper.

> ... we certainly have understood that one portion of the amount required to establish the *New Zealand Gazette* ... was furnished by intending colonists, of whom the editor of the *Gazette* was one, and that the remainder was advanced by the New Zealand Company.
> (*New Zealand Colonist and Port Nicholson Advertiser*, 9 August 1842)

The situation was similar in Nelson where the "ostensible proprietor"[13] of the *Nelson Examiner* was Charles Elliott, a man who previously had a printing business in London. Again the common belief was that the plant and paper were really the property of the New Zealand Company. On this point an acknowledgement is made in the first issue. It also indicates a too easy coincidence of interests with the Company.

> It only remains for us to state that with respect to the New Zealand Company, under whose direction this settlement has

---

12   (1958), p.25.
13   Ibid, p.156.

## The New Zealand Newspapers of 1840-1844

been planted, we are wholly independent of its influence. It is indeed satisfactory to know, that the opinions, as well as the interests of that association, are, in all matters of importance to the colony the same as those of the majority of our fellow-colonists. If, however, questions affecting the public welfare should arise, on which we cannot conscientiously support the Company, we shall call upon the public to redeem a pecuniary obligation to that body under which we are known to be, for the means of establishing this journal.
(*Nelson Examiner and New Zealand Chronicle,* 12 March 1842)

Charles Elliott controlled the *Examiner* in partnership with his brother James. Both Revans and the Elliott brothers, in spite of their loans from the New Zealand Company, were the owners of their respective newspapers. The loans were repaid, Revans' by 1844 and the Elliotts' by 1847.

The officials of the New Zealand Company had early determined on the importance of newspapers. Their initial settlement planning was to include provision for a press and ancillary equipment, and for competent personnel to run a newspaper. This applied particularly to Wellington, which, being the principal Company settlement, was the obvious site for a newspaper to champion the Company's interests in New Zealand[14]. In the Nelson case, Elliott had already decided to emigrate and the Company was requested, successfully, to assist him financially when other arrangements he had made failed. The later settlements of Lyttelton and Dunedin, founded by offshoots of the New Zealand Company, were also to follow in this pattern. New Plymouth was to be the exception. A press was not part of original settlement equipment there and not until 1852, when a second-hand Albion press was obtained from Auckland, taken by bullock dray to the Manakau and then shipped south, did the *Taranaki Herald* begin.

The *New Zealand Gazette and Wellington Spectator* is noted for its unbending, and often strident, support for the New Zealand Company and its policies. Revans had been a thorn in the side of authority both in Canada and England. In New Zealand his barbs were directed towards the Auckland based Crown Colony Government, which, at that

---

14 The New Zealand Company also had its *New Zealand Journal,* a London based fortnightly which published its first issue on 8 February 1840.

distance, was unable to subject him to the pressure placed on the northern press. Locally, however, he was content to remain a staunch advocate for the New Zealand Company. The newspaper was often accused of being under the control of the New Zealand Company but a dichotomy between a controlled and independent press is largely irrelevant in regard to the relationship between the *Gazette* and the New Zealand Company. The *Gazette* was an uncoerced and willing supporter of the New Zealand Company.

As will be discussed later, the New Zealand Company officials saw newspapers as components of their plan of colonization. Revans had financial obligations to the New Zealand Company for the initial establishment of the paper but there is no record of this being used to pressure him to support the Company. The ties between the Gazette and the New Zealand Company, however, were such that any pressure or control was unnecessary. There was a coincidence of inclination and an interchange of personnel which linked the newspaper and the Company. Revans was the first appointee as secretary to the Council, the committee of colonists in charge of the settlement. Colonel Wakefield, being the New Zealand Company's principal agent, was automatically the president. Similarly, two of the Gazette's editors moved on from the editorship to hold important Company posts. J.T. Wicksteed, in March or April 1842, resigned as editor to become the New Zealand Company Agent in New Plymouth. William Fox resigned as editor in September 1843 to become the New Zealand Company Agent in Nelson.

Where New Zealand Company and Wellington settler interests were one, the *Gazette* was to be a forceful champion. Nowhere is this more noticeable than in the criticisms of attempts to entice away settlers. The two following extracts illustrate this:

> An advertisement by the Government will be found in today's paper for mechanics to proceed to Auckland[15]. We are not monopolists, nor do we advocate monopoly in any shape, but we do think that it is very unfair for the Government to send here for labour imported at the expense of parties who have purchased land in this part of the Island. None would murmur at Government seeking labour here to improve Port Nicholson; but to take our labour away to improve a district as distinct

---

15 The advertisement was for four first-rate carpenters, six second-rate carpenters, six pairs of sawyers, three bricklayers and two stonemasons.

from this place as Barbados is from Trinidad, we fear shows a determination to wield the powers of Government for the especial benefit of a single district, and against which monopolising proceeding it becomes our duty in the name of the settlers in this part of New Zealand to protest.
(*New Zealand Gazette and Britannia Spectator*, 7 November 1840)

We hear that the *Patriot* before leaving Launceston, received instructions to obtain here and take back with her a considerable number of the working class. The report was abroad that free passages were offered, that no restraint of any kind was to attend this supposed boon. Considering it our duty to make ourselves acquainted with the matter, we have found upon inquiry that the boon of a free passage is only attended with a slight disadvantage of being bound by indenture to serve for two years at wages considerably lower than the lowest rate ever yet paid in Port Nicholson, and to submit to a deduction from the first years wages of only eight pounds, as a slight acknowledgement to the kind Captain for having transferred the free man from the state of independence and self-respect, to the blessing of herding with the miserable and the wicked in the sink of the Southern seas.... How ignorant, how disgustingly besotted, or vicious, must that man be who would not shrink with horror at this moment from asking the working man and his family to become the daily companion of every crime for which transportation is the reward!
(*New Zealand Gazette and Wellington Spectator*, 19 December 1840)

The comparatively mild language used in the first extract was an attempt by Revans to be civil to Hobson who was in the process of choosing a site for his capital. Once Auckland had been chosen the *Gazette* returned to calling members of the Administration the "Thames River Functionaries" and Hobson became "Captain Crimp" for his labour recruiting expeditions. Bellicose attacks on the Crown Colony Government constituted a topic Revans could pursue without fear of offending either the New Zealand Company or the Wellington settlers.

However, there were to be areas in which Company and settler interests were to be at odds and in these areas the *Gazette* became a Company rather than a settlers' paper.

Revans set out to serve the interests of the Company, clearly believing such a policy would also serve the interests of the settlement. He attempted to quieten discontent, not always allowing criticism of the Company to be published. This was in marked contrast to some settlements. For example, both in Nelson and later in Lyttelton the controllers of the first newspapers prided themselves on never refusing publication to letters.

During the *Gazette*'s four years of New Zealand publication its championing of the Company became less and less acceptable to the settlers as their own and the Company's interests diverged. As in Auckland the major area of discontent was to be in regard to land. The first published rift can be seen in early 1841 when a letter of protest at the manner of conducting the land sales received short shrift from Revans who steadfastly followed the Company line in this matter.[16]

The *Gazette*'s factional position within Wellington led to it being countered by an opposing press. The first was the *Victoria Times* of which only the first issue survives and it is possible only the one issue was ever published. The paper was printed and published by Thomas Bluett, its proprietor. It planned to be a weekly and was offered on the same terms as Revans' paper. Like the *Gazette* it was a four page paper but unlike the *Gazette*, or any other early paper, it was a lithographed newspaper with the contents being handwritten rather than typeset. At least now, it is scarcely legible in parts. (Page four of the first issue was completely given over to a plan of the City of Wellington; this is the first New Zealand newspaper illustration.) Bluett was open about the fact that his paper was to counter the *Gazette*.

> Some public organ is required to represent the interests of the public without the exaggeration and misrepresentation which papers got up for party purposes are so want to indulge in .... The *New Zealand Gazette* has hitherto been considered as infallible as the Delphic Oracle of old; it has (?) forth its thunders against the Colonial Government, and attacked the characters of private individuals with the most unrelenting and cruel spirit...
> (*Victoria Times*, 15 September 1841)

---
16 *New Zealand Gazette and Wellington Spectator*, 9 January 1841.

## The New Zealand Newspapers of 1840-1844

Nothing more, however, is left of the *Victoria Times* and the *Gazette* was to be unchallenged for almost another year before its second opponent was to appear. This newspaper was the *New Zealand Colonist and Port Nicholson Advertiser*. The *Colonist* was also started in deliberate opposition to the *Gazette* which it saw as increasingly antagonistic to the settlers' interests.

> This is emphatically a colonists' paper. It has been established by and for the colonists. It had its origin in the growing perception of the settlers at this place, that the *Gazette* neither advocated the interests nor expressed the sentiments of the community. Many ... considered ... that our contemporary took a narrow and inaccurate view of the position and interests of this place, and that it was intended to advance the cause of a party in defiance alike of justice and policy ... And if there had been no alteration in its original course—no uncalled-for and unworthy suppression of truths which it was feared might prove offensive to parties whom our contemporary, on whatever account, did not choose to offend—no exaggerated or groundless accusations—no habitual postponement of the interests of this settlement to the feelings and prejudices of one, and that a very small portion of the inhabitants, this paper would never have existed.
> (*New Zealand Colonist and Port Nicholson Advertiser*, 2 August 1842)

The *Colonist* was established by a group of settlers, who appointed R.D. Hanson as editor. The paper's financial position was always difficult and was exacerbated by the lack of support it received from the New Zealand Company. Neither advertisements nor subscriptions were to be readily available from that source. The paper ended, a year after it began, showing some anger towards its apparently numerous debtors.

> ... our own circulation, which was at first greater than we had anticipated, has continued steadily to increase. And had the amount of money received been as satisfying as the list of subscribers, we should have long continued our publication.
> (*New Zealand Colonist and Port Nicholson Advertister*, 2 August 1843)

## The Making of the New Zealand Press

During its year of existence the *Gazette* and *Colonist* kept up a verbal battle with the main focus of the *Gazette*'s attack being that the *Colonist* was a Crown Colony Government supporter and prejudicial to the interests of the Wellington settlers.

> The *Colonist* seems determined to do its best to cause the settlers to lose confidence alike in themselves and their property. Truly Auckland is well backed now in Port Nicholson. Though the Government have been unable to maintain an organ expressing opinions in its favour at the capital, it has succeeded in securing able advocacy in this place.
> (*New Zealand Gazette and Wellington Spectator*, 24 September 1842)

While Hanson did hold the post of Crown Prosecutor as well as *Colonist* editor, it is an exaggeration to see the *Colonist* as pro the Crown Colony Government and anti the New Zealand Company. It was Revans' simplification to see the matter in such black and white terms. The major reason for the establishment of the *Colonist* was, as stated, to oppose the *Gazette*'s one-sided and exaggeratedly pro-New Zealand Company understanding of affairs in Wellington. While Hanson was, unlike Revans, not an unwavering New Zealand Company supporter, his policy was more anti the *Gazette* than anti the New Zealand Company. The failure of the small settlement to support a second newspaper against the established *Gazette* deprived Wellington of an able and largely disinterested voice.

With the demise of the *Colonist* the *Gazette* was again left alone. It was itself, however, only to last for another year. Towards the end of this year Revans ceased to be proprietor of the *Gazette*. The new owner is unknown. Revans' name disappears from the imprint on 7 August 1844 to be replaced by Edward Roe on 14 August 1844. The imprint refers to the printer and publisher, not necessarily the proprietor, but this change was followed by a statement in the issue of 4 September 1844.

> Edward Roe begs respectfully to inform the public that, the proprietorship of this establishment having been lately changed he is instructed by the present proprietor to request that all accounts due to it may be discharged as early as possible, and to intimate that in future no further credit can be given.

## The New Zealand Newspapers of 1840-1844

The major result of this change was a difference in attitude towards the New Zealand Company, as the following, less than obsequious, editorial quotation illustrates.

> At the present moment the settlers in the New Zealand Company's settlements are prevented from exercising the privilege of purchasing from the natives, which has been conceded to the inhabitants of other parts of the colony, because it would interfere with the monopoly of the New Zealand Company. But it is impossible to conceive that any Government can seriously contemplate persevering in a course so ruinous to these settlements, in order that the shareholders of the Company may not be disturbed in the enjoyment of a property which they can only retain in violation of a solemn contract entered into with their purchasers.
> (*New Zealand Gazette and Wellington Spectator*, 4 September 1844)

A week later the *Gazette* announced it was to cease publication and, in a rather confused editorial, saw its end as at least partly due to opposition from Company supporters.

> Since our last publication we have been informed of secret meetings having taken place with a view to endeavouring to establish another journal ... Another paper would diminish our present small support, which is not sufficient to pay our expenses ... We beg now in conclusion to inform our fellow settlers that the *New Zealand Gazette and Wellington Spectator* will be discontinued on the 1st of October next; another paper may, or may not be established immediately, but we wish it to be understood, that if it be not the merit or demerit of this settlement being henceforth without an organ of discussion, and communication, will be due to the holy alliance of the Wakefield clique, small, miserably small though it be; of the representatives of the absentee interest; of the thoughtless, and of those who think they can influence the policy of the present government, relative to the mode of dealing with natives and the land and other questions more advantageously than they consider we are able to do, though they were not able,

when challenged by us, to state the mode in which they would proceed.
(*New Zealand Gazette and Wellington Spectator*, 11 September 1844)

It may be that the "Wakefield clique" was influential in the ending of the *Gazette*. The sudden closure of the paper, finally rebellious after four years of faithful service is difficult to explain otherwise. The fear of competition from another paper was real but it was by no means certain that the *Gazette*, rather than the newcomer, would lose out in such a competition. Certainly it was not necessary for the *Gazette* to fold before the battle had begun.

The politics of the settlement had become such that no longer were the Company and settlement interests one. Absentee and resident landowner interests had long diverged and the Company's interests had also ceased to coincide with those of the settlers. In regard to local newspaper support for the New Zealand Company, the collapse, when it came, was sudden and total. The *Gazette* suddenly rebelled against the Company and then equally suddenly stopped publication. The new paper was never to be a New Zealand Company champion.

The new paper was the *New Zealand Spectator and Cook's Straits Guardian* and it was to demonstrate early its separation from the New Zealand Company. Its second issue, that of 19 October 1844, carries a strong editorial advancing the claims of the settlers against both the New Zealand Company and absentee interests. The *Spectator* represents a change in Wellington newspapers for it marks the end of New Zealand Company advocacy in editorial and general newspaper policy.

The other New Zealand Company settlement was Nelson and its newspaper began with similar characteristics to its Wellington counterpart. As mentioned, Charles Elliott, the printer of the *Examiner*, was obliged to the New Zealand Company for financial assistance in starting his paper. The paper which was first issued on 12 March 1842, two months after the settlers' arrival in Nelson, began, as in Wellington, in debt to the New Zealand Company. There was also, as in Wellington, a broad initial agreement with New Zealand Company philosophy and practice and the *Examiner* also began life as a champion for the interests of the New Zealand Company. According to Saunders:

## The New Zealand Newspapers of 1840-1844

... both the land purchasers and the labourers felt that the Nelson press would offer no facilities to ventilate their grievances against the New Zealand Company.[17]

The *Examiner* was, however, the Nelson newspaper and Nelson, while being a New Zealand Company settlement, was not the principal settlement. The point of the distinction for the *Examiner* was that while it was expected to be a New Zealand Company supporter, it was the *Gazette* in Wellington which was the New Zealand Company mouthpiece. While Revans in Wellington was prepared to censor criticism of the New Zealand Company, Elliott was able to point to his record of never having refused publication to letters[18]. Elliott was a New Zealand Company supporter but not the slavish one implied by Saunders. The *Examiner* was able to show more independence than its Wellington counterpart and, unlike the Auckland papers, did not have to fear closure for expressing its opinions.

Prior to 1844 the *Examiner* was the New Zealand newspaper least affected by the authority of either the Crown Colony Government or the New Zealand Company. It soon became the major New Zealand newspaper with the early and mid 1840s being the period of its major status and influence. The Auckland press, locked in internecine conflict with the Crown Colony Government and the *Gazette* in Wellington, with its strident and unvarying defence of the New Zealand Company, presented little competition. But the *Examiner* would have shone in any assembly.

**Press Independence:**
During the early 1840s there arose differences between the concerns of the settlers and those of their leaders. A principal problem topic was land and the methods of acquiring it. Both in Auckland and the Company settlements, settlers discovered that the Crown Colony Government and the New Zealand Company approached the topic from a different orientation to themselves. But land was not the only topic of contention. Particularly in regard to relationships with the Crown Colony Government, the topic of representative government early appeared and immediately indicated large differences between the settlers' views and those of the Governor and his Administration.

---

17   (1896), Vol. 1, p.180.
18   *Nelson Examiner and New Zealand Chronicle*, 15 April 1843.

## The Making of the New Zealand Press

Equally in regard to relationships with the New Zealand Company, there were important differences as the interests of the settlers separated from those of both the absentee landowners and the New Zealand Company. During the early 1840s the settlers learnt that their leaders were not their leaders.

The major public arena in which the conflict between authorities and settlers was staged was the press. While the New Zealand Company had more success than the Crown Colony Government in keeping the settlers' views out of print, both authorities were eventually to fail to keep opposition suppressed. In Auckland the conflict involved great antagonism between the Crown Colony Government and the press. A major aspect of Crown Colony Government authority over the local newspapers was the power held by virtue of ownership of the only available printing press. The exercising in Auckland of this ability to deny access to a press has been shown. While it did not bring an end to the antagonism between press and Crown Colony Government, independence for the press in Auckland began when the controllers of the *Southern Cross* obtained, from Sydney, a second printing plant. Although only the *Bay of Islands Observer* went so far as to write a clause into its rules prohibiting any Government officer from becoming a trustee of the paper's parent company, all newspapers from the mid 1840s were to be aware of the need to keep control out of the scope of local authorities.

While in Auckland a measure of independence for the *Southern Cross* was gained by obtaining a new printing plant, in the south the power and influence of the New Zealand Company itself was waning. Press independence came as an early manifestation of the power changes in the Company settlements. In Wellington the changes were revolutionary as new newspapers rose to challenge and eventually supplant the *Gazette*. In Nelson the process was evolutionary as the *Examiner* gradually shifted its allegiance away from the New Zealand Company. After their first few years the New Zealand newspapers began to achieve considerable independence from their local authorities. Over the next decade, those who controlled the newspapers were to take full advantage of their position and became among the most influential of the settlers' leaders in an attempt to gain self-government for the colony.

# 3. The New Zealand Newspapers of 1844-1853 and their Part in the Agitation for Self-Government

A ten year period of stability began for the New Zealand newspapers in the mid 1840s. The *Nelson Examiner* continued. In the other settlements new newspapers began and, after some initial difficulties, settled into an enduring period of publication. From the mid 1840s until the passage and implementation of the Constitution Act of 1852 the issue of self-government increasingly became the major concern of the New Zealand press. Newspaper personnel became of central importance in the New Zealand agitation for self government. My immediate aim is to indicate the newspapers which operated during this period, to discuss the circumstances in which they began and continued publication and to discuss their involvement in the movement towards self-government. This is done by arranging the chapter through regional areas. My contention is that the movement towards self-government was coordinated through the New Zealand newspapers, that press personnel were among the leaders of the settlers' agitation for self-government, and that press representation was an integral part of the settlers' *de facto* political representation during this period. With no recognized constitutional avenue for their political aspirations settler politicians engaged in journalism as a means of gaining their political goals. This was to define much of New Zealand journalism not only during the period of Crown Colony Government but also later in the years of self government.

A major aspect of my general argument is that newspapers came to occupy partisan positions within the New Zealand political system. Their political linkages were open and were accepted as proper. The commencement of this type of journalism is to be found in the involvement of newspapers in the agitation for self-government and particularly in the subsequent success of newspaper personnel in the political elections.

**Auckland**

The first long lasting newspaper in Auckland, the *Southern Cross*, began publication in April 1843. However, an enduring Auckland press did not begin with its advent for, after two years, it ceased publication until July 1847. The new journal was early acknowledged and assessed by the Nelson newspaper.

We have received from Auckland the first five numbers of a new paper, entitled the *Southern Cross* ... The *Southern Cross* is decidedly anti the present Colonial Government ... It is to be supposed we shall differ with him now and then, but he is too far off to wage war with, and far too clearly possessed of "the pen of a ready writer" not to be acknowledged as the best of the Auckland journalists
(*Nelson Examiner and New Zealand Chronicle*, 10 June 1843)

The founder, manager and proprietor[1] was William Brown and the editor was Samuel Martin, the final editor of the *New Zealand Herald and Auckland Gazette*. Willoughby Shortland was Acting-Governor and the *Southern Cross*, with its motto[2] signifying continuity with the past Auckland newspapers, carried on the antagonism with the Crown Colony Government. This antagonism became somewhat muted after Shortland's replacement by Governor FitzRoy in December 1843. Fitzroy and Martin enjoyed a good personal relationship and, importantly, the Maori policy of the *Southern Cross*, as advocated by the Wesleyan Martin, was closer than any other New Zealand newspaper to FitzRoy's own position. In 1844 both Brown and Martin were appointed Members of the Legislative Council (M.L.C.) by FitzRoy. However, these changes did not lead the *Southern Cross* towards supporting the Crown Colony Government. Although the attacks on the Governor were no longer personal the *Southern Cross* remained opposed to the Government. This was most apparent in regard to the matter of settler representation where both Brown and Martin were committed to the attainment of representative government. The committment was such that, for instance, in the article announcing Brown's and Martin's appointments to the Legislative Council, the paper still denounced the Council as "a mere mockery of the rights of the people."[3]

Late in 1844 both Brown and Martin went to Britain. Brown's journey was intended to be a temporary business visit. But Martin did

---

1   Possibly William Brown was co-proprietor of the paper with John Logan Campbell. Brown and Campbell were partners in the merchantile firm of Brown and Campbell, and Campbell did have considerable association with the paper. However Brown was the major figure of the two in the life of the *Southern Cross*.

2   LUCEO NON URO. "If I have been extinguished, yet there rise.
       A thousand beacons from the spark I bore."

3   Reprinted in *Nelson Examiner and New Zealand Chronicle*, 8 June 1844.

not return. John Logan Campbell took over as manager and Charles Terry, the first editor of the *New Zealand Herald and Auckland Gazette*, became Martin's successor. There were, in 1844, three papers in Auckland; the *Auckland Times* which had resumed publication on 7 November 1843, the *Chronicle* and the *Southern Cross*. But in 1845 "Heke's war fell like a plague upon the business world of Auckland".[4] The *Chronicle* folded in February and in April Campbell decided to suspend the *Southern Cross*. It was to remain out of action for 26 months, until after Brown's return.

The next Auckland paper, the *New Zealander*, took advantage of the relative lack of competition during the 1845 depression. It began on 7 June 1845. Its founder and proprietor, John Williamson, apart from seizing an opportunity to return to his trade of printing, saw his only competitor, the *Auckland Times*, as over preoccupied with the land claimants. As the title of his paper suggests, Williamson was an advocate of the Maori and because of this policy he was assisted by the Wesleyan mission to acquire a printing plant.

Falwasser's death at the start of 1846 meant Williamson had the newspaper field entirely to himself. By July 1847 when Brown returned to New Zealand and restarted the *Southern Cross*, the *New Zealander* was a well established bi-weekly publication.

With the resumption of the *Southern Cross* the Auckland newspaper pattern was set. There were to be few attempts to start newspapers until the 1860s and, of those that were attempted, none were to offer a serious challenge to the *Southern Cross* or *New Zealander*. There was to develop a conflict between these two which continued until and well beyond the granting of self-government. As the *Southern Cross* resumed its criticism of the Crown Colony Government, the *New Zealander* moved to defend Sir George Grey, the Governor who had succeeded FitzRoy, and the two newspapers became mouthpieces for the two political groups in Auckland. The *New Zealander* spoke for the official party, composed of the Crown Colony Government officials, the Military and their supporters, while the *Southern Cross* spoke for the opposition, known variously as the Radicals, the Senate or the Progress Party. In the case of the *Southern Cross* the newspaper was more than the mouthpiece for the opposition. In a sense it was the opposition. The focus of political opposition in Auckland had from the start been the

---

4   Scholefield, (1958), p.77.

press and this pattern continued with the *Southern Cross*. Brown, the leader of the Progress party, used his paper as the expression of opposition, it being by far the major form of opposition available. The newspaper gave coherence and strength to opposition.

Both Auckland newspapers were in favour of self-government but the *New Zealander* accepted Governor Grey's timetable for its introduction. Opposing views were most apparent from September 1848 when it became clear that Governor Grey intended to oppose the introduction of Earl Grey's, the Secretary for War and Colonies, Constitution and to defer full representation. This was the turning point throughout the New Zealand settlements. From this time the majority of settlers, and newspapers, broke with the policy of their Governor. Agitation for self-government became for the *Southern Cross*, as for the southern newspapers, the dominant issue. The Auckland agitation for self-government was coordinated and given expression by the *Southern Cross* and its senior personnel were clearly the leaders of the political opposition to Grey.[5]

As observed by numerous writers, the Auckland settlement, for its origins, owed much to Sydney.[6] Using the press to oppose the Governor as a staging point on the road to self-government was a tradition first nurtured in New South Wales which developed independently in Auckland. It owed nothing to the Wakefield settlements.

## Wellington

In Wellington a similar opposition of newspapers was to emerge though its manner of development was to be distinctive. The *New Zealand Spectator* and *Cook's Straits Guardian* began after fifty settlers each contributed towards its establishment costs. It saw itself as a settlers' newspaper with its affairs being "conducted by a committee of half a dozen of the principal gentlemen in the settlement".[7] This managing

---

5   Sir William Fox, in his *How New Zealand Got Its Constitution*, names only three Auckland figures in his listing of those who obtained representative government. They are William Brown, John Logan Campbell and Hugh Carleton. All three were associated with the *Southern Cross*.

6   "A mere section of the town of Sydney transplanted to the shores of New Zealand" was Fox's unfriendly description, (1851), p.40.

7   Hocken, (1901), p.103.

committee was subject to election at half yearly meetings.

In spite of the closing of the *Gazette*, the *Spectator* was not free from Samuel Revans's influence. He was to be the catalyst which gave rise to the *Independent*, the *Spectator*'s rival for twenty years. The act which set this in motion was the insertion of a somewhat scurrilous advertisement by Revans in the *Spectator* of 29 March 1845.

Revans' advertisement consisted of a copy of a deposition from Daniel Wakefield, a lawyer and the younger brother of Edward Gibbon Wakefield, that "I was in the Billiard Room at Barret's Hotel when Mr. Samuel Revans came into the room, and in the presence of several persons said, "I have long sought you to tell you that you are a liar, a scoundrel and a coward"". Wakefield's deposition continued with a request that Revans be bound in recognizances to keep the peace. Revans concluded the advertisement with a statement that provocation was given by Wakefield and supported by "gross and deliberate falsehoods."

Wakefield's reply was published in the next week's edition.

... Much against my inclination, therefore, I feel compelled to state what took place between Mr. Revans and myself. A trial was held at the late sittings of the Supreme Court, Smith V Betts and another, involving a question as to the validity of a deed, by which Mr. Revans conveyed the whole of his property to Capt. Smith,[8] to the exclusion, among others, of Messrs Betts and Co., of Sydney, to whom Mr. Revans is indebted. I was of Counsel for the Defendants, and a verdict was returned for the plaintiff, on which a new trial was applied for, and a Rule Nisi obtained. On the day on which this happened, that is Tuesday the 18th March about four o'clock in the afternoon, I met Mr. Revans on the beach, close to the Scottish Church, in company with James Smith and I said to him, "We have got a Rule Nisi in that case, meaning Smith V Betts." Mr. Revans replied, "Oh, a Rule Nisi is nothing." Upon which I said, "It is a first step." Mr. Revans immediately said, "Well, I will bet five to one I win it. I know Chapman, (meaning the Judge) I can trust him, or he

---

8   Was Smith then the final proprietor of the *New Zealand Gazette and Wellington Spectator*? See page 30 above.

will take care of it. I know Chapman; we kept two sisters together for three years." then stating other circumstances not necessary to be mentioned.
(*New Zealand Spectator and Cook's Strait Guardian,* 5 April 1845)

A result of the ensuing scandal was that the committee in charge of the *Spectator*, angry at their printers for not clearing such an advertisement with them first, dispensed with their services and arranged to have the *Spectator* printed elsewhere. In retaliation, the printers immediately started a new paper, the *Wellington Independent*.[9] The *Spectator*'s committee successfully attempted to stop their rival by secretly purchasing its premises and plant.

Engaged as we have been almost from the landing of the first settlers in working the press first established in New Zealand, we were by the sale of that press, at the notice of only a few hours, deprived of our accustomed means of earning a living.
(*Wellington Independent,* 26 November 1845)[10]

However, the *Independent* was only suspended rather than retired. Closed down at the start of August 1845, new plant was obtained from Sydney and it resumed publication in November 1845.

The two Wellington newspapers were to develop opposing viewpoints similar to those offered by the Auckland newspapers. The *Spectator* was to become a supporter of the Crown Colony Government while the *Independent* was to become the Government's leading opponent newspaper. As in Auckland the dominant concern was to be the topic of representative government.

---

9  The printers were a quintet; Edward Roe, William Edward Vincent, James Muir, George Fellingham and Thomas McKenzie. The major figure is McKenzie. He was eighteen when the *Independent* began and had first been employed in Wellington as an apprentice on the *Gazette*. Roe's name does not appear on the imprint after the 1845 suspension. The other partners also one by one left the partnership until, in February 1865, McKenzie was sole proprietor.

10 The above is the generally accepted sequence of events in regard to the start and suspension of the *Independent*. See Hocken (1901) and Scholefield (1958). Burns (1957) Vol.2, pp. 157-161 questions, however, whether the printers did not in fact wish to leave the *Spectator* and branch out on their own. She also argues that the *Spectator* committee were not involved in the purchase of the *Independent*'s premises and plant.

## The New Zealand Newspaper of 1844-1853

The *Spectator* had begun with a pronounced anti-Government policy. Its opening editorial, for instance, is a bitter attack on FitzRoy and his Administration ending with a Revans like lamentation on Wellington's woes.

> ... as respects the interests of Cook's Straits, we have no Government at all ... We certainly have a gentleman of a noble family as a Governor, and perhaps, fifty officials, some of whom wear uniforms, and all of whom receive salaries. We have clergymen too in abundance, with a Lord Bishop at their head, but we have no one who knows our wants or concerns himself with our welfare.
> (*New Zealand Spectator and Cook's Straits Guardian*, 12 October 1844)

A major facet of this anti-Government stance was the attitude towards the Maori. Again this was in decided opposition to the official policy.

> From viewing the Maories as a civilized race ready to perform the duties, and therefore entitled to the rights of British subjects arose the calamity at the Wairau, and the present almost insuperable difficulty of acquiring and possessing land.
> (*New Zealand Spectator and Cook's Straits Guardian*, 19 October 1844)

But after the *Spectator* had been publishing for almost two years there was a change in both the control and policy of the newspaper. For their part the Committee in charge of the *Spectator* tired of their involvement with it and its attendant difficulties. One of their number, Robert Stokes, had become the paper's editor. Total responsibility for and eventual ownership of the *Spectator* were given to him.

> The readers of the *New Zealand Spectator* will perceive that, by a resolution passed at the halfyearly meeting of the subscribers, the duties of the Superintending Committee have ceased, and the responsibility of conducting this Journal will in future solely devolve on its present editor.
> (*New Zealand Spectator and Cook's Straits Guardian*, 23 September 1846)

Stokes also took this opportunity to announce publicly a change in policy for the paper which had been gradually emerging; that of support for Governor Grey and his Administration.

> The *New Zealand Spectator and Cook's Straits Guardian* was originally established by the settlers as an organ for the expression of their opinions at a period of unusual difficulty, and the responsibility of its management was entrusted by them to a Committee of five of the oldest settlers. The settlers were then contending against the bitter hostility of the Colonial Secretary, and his willing agent Captain FitzRoy. They have outlived the contest, their adversaries have been removed and we may hope this place will know them no more ... The settlers have now had sufficient experience of their new Governor to feel confident that he will strenuously exert himself to promote the real interests of the colony, and the permanent welfare of both races of its inhabitants.
> (*New Zealand Spectator and Cook's Straits Guardian*, 23 September 1846)

This pro-Grey policy was to be the continuing hallmark of the *Spectator* and was to mark it from the majority of the country's press. Grey was supported only by the *Spectator* and, in Auckland, the *New Zealander*.

The *Independent* was also generally supportive of Grey at the start of his Governorship but went against him as the introduction of self-government was delayed. As with the Auckland newspapers the turning point was in September 1848 when Grey's intention to defer full representation became obvious. Again, as in Auckland, both newspapers advocated self-government but the *Spectator*, as with the *New Zealander*, accepted the Governor's timetable for its introduction. The *Independent*'s opposition was led, not by its proprietors, but by Isaac Featherston who was the first editor of the paper and the major formulator of its policy.

It was at this point, from late 1848, that the Settlers' Constitutional Associations were formed in all settlements but Auckland, with the object of obtaining immediate action on the introduction of the "great prize of Self-Government".[11] The formation of the Settlers' Constitutional Associations was important for the political role of the New Zealand newspapers, both in the way the newspapers and the Associations were

---

11   *Wellington Independent*, 3 March 1849.

## The New Zealand Newspaper of 1844-1853

linked, but, more importantly, in the way these links forged and foreshadowed alliances between the press and political spheres after the introduction of self-government. This is so for, as well as agitating for self-government, the Associations served the purpose of both training and bringing into public prominence the future political leaders of the country. "The greatest value of these associations lay in the training they provided for public life in a colony lacking even a rudimentary form of municipal government. In a very real sense, they were the political nurseries of their day."[12] If the Settlers' Constitutional Associations were the political training grounds prior to independence, the administration and coordination of this training was carried out within those New Zealand newspapers which supported their aims.

Both the Settlers' Constitutional Associations and the New Zealand newspapers provided independently a public political forum. But the two institutions were given an interactive relationship by their common personnel and common purpose. The Settlers' Constitutional Associations "unquestionably captured the public imagination"[13] and were the expression of the political aspirations of the settlers. But this expression was given voice through the network of supporting newspapers which gave themselves over enthusiastically to what they saw as their great task. In each settlement it was not possible to divide clearly the association from the newspaper. In each case the association was supported and given voice by a local paper. The various leader writers kept up a correspondence within the limited means of communication possible. Being of the same political persuasion they reprinted from one another and commented on each others articles. Generally the journalists were major figures in their local association and it was their coordination which tied the various associations together.

In the case of Wellington, Isaac Featherston was the person who embodied the identity of purpose between the *Independent* and the Settlers' Constitutional Association. In no sense was the *Independent* an impartial observer and recorder of proceedings. All the printer proprietors of the newspaper were members of the association. But it was the editor, Featherston, who, as well as being the dominant force

---

12   McLintock, (1958), p.298.
13   Ibid, p.301.

behind the *Independent* during this period, was also, for the association, the "mainspring of the movement".[14]

From 1849 the *Independent* and the Wellington Settlers' Constitutional Association spoke with the one voice. On occasions Settlers' Constitutional Association statements and *Independent* editorials were one and the same. Under Featherston's editorship the *Independent* took over from the *Nelson Examiner* the position of leading New Zealand newspaper. Featherston's polite writing style had none of the coarseness of the earlier Wellington editorials of Samuel Revans but it was no less forceful. The *Independent* was Grey's leading press opponent in the battle for self-government.

**Nelson**

In Nelson the *Examiner* was throughout the period to remain the first and only newspaper. As in the North Island settlements the introduction of representative government had always been desired and argued for. In Nelson, as elsewhere, it was to grow in importance to become the paramount issue of press concern. Charles Elliott, the *Examiner*'s co-proprietor, had warmly greeted Grey's Governorship but was gradually to turn against him. As elsewhere, September 1848 was the month from which the paper settled on an anti-Grey policy with the introduction of representative government being the chief concern.

While not being as prominent in the Nelson Settlers' Constitutional Association as was Featherston in the Wellington counterpart, Charles Elliott was to the fore in the Nelson agitation. He was on the committee appointed during the first Nelson public meeting which regretted the nominee system and desired representative government.[15] He was also one of the leaders of the Nelson Settlers' Constitutional Association. The columns of the *Examiner* were open to the Association. Other Nelson leaders such as Francis Jollie, an earlier *Examiner* editor, and Edward Stafford were frequent contributors to the newspaper.

---

14   Ibid, p.299.
15   *Nelson Examiner and New Zealand Chronicle*, 6 January 1849. The nominee system followed the suspension, under Governor Grey's urging, of the New Zealand Government Act 1846. In the nominee system the planned Provincial Legislative Councils were retained but all members of the Councils were to be nominated by the Governor. From this point the majority of settlers began referring to themselves as the "factions", so as to distinguish themselves from the "nominees", those who accepted Grey's system.

Connections with other settlements, on the issue of representative government, were maintained by the *Examiner*. This was particularly so in regard to Wellington where the *Examiner* acknowledged an alliance with the *Independent* and an opposition to the *Spectator*. The Examiner maintained a high level of understanding in Nelson of Wellington Settlers' Constitutional Association members' views by giving many *Independent* columns a reprinting. It was also to follow a similar policy with regard to the views of the members of the Settlers' Constitutional Associations of the later settlements of Otago and Canterbury.

**Otago**

The Otago settlement began with the arrival of the first settlers in March 1848. Although it will take us away from our immediate purpose that of discussing the role of the press in the agitation for self-government it will be instructive to review the history of the first newspaper in Otago. Not only did it determine the policy of the next, and first enduring, newspaper in Otago but it also is a further illustration of the events that had occurred in the other settlements; that of conflict between the settlement authorities and the press.

Otago's newspaper history was to begin with strong conflict between the newspaper and the Otago Association, the offshoot of the New Zealand Company responsible for the initial planning and colonization of the settlement. The Otago Association did not have a newspaper as an immediate priority on arrival in Dunedin. Not until 9 months after arrival was the *Otago News* published. And then, rather than supporting the Association, the *News* was in opposition to it. Its proprietor and editor, Henry Graham, had not been among the first settlers but had arrived in Otago in September 1848. He lacked both the social status and personal connections to place himself among the community leaders and added to this a personal dislike of both the class nature of the New Zealand Company settlements and the religious exclusivism of Otago. Graham was an Anglican who opposed the Presbyterian dominance in the settlement. Graham reported the Rev. C.R. Creed's initial Church of England service in Otago.[16] Creed's service and Graham's reporting of it provoked strong disapproval in the Presbyterian settlement particularly from Capt. W. Cargill, the powerful Association

---

16  *Otago News*, 7 February 1849.

*The Making of the New Zealand Press*

leader in Otago. Cargill first expressed himself in a letter to Creed, which Graham published.

> ... I would now frankly put it to yourself how far is it either seemly or called for that you should postpone your own charge as a missionary to the heathen for the purpose of giving at least half your time .. to a people so carefully and amply provided for as our little community here?... You may perhaps say that we are not all Scotch Presbyterians that we have a minority of English amongst us; but be it observed that these parties joined us at their own request, in the full knowledge of our being a class settlement, and quite willing to avail themselves of our worship until such increase of their numbers as should lead to their being otherwise provided for by their own Bishop (*Otago News*, 2 May 1849)

In spite of Cargill's disapproval Graham continued to give publicity to Anglicanism. Cargill's "uncalled for interference" Graham judged to be "an attempt at religious persecution and intolerance worthy (of) the sixteenth century." (*Otago News*, 16 May 1849).

Of at least equal importance, Graham also set out to champion the cause of the labouring class in Otago. In his fourth issue (24 January 1849) he published the Petition from the working men of Dunedin to William Fox, Acting Principal Agent of the New Zealand Company, in which they asked for changes in their working conditions, including a pay rise and a reduction in working hours from ten to eight per day. In the same issue he published Fox's negative reply. The editorial is on the topic and takes the labourers' side. Graham also laid the blame for the over-supply of labourers squarely with the New Zealand Company. This provoked, in issue five, two strongly critical letters from "A Land Purchaser" and "A Land Proprietor", but Graham continued the attack and the leading article in this issue quarrelled with the basic plan of colonization in Otago. Graham asserted the Otago area was suitable for the grazing of cattle and sheep but not for horticulture. He contended that the New Zealand Company should cease its concentration on town development. The free passages should be given to farm labourers rather than to tradesmen and city labourers. As a corollary, the propertied men should also go out into the rural areas.

> We have nothing in Dunedin for capitalists to speculate in with advantage; their proper sphere is the rural districts.
> (*Otago News*, 7 February 1849)

Captain Cargill, in a letter of 6 March 1849, published with a lengthy rejoinder in issue 8 of 21 March 1849, withdrew the subscriptions of the Free Church Association for 20 copies, and the subscriptions of the New Zealand Company for 20 copies, "because of the capabilities of the Otago block and its settlers being so grievously misrepresented in the editorial articles, beginning with No. 5".

I am unable to ascertain the circulation of the *News*, but the loss of 40 subscriptions must have been a heavy blow.[17] The *Otago Witness*, the successor to the *News*, for example, had only 120 subscribers in its early days. Graham, however, had responded to the first criticisms by promising both a larger format and weekly, rather than fortnightly, publication.[18] He was to keep to this promise but the first editorial on assuming weekly publication shows awareness of the difficulties. The original cheerfulness of the paper, shown in its Shakespearian motto "There's pippins and cheese to come" has become a more serious and combative stance.

> We have to urge upon our friends and the public the necessity of sending their names and subscriptions for the *News* as early as possible. Considerable additional expense is incurred, and a much greater amount of labour required for the publication of our present enlarged weekly paper than our former fortnightly sheet; and we call upon every lover of "FREEDOM, JUSTICE AND TRUTH", to help us for their cause. To those who consider 6d a week too much to expend on a newspaper, we say, combine together, and in two's and three's you will easily obtain your point of cheapness, and confer an additional advantage upon the publisher. Co-operation has done much for the labouring man at home, and it is a system which may be pursued with still greater advantage here.
> (*Otago News*, 9 June 1849)

---

17 Newsam estimates it at "about 80 copies at the most." (1979), p.18.
18 *Otago News*, 7 February 1849.

Graham, however, was an ill man and the end of the *News* came with his declining health. He was forced, in October 1850, to revert to publishing every tenth day,[19] and, on 21 December 1850 to cease. The final editorial includes comment on both the financial and health aspects.

> ... Matters more personal to ourselves, and which should, in some cases, never have appeared brought us into collision very early in our career with the heads of the Church and the Company here, and our pecuniary prospects have borne a tinge of darkness in consequence; but we have been upheld by the heartfelt encomiums of others who have pressed around us with their congratulations.However, 'man cannot live upon grass alone'. So long as health lasted, the struggle was not unequal, or its results depressing; but when sickness laid its heavy finger upon us, it was time to say the word 'Adieu', and to draw our labours to a close.

Henry Graham died two months later, in February 1851. In an obstreperous career, which saw him normally at odds with at least the more influential section of the settlement, he received overwhelming support from the local community on only one issue, that of self government. From the start he was an advocate for its introduction. It is significant that although Graham's *News* was, among the other Company settlements, allied only with the *Spectator* in opposition to the New Zealand Company, in no way did this alliance lead Graham to accept the *Spectator*'s support for Grey's nominated Legislative Councils. Although Fox omits him from his listing of those who obtained self-government for New Zealand, Graham was an advocate for self-government. Nor could he imagine "a 'man with soul so dead' as to refuse his aid in the great work."[20]

The successor to the *News*, the *Otago Witness*, began in the month of Graham's death. This paper eventually became the weekly stablemate

---

19 "The proprietor is sorry to have to notify that, on and after this present number of the *News* the papers for the remainder of the quarter, will appear every tenth day, or every alternate Wednesday and Saturday. However unwilling the proprietor may be to make these changes, he is compelled to adopt the present method as the only likely means of finishing the quarterly copies of the subscribers, and, at the same time, giving him a chance of recovering his health". (*Otago News*, 19 October 1850)

20 *Otago News*, 7 September 1850.

of the *Otago Daily Times* and lasted well into the twentieth century. It was started by a group of resident land purchasers. Editorship of the paper was entrusted to Cargill's son-in-law, William Henry Cutten. As noted by Saunders, Cutten "had a good deal more of the lymphatic in his temperament, and was altogether more likely to be orthodox, than Mr. Graham".[21]

The first editorial indicated a desire to support majority religious and political feeling in Dunedin. It also promised to avoid a one man championing of contentious causes.

> The principles of the *Otago Witness* are to be in harmony with the Scheme of the Otago Settlement, as propounded by its originators, and set forth in the 'Terms of Purchase' and 'Institutes'. In religion, evangelical; and in Politics, adhering to the principles of the British Constitution maintaining the rights and privileges of Local Self Government, and of civil and religious liberty in the widest sense ...
>
> ... (the proprietors) also hold, that where there is but one newspaper, the guardianship of these views and principles is too much to be entrusted to any one man, and it will therefore be placed in the hands of a Committee, responsible to themselves and to the public for giving fair effect to this Prospectus.
>
> (*Otago Witness*, 8 February 1851)

The *Witness* was to keep to only one of these proposals. The intention to support the peculiar national and religious character of the foundation of the settlement was to bend to the situation in New Zealand. A more moderate course was advocated. Nor was the desire to keep control out of the hands of any one person to last. The paper paid no dividends and was generally "a source of trouble and anxiety to the other proprietors"[22] who eventually presented the property to the editor. Cutten's name appears as sole proprietor of the *Witness* from 23 April 1853.[23]

Only in regard to advocacy for self-government was the *Witness* to keep to its original principles. The *Witness* began rather too late in the Crown Colony Government period to be of major importance in the attainment of self-government in New Zealand. It did, however, join

---

21  (1896), Vol.1, p. 261.
22  Paul, (1924), p.10.
23  Cutten had been sole editor of the paper from the eighth issue.

forces with the *Southern Cross*, the *Independent* and the *Examiner* and, through these alliances, both kept the Otago settlers aware of agitation for self-government in the other settlements and coordinated the Otago protest with the colony wide movement. As elsewhere, the *Otago Witness* was closely allied with the agitation for self government. Cutten was a foundation member of the Otago Settlers' Association the organization which "by 1852 ... was recognized as the voice of Otago, speaking with authority on all matters concerning self-government."[24] If the Association was the voice of Otago the *Witness* was the province's mouth. It actively supported the agitation and gave the Association's leaders liberal access to its columns.

### Canterbury

Further north, in Canterbury, a final ally for this group of newspapers was to emerge.

The *Lyttelton Times* began as a planned part of a planned settlement. It received the greatest pre-publication support of any of the colony's newspapers and the first issue was out within a month of the settlers' arrival. J.E. FitzGerald, who had offered to edit the paper until Ingram Shrimpton, the owner, came out to New Zealand, in a full and thoughtful first editorial considered it:

> ... wiser to leave our politics to develop themselves in the course of time, devoting our whole energies to the far more important part of our task; namely that of making our weekly journal as useful as possible to the colony as a source of general information and mutual convenience. There are, however, one or two points upon which it is right we should at the outset indicate the line to which we shall in future adhere. First, we entirely believe in the soundness of the general principles upon which the Association have hitherto acted, and without pledging ourselves to uphold their future policy, or to defend every individual action of the Committee, or of its agents, we shall always give our cordial support to the general principles upon which the colony has been founded.
>
> Secondly, with respect to the question of Government. Without indulging in any unjust hostility to the officers in whose hands the executive of the present Government is

---

24 McLintock, (1949), p.286.

placed, or visiting their acts with undue censure, we shall never cease to oppose the continuance of the present form of Government in New Zealand, and to insist upon the introduction of a constitution such as that under which we and our fathers have lived, and in which the great principle of British law shall be recognised to the full, that no Englishman shall be taxed without his consent, signified by his representatives.
(*Lyttelton Times,* 11 January 1851)

The *Lyttelton Times,* at first content with the Canterbury Association's ideas, soon moved from them. Although a complete break did not come until 1856 when the paper changed hands, the divergence is apparent even during FitzGerald's editorship. The point is well made by FitzGerald's would-be biographer:

> ... the files on the *Lyttelton Times* in its first year are witness that his (FitzGerald's) gifts were real and substantial. It is further significant that although the Canterbury Association's membership was overwhelmingly Tory and High church, the *Lyttelton Times* was neither. In politics it was liberal; in church matters it had no perceptible party bias. Its columns show that from the first the ideas of the Canterbury colonists had little affinity with the ideas of those who had conceived and organised the settlement.[25]

As in Otago, where neither of the newspapers were able to buttress the religious and national exclusiveness of the Otago Association, so in Canterbury the *Lyttelton Times* found its espousal of the Canterbury Association philosophy had to be tempered with an acceptance of the circumstances in New Zealand. In regard to the topic of self-government, however, there was accord between the Canterbury settlers, the *Lyttelton Times,* and the Canterbury Association. All advocated its urgent introduction and the *Lyttelton Times* immediately become allied with those other settlement newspapers that opposed Governor Grey on this matter. As elsewhere, the *Lyttelton Times* maintained a liaison with allied newspapers in other settlements and coordinated the Canterbury protest with the movement. As elsewhere the newspaper personnel were to the fore of the settlement leadership in the movement for representative government. In Canterbury this applies particularly

---
25 O'Neill manuscripts, Canterbury Museum.

to James FitzGerald but Fox also mentions Crosbie Ward and W.G. Brittan as being among those who obtained representative government for New Zealand.[26] Both Ward and Brittan were of assistance in the establishment and early running of the *Lyttelton Times*. They were to have subsequent and important connections with Canterbury journalism.

In spite of its relatively late start Canterbury was an important settlement in the agitation movement. This was largely due to the powerful support the Canterbury Association could muster in England among the clergy, the aristocracy and parliamentarians. In New Zealand this influence was reflected onto the *Lyttelton Times* which, as the voice of the Canterbury reform movement, had an importance not adequately measured by the fact that it began publication only in the year preceding the granting to New Zealand of its form of self government.

### The Press and Political Representation

The settlers who were agitating for self-government considered themselves to be without political representation. They were not prepared to accept that form of representation offered. Earlier, while never accepting the offered representation as adequate, they had been prepared to avail themselves of it. But, increasingly, this practice lessened and, particularly in regard to the nominated Legislative Council, the settlers saw acceptance at best as prejudicial to honour. The settlers, however, lacking neither political aspirations nor political supporters, did have a *de facto* political representation. Emissaries were a feature of this. Several prominent settlers, while on visits to England at various times, acted as representatives of such organizations as the Settlers' Constitutional Associations.

But, for the settlers, their newspapers were the most visible aspect of their *de facto* political representation. They were a forum for the settlers' political expression and the major means of communicating that expression both to relevant authorities and to other settlements. Holding a strategic position in the communication of information within and among settlements, the press was the obvious medium to communicate and coordinate the settlers' political ambitions. Private letters were the main available alternative but while they were often superior to the newspapers in regard to speed, by their private nature, they never had the breadth of readership courted by the press.

---

26  Fox, (1890), p.11.

The other major aspect of the settlers' *de facto* political representation were the Settlers' Constitutional Associations with their elected leaderships. These Associations were not properly constituted, representative bodies and were always subject to questioning as to the adequacy of their representation. In a typical argument, the partisan Richard Wakelin, a supporter of Governor Grey, described the Wellington Association as "in no sense of the term a representative body; it never had the confidence of the working settlers; and its proceedings were opposed from the first by a large majority of the more influential citizens of Wellington".[27] The Associations, however, were accepted by the settlers as being an avenue by which they could express their political desires. They are generally accepted as having reflected majority opinion. Only in Auckland was there no clear majority opinion.

While there were instances of strong support for reform, only in Auckland was there no Settlers' Constitutional Association. Nor did the Progress Party, which advocated reform, enjoy in the later years of the Crown Colony Government an outright majority support against the Officials.

While the Settlers' Constitutional Associations and the New Zealand newspapers were distinct entities it is not possible to clearly separate their political effectiveness. The political activities of the newspapers were coordinated with one another and with the other avenues of political expression, particularly the Constitutional Associations, available to the settlers. The liaison between the Settlers' Constitutional Associations and the settlement newspapers, with the exception of the Auckland newspapers and the *Spectator* in Wellington, was strong and recognized in all settlements. In each settlement the newspaper was recognized as the voice of the Association. The press action was more than a reporting of Association activity. It was itself a partisan feature of the decision making process and agitation of the Associations. In each settlement, the leaders of the newspaper were among the leaders of the Association. In each settlement just as the newspaper leaders became involved in the political agitation, so did the other political leaders become involved in journalism which they saw as an important method of promulgating and achieving their aims.

This intermingling of journalistic and political activity applied to Auckland, the only settlement without a Settlers' Constitutional Association, as much as it did to the southern settlements. Auckland,

---

27 (1877), p.12.

distinguished from the rest of the colony by the experience of an Imperial rather than Wakefield scheme of colonization and by the influence of a large military-official establishment, also experienced a *de facto* political representation in the form of newspaper agitation. In Auckland it was the press that was the real opposition to the Crown Colony Government. In Auckland, as elsewhere, political and journalistic prominence went hand in hand.

The special status of the press in a colony without representative government was increasingly recognized by the Crown Colony Government. That Government, which earlier in Russell was ready to apply Darling's press laws, developed during the Governorships of FitzRoy and Grey an appreciation that a colony deprived of self-government should in its stead at least enjoy a wide freedom of the press. Probably the clearest statement of this was given by the Attorney-General during a libel hearing between the two Auckland papers.

> During the period for which I have the honour to hold the office of Her Majesty's Attorney-General for the Colony, in no single instance have legal proceedings been taken on the part of the Government against the Press for the publication of a libel not, gentlemen, that gross libels have not appeared in the public prints; but because it has been thought more for the advantage of Her Majesty's subjects in these Islands that there should be occasional excesses on the part (of) the Press rather than continual restraint, and that, so long at least as the people of New Zealand had no direct voice in the government of the country, they should enjoy, without limitation or restraint that true liberty that "Free-born men, having to advise the public, might speak free".
>
> (*New Zealander,* 10 September 1853)

The political activity of the New Zealand newspapers during the years of Crown Colony Government had important consequences at the time for journalism and the press generally. Journalism was early recognized as a partisan political activity and one accepted as an essential component of that *de facto* political representation the settlers did experience. Those engaged in journalism received a personal political prominence because of the political nature of journalistic activity. This applied not just to those men, such as Featherston and Brown, whose

## The New Zealand Newspaper of 1844-1853

motivation had from the start been primarily political, but also to printers, such as Williamson and Elliott, who found that, in New Zealand, their profession made them prominent public figures. This influence on the press and the nature of journalism was to continue after self government was gained. This will be examined in Part Two. Because of their political prominence newspaper personnel were to be heavily represented among those winning official positions in the first elections. After self government there were to be notably close links between press and government.

# 4. Newspapers and Journalism in the Crown Colony Government Period

During the Crown Colony Government period the New Zealand press comprised some eighteen newspapers. They were not, however, all publishing at the same time and there were major variations in their publication records. The *Nelson Examiner*, with regular publication through the Crown Colony Government period from the paper's start in 1842, is the most consistent newspaper, while at the other extreme the *Victoria Times* appeared only once. At the end of the Crown Colony Government period seven newspapers were in publication. There were two each in Auckland and Wellington and one in Nelson, Canterbury and Otago.

The idea of journalism as being concerned with political advocacy was by no means confined to New Zealand. But the political advocacy that was so essential a part of journalistic activity, in New Zealand had two unusual features. Firstly, it was successful. Self-Government was gained and the Factions, those organized around the Constitutional Associations and the newspapers, became the major political power in New Zealand. Press personnel were disproportionately over represented among those gaining official positions in the ensuing political institutions. This itself led to increasing links between the journalistic and political institutions and will be examined in subsequent chapters. Secondly, this politically active style of journalism was in New Zealand combined with an emphasis on news and a commercial orientation that were to have long term effects on the New Zealand press.

My intention in this chapter is to indicate the importance that New Zealand newspaper proprietors attached both to political advocacy and to the provision of news and advertising space. Such a combination was to have long term effects on the survival and influence of political advocacy as a journalistic activity. For when the daily newspaper, oriented around news and advertising, finally became ascendent in New Zealand, it came not, as in many other countries, as a replacement for an earlier politically active journalism but as an extension and continuation of the existing style which combined political involvement with commercial journalism.

I shall also discuss matters which operated to make the New Zealand newspapers class newspapers, newspapers which advocated the interests of a particular section of the community rather than of the community in general. The class allegiance of the newspapers was to a developing

## The Crown Colony Government Period

upper class which derived its coherence from ownership of property. Property ownership in nineteenth century New Zealand was not an absolute distinction for a high proportion of the population owned land. But domination in land ownership increasingly became the preserve of a small upper class. The dominant landowners should not be seen as opposed to any merchant and trading group in New Zealand. As a minority became the dominant land-holding group in the Wakefield settlements so also were they prominent in developing and controlling those business enterprises which comprised the commercial sector of the settlements. A similar identity of major landowners and urban businessmen was apparent in Auckland, the main non-Wakefield settlement. In both the North and South Island settlements control of commerce and the ownership of land were the preserve of the one group.[1]

During the Crown Colony Government years the developing upper class, because of the limited contact between the scattered settlements, had little national coherence. But within each separate settlement a small upper class came to the fore. As well as superiority in commerce and land ownership this class also gained political power in New Zealand. Over the 1840-1880 period control of land, commerce and the political order became concentrated within a developing upper class and mobility into this class became increasingly restricted. The control of newspapers is itself a part of the development of this upper class. Newspaper ownership was part of the developing commercial dominance of the upper class. The identification of newspaper policy with the interests of an upper class is important for it was this class which won political power after self-government. It was because of the support for this class, developed during the Crown Colony Government period, that the newspapers were to be so closely linked with the Provincial and General Governments after 1853.

There were four main matters that led to the New Zealand newspapers becoming class newspapers. These were the class nature of the settlements, the price of newspapers, the cost of establishing and maintaining newspapers, and the voluntary nature of newspaper work. They operated to make newspaper ownership, involvement in journalism and even newspaper subscription, the preserve of the wealthier and high status settlers. It was these settlers who, after self-government

---

1 Such a conclusion has been reached by writers in regard to various settlements. Cf. Campbell (1972), Eldred-Grigg (1980), Fairweather (1985), Stone (1973).

was gained, were to be politically dominant. It was their membership of an upper class, along with their leading involvement in the agitation for self-government, which brought so many individual journalists to political prominence in New Zealand.

## The Multiple Roles of the New Zealand Newspapers

The New Zealand newspapers were, from the start, seen not only as journals enabling a public discussion of political and other concerns but as objects of general use to the new settlements. As the *Lyttelton Times* phrased the matter;

> ...the position which a newspaper occupies in a new colony is somewhat different (to that in a populous and wealthy country). The importance of a newspaper to Canterbury will depend far less on the opinions expressed in its leading articles, than in the great convenience it will afford the inhabitants, and in its general utility as a medium of public intelligence in local affairs.

(*Lyttelton Times*, 11 January 1851)

Even the *Otago Witness*, a newspaper carefully tailored to be more politically acceptable than its unruly predecessor, saw itself as firstly a medium for news and advertising.

> The objects of the proprietors are, in the first place, to supply the settlement with the means of advertising, and with the news from home and other quarters.

(*Otago Witness*, 8 February 1851)

Such a combination was unusual. The English experience during the same period was one where the political character of the press was usually limited by commercial considerations, with the provision of advertising acting as a strong disincentive to the expression of political views. Neither did the early nineteenth century newspapers in the United States combine political expression and advertising. They were firmly attached to political parties, were purchased by subscription, and their political role was not combined with the provision of space for advertisers.

The New Zealand settlements were different from the well-established towns of more populous countries. With little fear of competition from alternative styles of journalism and with a clear need to be of wide use

## The Crown Colony Government Period

to their community, the New Zealand newspapers were to combine in their tiny settlements the roles of different types of newspapers. They had a wide topic range. Social and fashion reporting, literary columns, literary and dramatic criticism and feature articles were to be part of their makeup. The major components, however, were advertising, news and public discussion. These were to be combined to form a distinctive journalism.

### An Illustration

While there is no one typical issue of a typical newspaper the combination of roles can be illustrated by detailing one issue of one newspaper. The *Wellington Colonist* of 18 July 1843 had the usual four page format of the time with four columns per page. All of page one plus the first column of page two were filled with advertisements. Shipping Intelligence took half a column then came three columns of leading articles. The leading articles dealt with two topics. One was the British Government's New Zealand responsibilities while the second was a dispute with the other Wellington newspaper. It began:

> The *Gazette* of Saturday has surpassed itself...in the article of Saturday there is a naked vulgarity of style, a coarse malignity of spirit, and a hardihood of mendacity in the assertions, which it would be difficult to parallel in the most unscrupulous specimens of political and personal virulence that occasionally disfigure the more violent portions of the English press.

The leading articles finished half way down the first column of page three to be followed by a half column report on a Municipal Council meeting in Wellington. Two columns of English news followed. These were reprinted from the *Colonial Observer*, a British newspaper. A further half column was a reprinted article on the Tahiti and Sandwich Isles. Two columns, the final on page three and first on page four, were devoted to a reprint of an English article on the corn laws. Two columns extracted from the *Weekly Chronicle* were on European news while the final column was, as usual, given over to Wholesale Prices Current. While this issue had, unusually, no light or amusing material at all, it is generally representative of the layout and content of its contemporaries.

## The Provision of News

The dissemination of news was from the start considered by the controllers of the New Zealand newspapers to be a major part of their role. It proved, however, on account of the isolation of the settlements a difficult role to perform. "We are now nearly four months without news from the seat of Government..." lamented the Nelson Examiner on 30 July 1842. The situation was to be a feature throughout and after the Crown Colony Government period. A concentration on events in the local settlement was not considered enough.

> The absence of regular communication renders the conducting a newspaper a matter of extreme difficulty, and must be our apology for not presenting our readers with such a number as we could wish. There is but little going on in the settlement of local interest...
> (*Otago Witness*, 25 June 1853)

The "absence of communication" had the consequence that for all practical purposes New Zealand was not one community but many. Identification with a regional rather than a national community was to be a long-term feature of New Zealand. At least when it was politically expedient to do so the dominant settler view was that they lived not in one colony but six.[2] But the settlers, or at least the newspaper writers, also took many opportunities to consider themselves part of one colony. They were interested in news from other settlements, accepting that it could have repercussions on their own lives.

> We are this week without arrivals of any kind, and are therefore in total ignorance of what may be going forward beyond the limits of our own little world. The anxiety for news from the north is very great, for on the course which the Governor now takes will the future existence of the colony depend.[3]
> (*Nelson Examiner and New Zealand Chronicle*, 17 April 1845)

The arrivals referred to are ship arrivals. Within the two islands land routes were available and used. But communication was generally by sea and was irregular. Acknowledgement of a lack of news was common.

---

2   Fox, (1851).
3   The Nelson settlers knew of Hone Heke's burning of Kororareka but not of subsequent events, including FitzRoy's reaction.

> We have nothing to communicate this week as we are without news either foreign or domestic.
> (*New Zealand Spectator and Cook's Straits Guardian*, 7 December 1844)

Receiving news was itself news.

> The receipt of news since our last paper has been great and of an interesting and satisfactory nature. We have endeavoured to make the number really a newspaper.
> (*Wellington Independent*, 23 April 1845)

The isolation of the settlements was to make it impossible for the newspapers to provide a news coverage on anything other than an intermittent basis. The desire to do so was always present and, in so far as circumstances permitted, the newspaper controllers were conscientious news reporters.

Communication among settlements was at best irregular. In 1851 Canterbury had no news from Otago between April and November. In mid 1852 Nelson was three months without news from Wellington. These are not extravagant examples for they occurred between neighbouring settlements and towards the end of the Crown Colony Government period. Such conditions prevailed throughout the years of Crown Colony Government and, in the circumstances, newspaper controllers had little choice but to avail themselves of whatever variety of news was at hand even if the sources were less than reliable. Other newspapers were eagerly sought. As in other countries it was accepted that newspapers would copy from one another and much news reporting was by judicious use of scissors. The Wellington settlement, typically, was "accidently informed" of the arrival in New Zealand of Governor Grey through "a stray newspaper".[4] Such haphazard news transmission not only gave little chance to check the authenticity of reports but also forced a reliance on sources that were often considered unreliable. Newspapers from Auckland had little trust in those from the Wakefield settlements and vice versa but both were forced to use one another's copy if they wished to print any news of the other settlements. Similarly, private letters, which along with official despatches and word of mouth were the only alternative means of communication, were used in a spirit of suspended judgement. The following inaccurate news is an example.

---
4  *New Zealand Gazette and Wellington Spectator*, 3 January 1846.

## The Making of the New Zealand Press

> We have heard, from a quarter which we have no reason to doubt, that private letters have been received in the colony, stating that the English Government had recalled Mr Shortland from the office of Colonial Secretary. We give the above as a rumour, but we do not vouch for its authenticity.
> (*New Zealand Colonist and Port Nicholson Advertiser*, reprinted in *Nelson Examiner and New Zealand Chronicle*, 26 November 1842)

Again the situation was long-term. Newspaper controllers became more adept at gauging the reliability of their information but the reliance on irregular channels continued.

> We may shortly expect some additional European news, which seems already to have reached Wellington; as a private letter which crossed the Straits to the Wairau speaks of intelligence that the Emperor of the French had been shot at during his visit to our Queen at Osborne.
> (*Nelson Examiner and New Zealand Chronicle*, 2 December 1857)

The New Zealand newspaper controllers, in their search for news, were forced to use whatever snippets of information should come their way. Their desire to offer a news service, often had them involved in a reliance on dubious sources and the process of news dissemination was one in which an assessment of the accuracy of rumours was a major part of journalism.

### Newspapers as Community Advocates

In the absence of a regular news flow to fill the pages there was little option but to open newspaper columns for discussion. But the idea of a newspaper being both a forum for public discussion and a vehicle for political expression and political action was one the settlers brought with them to New Zealand and expected to implement. The English press at the time the settlers left for New Zealand was becoming a daily and commercial press. But the tradition the settlers brought with them was one whereby "a newspaper is usually the organ and voice of some political or other section of the community".[5] This tradition was to be continued in New Zealand with the major difference that the newspaper

---

5  *Lyttelton Times*, 11 January 1851.

*The Crown Colony Government Period*

was argued to be the voice of the community rather than of a section of a community. The point is, for instance, implicit in the following extract from a letter addressed to Governor Hobson by "An Englishman".

> ... it is not a noisy band of democrats and demagogues who call for your dismissal: a whole community, composed of all sorts and conditions of men, varying infinitely in opinion, need and character, upbraids you with one accord...
> (*Nelson Examiner and New Zealand Chronicle*, 16 July 1842)

In this respect the newspapers were seen as a form of political action and were often directed not at the local community but at a different audience. While much rhetoric was aimed at the representatives of the Crown Colony Government in New Zealand, English authorities, especially the Secretary for War and Colonies, were also a common target.

> ... we had on a late occasion the disagreeable task of narrating the unhappy effects of the policy of this Government towards the natives. We have now to narrate, for the information of the Secretary of State for the Colonies, the history of a financial transaction between this Government and a Mr Boyd of Sydney; and if, in the former, we had to speak of matters which claimed the sympathy and pity of the humane towards the oppressed and deeply wronged natives, we have now to speak of matters which must astonish the man of business, and, we doubt not, very much displease the nobleman who presides over the genii who rule in colonies.
> (*Southern Cross*, reprinted in *Nelson Examiner and New Zealand Chronicle*, 24 June 1843)

A major illustration of this direction towards English authorities is from the *Nelson Examiner* where, on taking the editorship Alfred Domett's strategy of protest was to draw up a petition to parliament questioning FitzRoy's decision not to pursue further the matter of the Wairau. The petition was published in the *Examiner* on 15 June, 1844. It was signed by 597 male adults, a number, the paper was careful to point out, that meant the abstentions were almost entirely absentees and government employees. Couched in its careful language,[6] the petition was a factor in FitzRoy's recall.

Although not always as effective as the *Examiner*, this was common practice for the first papers. The first issue of the *Spectator*, for instance, was in such haste to catch the mail ship that it had to forego the traditional opening editorial.

> The first number of a new paper generally puts forth a sort of programme of its intended performances in the shape of a statement of its political principles. On the present occasion, however, we have neither time nor space to follow such a practice. The *Bella Maria* is about to sail direct for England, and it is of paramount importance that she should convey authentic and public intelligence respecting the position and prospects of the colony.
> (*New Zealand Spectator and Cook's Straits Guardian,* 12 October 1844)

**Newspapers as Class Papers**

The newspapers were ready to consider themselves the voice of the community. Their understanding of this, however, warrants investigation for, while they often advocated measures which received wide majority approval, they were the consistent voice of only a small section within each of the settlements. This feature links closely with their political success, for the class they supported gained political ascendancy in New Zealand. I now turn to consider those matters that operated to define and restrict the class allegiance of the New Zealand newspapers.

*1. The Class Nature of the New Zealand Settlements and the Practice of Journalism within them.*

Nineteenth century New Zealand was a society in which the divisions of social class were accepted as natural and proper. The class nature of the New Zealand press was much shaped by the intended nature of the first settlements. A majority, all but Auckland and the settlements at the Bay of Islands, were under the influence of Edward Gibbon Wakefield and were intended to be class settlements. Wakefield's objective was to reproduce in the colony the society left behind. As H.S. Chapman,

---

6 "Your petitioners therefore pray that your honourable house will be pleased to take such steps as in your wisdom may seem right, in order that Her Majesty may be moved to express her disapprobation of the conduct pursued by his Excellency, the Governor".
(*Nelson Examiner and New Zealand Chronicle,* 15 June 1844)

## The Crown Colony Government Period

Wakefield's friend and editor of the *New Zealand Journal*, phrased the matter, "Colonization has taken the place of mere emigration; the removal of society, that of mere masses; and men of refinement and education may now emigrate, without any material disturbance of their habits".[7] Wakefield quotes approvingly Hind's essay on colonization where the announced intention is for a colony that "would fairly represent English society, and every new comer would have his own class to fall into; and to whatever class he belonged he would find its relation to the others, and the support derived from the others, much the same as in the parent country."[8] The intention was from the outset confused. The intended society owes more to Wakefield's understanding of a pre-industrial arcadia than to the England of the mid nineteenth century. Karl Marx, who devoted a chapter of *Das Kapital* to Wakefield, argued that the outcome was modern and was to manufacture wage labourers in the colony and thus to reproduce the capitalist relations of the mother country.[9]

Nor did the execution of the plan allow it to succeed. Under Wakefield's plan settlers were divided into colonists and emigrants. Colonists were land order buyers who were to become the property owning upper class in the new settlements. Emigrants were the working class settlers who were to be employed by the colonists. The plan required a high proportion of land-order buyers to move to New Zealand so as to have the desired ratio of colonists to emigrants in the settlements. Emigrants did not pay for their passage to New Zealand, the funds for this coming from the money the land-order buyers gave as payment for their New Zealand land. However, colonists, land-order buyers who did emigrate, received a 75% rebate on the purchase price so as to pay for their own passage. They thus contributed little towards the cost of transporting emigrants. There was, therefore, a need to sell land orders to absentees, buyers who had no intention of emigrating, so as to fund the passage of the labouring emigrants. The outcome was that absentees considerably outnumbered colonists and Wakefield's desired class balance never eventuated in New Zealand.

While Wakefield himself devotes little attention to the role of the press in colonies, both he and the intending settlers saw a settlement newspaper as a desirable, if not essential, part of settlement. New

---

7  *The Quarterly Review*, 1841, Quoted in Turnbull (1959) p. 67.
8  E.G. Wakefield, (1914), p.114.
9  Marx, (1954), Vol.1, Chapter 33.

Plymouth was without a newspaper and the first Otago newspaper was begun in opposition to the Scottish and Presbyterian nature of that settlement. But in Wellington, Nelson and Canterbury the first newspapers received assistance from the founding associations and were conceived as aids to the successful establishment of the settlements. They were intended to maintain civilization with much of this lofty notion being regarded in terms of a continuation of an existing system of stratification. The point is well made in a quote from De Tocqueville's *Democracy in America* which, for many years, the *Nelson Examiner* published at the start of its leading articles.

> Journals become more necessary as men become more equal and individualism more to be feared. It would be to underrate their importance to suppose that they serve only to secure liberty; they maintain civilization.

The first New Zealand newspapers were considered to be public leaders with their writers needing a combination of ability and integrity which made newspaper work a matter of high public service.

> ... whilst a public press ... represents the public voice, it also acts directly and immediately as the teacher and guide of public opinion; and this action is powerful or feeble, according to the ability, beneficial or hurtful, according to the integrity and conscientiousness with which the task is performed.
> (*Lyttelton Times*, 11 January 1851)

This viewpoint is epitomised in the first editorial of the *Nelson Examiner* where, in the finest of the opening statements of the settlement newspapers, journalistic responsibilities take on the stature of a sacred trust.

> The office of a journal is to bind together by the ties of a common interest the various elements of a society; to awaken when supine, and to maintain when active, the habit of working in common for a common end; to remind men of what, as good citizens, they owe to the community; to remind them that, in the conduct of public business, they are bound to combine their influence, so that each may join his strength to the strength of all; jealously to watch for the earliest indication of apathy respecting the common good; to appeal to the nobler sympathies of men against the highest tone of sentiment; to encourage,

awaken and defend all tendencies to improvement and to good; to censure boldly and inflexibly every neglect or violation of honour, justice, and public faith; to impress upon our fellow colonists that success depends on the energy with which we strive to render industry most productive and capital most abundant; to uphold the necessity for local government and national representation; to assert the independence, to maintain the character, and to spread the influence of the press; to aid in the progression of society, and to be in charity with all. These are the legitimate functions of the press in a free country, but most in a community like this. We shall, to the best of our ability, endeavour to discharge them honestly.
(*Nelson Examiner and New Zealand Chronicle*, 12 March 1842)

Herron has noted that the English tradition where the educated, leisured classes had a duty to engage in politics was not lightly cast aside in New Zealand.[10] Such thoughts as those quoted above meant that in New Zealand journalism also came to be included among those activities which the educated considered to be not only their duty but also befitting their rank. In the utopian vision shared especially by the higher ranking settlers to the Wakefield settlements journalism was accorded a purpose and status which it was not granted in England. Journalistic activity was continued by such people because of its politically active nature but in New Zealand it was the understanding of a moral duty that first gave it acceptability. In the England from which they had migrated newspaper journalism had little respectability and less prestige; in New Zealand such work came to be the preserve of the higher ranking settlers who saw it as a combination of public service and political activity.

Auckland was the major settlement not begun under the influence of Edward Gibbon Wakefield. But, no less than its southern counterparts, Auckland shared the general nineteenth century European view of the propriety of the divisions of social class. And in Auckland, as elsewhere, an upper class became dominant. Similarly, Auckland shared with the southern settlements the attitude towards journalism as being a political activity worthy of the would-be settlement leaders.

---

10 (1959a), p.339.

*The Making of the New Zealand Press*

## 2. Price

While the class nature of the settlements influenced the newspapers the newspapers were also to be restricted to the more wealthy settlers purely by their cost. The price of the New Zealand newspapers, before the advent of the penny press, was high. There were variations but they were few. The two founding newspapers, the *New Zealand Gazette* in Wellington and the *New Zealand Advertiser* in Russell, both had a subscription price of 40s per annum payable in advance or 1s a single issue. This pricing structure was generally followed by the other newspapers though some, such as the *Auckland Standard*, allowed subscriptions by the quarter at 10s payable in advance.

Most of the variations in price came with changes in the frequency of appearance. But newspapers remained expensive. Most of the papers began with weekly publication. The *Auckland Times* started with twice weekly publication, and a price to match (15s a quarter or 1s a single issue) but kept to this only during its short period of use of the Government press. The Mangle and subsequent issues were published weekly. The *Otago News* began as a fortnightly but was a weekly from 9 June 1849 at the colony's lowest subscription price of 22/6 per annum or 6d. a single issue.

The Otago, Canterbury and Nelson newspapers, without competition, remained as weeklies while the Auckland and Wellington newspapers soon moved to twice weekly publication. The *New Zealand Gazette* in Wellington led the way, on 20 October 1841, preceeding the *New Zealand Herald* in Auckland by a mere four days. With this change the *Gazette* retained its 40s per annum subscription rate and halved the price of a single issue to 6d. It was the first newspaper to introduce this lower price. The *New Zealand Herald* changed its rates from 40s per annum subscription and 1s per single issue to 15s per quarter subscription and 9d per single issue.

These subscription rates represented a substantial fraction of the wages received by the majority of settlers. 1846 wages for labour were, for example, recorded as follows:

"Domestic, per annum with board and lodging, £14 to £20
Predial, per annum with board and lodging, £25 to £45
Trades, per diem, 5s to 7s."[11]

---

11  Grimstone, (1847), p.57.

An annual subscription to a newspaper, thus, would represent from one to two weeks wages for a tradesman and the money that a domestic would receive over approximately six weeks. In such circumstances price alone was sufficient to prevent the majority of settlers from being newspaper subscribers.

*3. The Cost of Establishing and Maintaining Newspapers*

The first New Zealand newspapers were not, in comparison with contemporary English newspapers, particularly expensive businesses to found. In an age when a high circulation daily press was becoming dominant in other countries, with a general change to the technology associated with the steam press, the cost of establishing a newspaper had risen, in England, from the £2000 to £5000 needed in 1790-1820 to £30,000 to £50,000 in the 1830s and on to six figures in the 1840s. In New Zealand, however, the older technology of iron framed, hand operated presses printing one side of the paper and capable of around 250 impressions per hour was sufficient. This technology was not expensive being readily available second-hand in Britain, Europe and the United States. After the difficult first few years it was increasingly available in New Zealand with hand operated presses being made in Australia as early as 1842.[12]

But the question of expense is relative. In New Zealand the establishment of a newspaper was considered financially onerous. The first New Zealand newspapers, with one possible exception, were not financially successful. The establishment and continuation of a newspaper was to be restricted to those who could afford the cost. These were men either of a wealthy background or beginning other businesses able to subsidise their journalistic activities.

**Auckland**

The *New Zealand Herald and Auckland Gazette* was set up for £600, the nominal capital being £3000 made up of £10 shares. The shares were issued on £2 deposit with the balance on call. The shareholding was largely among officials of the Crown Colony Government who, among other intentions, hoped to profit by their investment. The company should have been financially secure for it immediately obtained the Government printing contract. However the company experienced considerable monetary difficulties and, by the end of 1841, within six

---

12  See the "Sydney Extracts" in *Auckland Standard*, 22 August 1842.

months of commencement, all the money on call had been summoned. The difficulties of the company were illustrated in a balance sheet published on 27 November 1841 which indicated there was a total of £1398 in unpaid debts owing to the company. This was to be a continuing feature of all the early newspapers. The paucity of the white population meant that circulations were tiny. The general shortage of cash throughout the colony meant that even these few subscriptions were to include a high proportion of unpaid accounts. When the *Herald* was closed down in April 1842 the plant, land and buildings were purchased by Hobson for his Administration for £1425; a high price but one representing a considerable loss for the shareholders.

The three subsequent Auckland newspapers, the *Standard*, the *Times,* and the *Chronicle* were mainly printed on the Administration press. None of them, therefore, had high establishment costs but neither had they the return from a printing business to offset their losses. The financial status of all three is unknown. Circulation rates for all were probably low. Circulation rates for the early New Zealand papers are difficult to determine as proprietors were not required to publish them and generally preferred to keep them secret. The best indication of circulation for the mid-1840s is given by an unsigned but probably authentic document from the Auckland Old Colonists' Museum. This lists nine of the Colony's newspapers. Circulations given range from 100 to 300.

The next two Auckland newspapers, the *Southern Cross* and the *New Zealander,* were the first long standing newspapers in that city. Both of them were linked with printing establishments. In both cases the printing house was financially successful while the newspaper was a losing concern. The circulation rates of both papers are unknown.

The *Southern Cross* was owned by William Brown but, as we have seen, the financial establishment of the newspaper owed much to the first editor, Samuel Martin, the editor dismissed from the *Auckland Herald*. Brown, however, provided the continuing financial backing for the newspaper. He is recorded by Hocken, who had the advantage of extensive interviews with Logan Campbell, Brown's partner, as losing £10,000 on the *Southern Cross* during his ownership which lasted from the beginning until 1869.[13] However, the General Printing Office, from which the *Southern Cross* was issued, gained for Brown a financial

---

13 (1901), p.112.

return in keeping with the general success enjoyed by the other commercial concerns of Brown and Campbell.

The *New Zealander* was begun in 1845 by John Williamson, a printer who had arrived in Auckland in 1841 under engagement to the parent company of the *Herald*. In January 1848 he made a partner in William Chisholm Wilson, another printer who had also come to Auckland in 1841 to work on the *Herald*. These two began a general printing business and met with considerable success. The pro Grey policy of the *New Zealander* won them official support and Williamson and Wilson became the Government Printers. The printing establishment quickly became large and successful. The partners constructed the first gas works in Auckland at the rear of the printing office, to supply it with gas. They introduced the first printing machine into New Zealand, a "Caxton" by Myers, of Southhampton. They also introduced the first news folding machine and imported a complete lithographic plant with which they produced mining plans, show cards and labels. While Williamson and Wilson were prosperous as printers, there is nothing from the scant evidence available to suggest that the newspaper also enjoyed financial success. Almost certainly it was, like the *Southern Cross,* a losing concern carried by the rest of the business.

**Wellington**

In the case of the *Wellington Gazette,* sales in the first year did not exceed 110 copies per issue and this included 20 copies bought by Colonel Wakefield.[14] Eventually the circulation more than doubled that but, by its final year, Revans argued the newspaper "ran at an annual loss of some hundreds of pounds" while his printing establishment was "worth about £700 a year."[15] A successful printing establishment was carrying a low circulation and unremunerative newspaper. Revans also had other business concerns, being a landowner as well as establishing a wood yard, a meat company and becoming a director of the Steam Saw Mill Company.

The second paper, the *Colonist,* was not part of any wider business establishment but was an independent company, the first established in Wellington. It was expected to be self supporting and was closed down when it failed to be so. It represented a new way of establishing a

---

14 The first Wellington edition, however, that of 18 April 1840, sold all 400 copies printed plus a reprinting of a further 150 copies.

15 Burns (1957), Vol. 2, p.7.

newspaper being a cooperative effort by fifty settlers who contributed £5 each to establish the paper. After five months a call of 20s per share had to be declared. In the final issue the shareholders announced their intention of suspending the paper "for the present", citing the financial difficulties faced by the paper as the reason for closure.[16]

The other two Wellington newspapers of the Crown Colony Government years, the *Spectator* and the *Independent*, were both, after initial periods of instability, to become long-lasting newspapers attached to and supported by printing businesses.

The *Spectator*, like the *Colonist* a cooperative effort, published reports of the bi-annual meetings of its managing committee. For the first two years there is, then, a record of the paper's finances. The paper ran at a loss with a subscription list of somewhat less than 150. It was printed on the press used previously by the *Gazette*. and the printing of the paper came under the control of Robert Stokes, After the purchase of the printing press and plant he took on the business and became a full time printer.

In September 1846, two years after the paper began, the *Spectator* committee resigned. They cited their satisfaction with Grey's Governorship and thus did not see a need to continue their vigilance. They were also happy to be done with the financial inconvenience and the incurring of personal odium that was associated with the management of the paper.[17]

The newspaper appears to have been given to Stokes who then became proprietor, editor and printer. While at times breaking even, the paper was no success financially and Stokes's living was gained through the printing business. Here, he was aided by his newspaper's policy; the pro-Grey attitude of the *Spectator* earning him many printing contracts with the Government.

The *Independent*, begun by the printers of the *Spectator* when the *Spectator* committee dispensed with their services, was, at least initially, under considerable financial strain. More than once the printers who controlled the paper offered to work on a barter system.

> The Committee of the *Independent* beg to announce to parties cultivating land in the bush, that they are willing to take produce of any description in payment for their journal.

---

16 *New Zealand Colonist and Port Nicholson Advertiser*, 2 August 1843.
17 *New Zealand spectator and Cook's Straits Guardian*, 23 September 1846.

(*Wellington Independent,* 10 May 1845, reprinted 18 June 1845, 16 July 1845)

After being suspended from August to November 1845, new plant and a printing press were obtained from Sydney and the paper reappeared, attached to a new printing business. Rivalry between the two Wellington newspapers was understandably the most intense in the country and led to a notable decrease in advertising rates and prices for single copies of a newspaper. Both papers had begun with the same subscription and advertising rates as the *Gazette*. These rates, which were high, were generally comparable throughout the country. The subscription rates were 40s per year or 1s per single copy.

*Advertising rates were:*

| | |
|---|---|
| 1 to 6 lines: | 3/6 for first insertion and 1s for each subsequent insertion. |
| 6 to 10 lines: | 5s for first insertion and 1/6 for each subsequent insertion |
| Over 10 lines: | 5s for first 10 lines and 4d per line for the rest, for the first insertion. 2d per line for each subsequent insertion. |

By May 1846, with the *Independent* leading the way, both papers had increased their frequency to bi-weekly appearances with subscription rates unchanged. Single copies were down to 6d. each. All advertisements were priced at 3d per line for the first and 1d per line for subsequent insertions.

The *Independent*, like the *Spectator*, was not a prosperous concern and the proprietors' financial return was gained through their printing business. The business was extended to cover other commercial concerns. Most notably it also served as a land agency.

## Nelson

Whether the *Nelson Examiner* was or was not a financially successful newspaper is uncertain. The document in the Old Colonists' Museum records its mid-1840s circulation at 200. With 200 subscriptions prosperity is doubtful. But the Elliott brothers were not reliant on the newspaper for a living. They had a printing establishment which also served as office for a variety of commercial activities. They opened a circulating library and a trading establishment and were agents for several absentee landowners as well as themselves acquiring a run in the Wairau.

## Otago

Details of finance and circulation for the first Otago newspaper are unknown. Henry Graham, prior to departing from England appears to have received encouragement, and perhaps assistance from John McGlashan, Secretary of the Otago Association.[18] Any such assistance was, however, lost once Graham found himself at odds in Otago with Captain Cargill, the leader of the settlement. Graham had a subscription list of 50 when he issued his prospectus on 24 November 1848, and his circulation could not have climbed much above that. Nor was financial success available to the next Otago newspaper, the *Witness*. It had a mere 120 subscribers in its early days and by the end of 1855 it had risen to only 210.

The *Otago Witness* was begun after the printing press and plant used by the Otago News were purchased. The *Witness* also began as a cooperative effort by settlers though £150 of the £200 raised was paid by one settler, W.H. Valpy, one of the leading landowners. The lack of financial success coupled with the tempestuous nature of contemporary journalism tired the shareholders. In the newspaper's second year they presented the paper and plant to William Cutten, the editor.

Cutten was not dependent on the *Witness* being financially successful. He had been appointed Immigration Agent for the province and received £100 per year from that source. He was also an auctioneer and merchant with a growing business. To this was now added a printing establishment and job printing became a further commercial activity for Cutten.

## Canterbury

The details of the *Lyttelton Times*, the first Canterbury newspaper, are somewhat clearer. The principal financial backer was Ingram Shrimpton, an Oxford printer and member of the Canterbury Association. Shrimpton invested around £2500 to establish the paper in Lyttelton with machinery and type and a year's supply of paper and ink. The costs included

---

18 "The importance of a Printing Press I consider so great that I felt authorised to assure him that the Trustees for Religious and Educational Uses would do all in their power for him, and upon the faith of this assurance he goes out." Letter from MacGlashan to Cargill, 1 May 1848, quoted in McLintock (1949), p.274.

## The Crown Colony Government Period

equipment beyond the needs of the newspaper. Notably the plant included three presses, a Columbia for engraving, an Atlas for fancy printing and a Stanhope to print the newspaper. Shrimpton did not emigrate until 1854 but did send a foreman and a compositor as well as persuading his son and nephew to go out as cadets.

The printing business, at least, was sound and prosperous. In 1856, when Shrimpton sold out he received £5000 for the copyright to the *Lyttelton Times* and the lease of property and plant for twenty years. The newspaper's circulation is unrecorded. It is possible, however, that the newspaper itself was also profitable, with a circulation, because of English subscriptions, considerably higher than the rest of the New Zealand newspapers. Shrimpton's nephew, George Taylor, who operated the press for the *Lyttelton Times* is recorded as stating Shrimpton obtained guaranteed English subscriptions before undertaking responsibility for the newspaper. Shrimpton "represented so forcibly the impossibility of undertaking the responsibility without some guarantee that, ultimately, the members of the Committee [of the Canterbury Association in London prior to the first four ships departing] and some other members of the Association agreed to become subscribers for 1000 copies of each issue of the paper during its first year, the subscription being 21s per annum."[19] Though there would presumably be considerable non-renewal of subscriptions, if the *Lyttelton Times* did begin with so large a number of subscribers, it would have been the single profitable New Zealand newspaper of the period.

One result of the tempestuous circumstances and general lack of profitability throughout New Zealand was the tendency for newspapers to be owned by single individuals, or at most partnerships rather than by joint stock companies.[20] Meiklejohn discusses this in regard to Auckland where he argues that subsequent ownership patterns in the Auckland press were influenced by the Crown Colony Government's repressive tactics in the early 1840s.

> In the capital and at the Bay of Islands, in 1842, were all the men who were to achieve prominence as newspaper proprietors in Auckland for many years to come. John Williamson, of the

---

19 *Christchurch Times*, 29 June 1935, Souvenir Supplement.
20 Genuine joint stock companies were not possible until the passage of the Companies Act of 1860. I, and Meikeljohn, refer here to newspapers funded by shares purchased by a number of settlers.

*New Zealander;* William Brown and John Logan-Campbell, of the *Southern Cross;* William Chisholm Wilson, of the *New Zealand Herald;* and James Busby, of the *Aucklander.* In a period of less than two years they had seen the failure of three newspaper ventures, all founded by joint stock companies. ... The inference appeared to be that popular ownership of the press was a source, not of strength, but of weakness. The alternative was newspapers owned and controlled by single individuals or by partnerships. Not for more than a quarter of a century long after the first steps had been taken towards the establishment of responsible government was the public again invited to participate in the ownership of a major newspaper in the northern part of New Zealand.[21]

While there is some force in Meiklejohn's argument it must also be noted that after the demise of the *Standard* in 1842 the Auckland press, with its individual or partnership patterns, was merely coming into line with what was to be the usual practice elsewhere in New Zealand. Joint stock companies were also tried among the southern papers where the alternative to individual ownership was newspapers financed by shares held by a number of colonists and managed by an elected committee. This occurred with the *Otago Witness* and the Wellington papers, the *Spectator* and the *Colonist.* The *Colonist* was soon closed. With the *Witness* and the *Spectator,* shareholders and committee members tired of an unprofitable and tempestuous involvement and the papers were presented to single individuals who then each continued as editor and sole proprietor. Collective ownership, where it was tried, was to be a short-lived phenomenon in all New Zealand centres until the larger scale newspapers of the 1860's, with their larger financial requirements, made it a practical necessity.

The men who owned the various newspapers of the Crown Colony Government years were high status settlers (in New Zealand Company terms they were colonists as opposed to emigrants) in the process of building up commercial concerns. In spite of their small scale on an international comparison, the New Zealand newspapers were regarded locally as substantial undertakings and often represented the start of what were to become big businesses. The commencement of the various newspapers, along with the printing and other trading establishments

---

21 p.114.

associated with them, was itself an important initial aspect of commercial development in New Zealand. However, as is particularly indicated by those newspaper concerns that were given away, they were also seen as unprofitable and troublesome undertakings. Newspaper proprietors ran enterprises that had tired many of their fellows. The proprietors hoped eventually to profit financially from their newspaper investment and most did prosper from their allied activity. Cynically, newspaper production could be viewed as the price that had to be paid so as to have access to a profitable printing establishment. But more charitably it must be acknowledged that newspaper proprietors viewed their activity as worthwhile community work. They saw their newspapers as necessary for the efficient continuation of the settlements and as advocates for what those settlements should become. They viewed their labour as a public service performed out of duty.

## 4. The Voluntary Nature of Newspaper Work

As a consequence of the generally unprofitable nature of journalism the staff of the newspapers were also often unpaid. There was a division between the editorial and manual aspects of newspaper work with the manual work being more commonly paid employment. Editorial involvement was more commonly unpaid and this worked to restrict such involvement to those settlers who could afford to engage in unremunerated activity.

Many proprietors were competent printers but only Henry Graham of the *Otago News* worked entirely without a staff, doing all the editorial and printing work himself. Most employed compositors and press men with both the production of the newspaper and job printing being part of the duties required. While proprietors did assist in the manual work associated with the production of their newspapers, there was from the beginning a generally accepted division of labour between the editorial and manual areas of newspaper work. The proprietors, who were themselves so often competent compositors and press men, were the major exception to this division of labour but they also gradually specialized and came to concentrate their attention on the editorial side. While there was this division of labour a professional approach to work did not necessarily follow. The following quotation is unusually frank but is representative of a general acceptance that, in New Zealand, standards set elsewhere could not always be applied.

## The Making of the New Zealand Press

> We are in a young colony, and printers will at times get drunk as well as ill, and at these periods our paper cannot be turned off in that workmanlike style that we could wish.
> (*New Zealand Herald and Auckland Gazette*, 22 January 1842)

On the editorial side of newspaper production there was an initial intention to pay journalists but within a few years such work became voluntary. The financial status of the New Zealand newspapers was so precarious that payment for editorial involvement became regarded as inappropriate.

There is no record of a salary being paid to Charles Terry, William Corbett or Dr Samuel Martin, the three men who successively edited the *New Zealand Herald and Auckland Gazette*. But as Martin, the final editor, successfully sued for the balance of his contract after the paper was closed down, it is possible to assume he and the other two were paid editors. In Wellington, Samuel Revans, proprietor of the *Gazette,* edited the paper himself in 1840 and 1841. J.T. Wicksteed edited the paper at a salary of £150 per year but remained in the position only for a few months in early 1842. He was succeeded for, at most, ten months by Dr Frederick Knox who was also paid. George White, the third editor until he was fired for his editorial on the Wairau Massacre, was presumably also paid. William Fox succeeded White, editing the paper from July to September 1843. The final editor is unknown. Nor is it known whether Fox and the final editor received a salary.

These two newspapers seem to be the only two to have paid their editors. In Auckland there is no record of the editors of the *Chronicle* being paid. William Swainson was Attorney-General while editing the *Standard* and his editorship was accepted as part of his official duties. Henry Falwasser edited his own unprofitable *Auckland Times*. The *Southern Cross* was edited without pay by Samuel Martin and then Charles Terry, before Logan Campbell suspended the paper. When Brown restarted it he edited the paper himself until 1849 to be followed by the unpaid Hugh Carleton. The editorship of the *New Zealander* was similarly unpaid. Not all the editors are known but they include Thomas Forsaith, Hugh Carleton and Dr John Bennett. In Wellington, R.D. Hanson was the unpaid editor of the *Colonist* during its year of publication. The two long lasting Wellington papers both had longterm and unpaid editors with Robert Stokes, the eventual proprietor, editing his *Spectator,* and the *Independent* being under the editorial control of Dr Isaac Featherston.

## The Crown Colony Government Period

Not all the editors of the *Nelson Examiner* are known. The first four were George Rycroft Richardson, Francis Jollie and Alfred Domett as well as Charles Elliott, the proprietor. Other editors and contributors included Francis Dillon Bell, Edward Stafford, and William Fox. Again contributors and the editors were unpaid. This was not always the intention. Domett, for example, was to have been paid a guinea a week but did not receive this salary. In Otago, both Henry Graham and William Cutten were proprietor editors. In Canterbury, J.E. FitzGerald edited the *Lyttelton Times* from the beginning until 1853. Again the work was voluntary.

There was with the first newspapers in Wellington and Auckland an attempt to continue in New Zealand a pattern that had emerged in England in the early nineteenth century; that of paying editors and other editorial staff who then became salaried employees. This was soon abandoned. Editorial staff in New Zealand newspapers became men involved in journalism not for pay but because of their belief in the worth of their involvement. A similar pattern also applies to those who were contributors to newspapers. Again there was a general inability to pay contributors and there grew an acceptance that such work was of a voluntary nature.

This voluntary nature of journalism had a major implication concerning the management of newspapers. While the proprietors retained overall control of their newspapers they are not to be seen as employers directing the activity of their employees. Rather, the production of a newspaper was an activity shared, often, by many individuals who were all concerned about and who all contributed to the editorial content and general policy of the newspaper.

The unprofitable nature of the early newspapers combined with the value accorded to journalism as a public duty served to limit involvement in journalism to the higher ranking settlers. Not only was such work considered appropriate for men of their social position but they were the only people who could afford to engage in activity which offered no financial return. The result of this was that, during a period when in other countries journalism was becoming an employee profession, New Zealand newspapers came to be controlled by a group of men who embraced journalism without regard to financial remuneration. This is not to say that they were unaware of the financial possibilities latent within journalism. FitzGerald of the *Lyttelton Times,* for instance, was absorbed with thoughts of the livelihood to be made from the business,

*The Making of the New Zealand Press*

and William Brown, one of the more successful Auckland merchants, was certainly aware of the use he and his partner Campbell could make of the advertising columns of the *Southern Cross*. But FitzGerald remained impecunious and the *Southern Cross*, unlike Brown's trading concerns, did not return a profit. While there was a profit to be made in businesses associated with journalism, especially that of job printing, the publication of newspapers was not only unremunerative but costly. Fortunately, the settlement understanding of journalism as an activity of public service meant those involved in journalism need scarcely expect payment for the performance of such a task. Their appreciation of their task gave themselves a higher purpose.

**Crown Colony Government Journalism**

When the first newspapers began in New Zealand, they began under one of two dominating influences; the Crown Colony Government in the north or the New Zealand Company in the south. While relationships between the New Zealand Company and the newspapers of Wellington and Nelson were relatively amicable, the same cannot be said of the situation in the north concerning relationships between the Crown Colony Government and the newspapers of Russell and Auckland. These relationships were soon characterized by mutual mistrust and antagonism. But, even in the south, the interests of the press, or of those settlers who controlled the press, became distinct from the interests of the New Zealand Company.

The Crown Colony Government was the officially recognized political and administrative authority in New Zealand but the press, with the exception of the *New Zealander* in Auckland and the *Spectator* in Wellington which, after the arrival of Governor Grey, came to support the Crown Colony Government, became a resident landowners' advocate. It was distinct from the Government both in terms of ownership and policy. Initially there were close links between press ownership and the Crown Colony Government. These links had, by the mid 1840s, been terminated and, as ownership of the press becamne separated from the Crown Colony Government, so did press policy. Press policy became that of doing all possible to force the pace towards self-government and the ending of the Crown Colony Government system.

There began during the period of Crown Colony Government, a marked political purpose to journalism. Those men who led the movement towards self government chose journalism as the activity in which they could best publicize their endeavours. The newspapers were not the only means of advocacy for self government. Towards the end of the Crown Colony Government period the internal agitation for self-government was led by the various constitutional associations. But in each case the association was supported and given voice by a local paper. Generally the journalists were major figures in their local constitutional association and it was their coordination which linked the associations. In the absence of elected political representation the press became the political voice of the colony and the journalists the *de facto* political representatives.

Reeves was to call "an oligarchy" that group which ruled New Zealand from 1853 to the advent in 1890 of the Liberal Government and he was to describe this oligarchy as "a minority who, possessing better education and on the whole more knowledge and ability possessing, too, land, money and the control of commerce and the professions ruled the country."[22] Whereas journalism was not always considered a proper activity for men of such rank in the England from which they had migrated, their entry into it in New Zealand had been inevitable in terms of the high value the colonists accorded to journalism. The mere fact that newspapers were established so early in the history of different settlements with, in some instances, the first issues being published within weeks of the first arrival of colonist ships, attests to the importance in which they were held in the plans for the nascent communities. Particularly in the southern settlements, newspapers were an essential component of the utopian vision shared by the colonists. The newspaper's practical ability to spread news and offer advertising space was always recognized, but of first importance was what was argued to be its aid to "the development of civilization" in the new colony. An ideological dimension to the power of the newspaper press was early recognised. New Zealand in general and each settlement in particular was seen as a society in the process of becoming. Colonists saw the newspaper press as an important instrument to ensure the future would be one compatible with their values and ambitions. This is a view that sees the press as not only actively involved in the pursuits of a nation but also providing direction to and leadership in those pursuits. This moral purpose given to the press is not peculiar to the first New Zealand Company settlements. The later settlements also shared it. This view, of the press as an instrument of civilization, shared in common by the New Zealand

---
22 (1898), p.271.

settlements, ensured, at least at the start, that men who entered into journalism were drawn from those upper echelons of society from which later would emerge the political rulers of the country. There was no social barrier inhibiting the political careers of journalists in New Zealand.

The economic history of the newspaper in New Zealand in the 1840-1880 period may conveniently be analysed as having two phases, the second being introduced with the start of the *Otago Daily Times* in 1861. Until then the economic and organizational nature of newspapers was such as to restrict participation in journalism largely to the wealthy. Participation here refers to involvement ranging from ownership of newpapers, to assistance in the preparation of issues, to subscription to newspapers. The initial arrangement involved both high capital investment and high running costs and combined these with a general lack of profitability. With few exceptions, the first newspapers were among the more substantial economic concerns in the new communities. When allied with job printing, the total enterprise was often profitable but newspapers alone failed to offer a return on their initial investment. Ownership of newspapers was restricted to those who could afford the initial investment and the limited return. Participation in journalism was likewise restricted to men of independent means who were able to devote so much of their time to an economically unrewarding activity. A paid staff to cope with the manual aspects of newspaper production was a feature, but not a universal one, of the early newspapers; their association with more general printing services tended to encourage this. But work at the journalistic and editorial level was different. It was voluntary work performed, not for a salary, but for a cause. Even subscription to newspapers was similarly restricted for their cost was prohibitive to all but the financially secure.

The early newspapers began with participation and circulation restricted to an emerging upper class and were to voice the political divisions and aspirations of members of that class. Journalists' appreciation of the "higher purpose" of journalism was also consistent with their own interests and newspaper allegiance moved during the Crown Colony Government years with the changing fortunes of the men who controlled the newspapers. From the start the newspapers had taken a landowners' perspective. Witness for example, the attitude to "our labour" in Revans' editorial.[23] Even Henry Graham, the champion

---

23 Cf. p. 26 above.

of the working class, operated from a perspective of superiority. He saw himself not as a member of the working class but as its teacher.[24]

The newspapers' emphasis on matters political was strengthened by their isolation and lack of a regular news flow from outside their local settlements. This hindered the presention of new information. Instead they concentrated on being political forums. The shift in allegiance was one of movement with the newspaper controllers as they became part of the dominant, white landowning group in New Zealand. With the exception of the two papers which came to support Grey, all were allied with the resident landowners. In all the settlements were of historical rather than demographic importance. The majority of the original settlers moved on. But these settlements did have lasting influence on New Zealand, especially in the political sphere. The country was to be ruled for much of the nineteenth century by a handful of the 'gentry' from the original settlements. These men won political power after the gaining of self-government but it was during the period of the Crown Colony Government that they came to public prominence. Here the newspapers are of importance for journalistic involvement was for these men a major avenue by which they gained political prominence. Those who dominated newspaper work were upper class colonists who were politically involved and active. They led and coordinated the self-government movement and, on the success of that movement, were to be prominent among those gaining the elected political offices. Their links with the press were not curtailed after the gaining of self-government and the active political involvement of the press was to continue.

---

24 We have always considered it the special duty of the press, and more particularly of the newspaper press, to endeavour to raise the working class in the scale of civilization to draw them up to a higher standard, instead of lowering their tone to pander to traits that are to a certain extent vitiated, because derived from an impure source. (*Otago News*, 21 July 1849)

In the cause of the labourer the working man we have attempted to guard him from hidden treachery, and to act as his champion when might seemed likely to crush him. Mentally we have endeavoured to raise him to that standard which every thinking man should try to attain... (*Otago News*, 21 December 1850)

PART TWO

# GOVERNMENT AND BUSINESS —THE PRESS IN THE PROVINCIAL YEARS

# 5. The New Zealand Newspapers in the Early Provincial Period.

Self government came to New Zealand after the passage by the British Parliament of the Constitution Act of 1852. The political elections in New Zealand following from that Act were held in the different provinces between July and October 1853. These first elections were to select representatives to Provincial Councils and a General Assembly. Each province was also to elect a Superintendent. A Superintendent was recognized as the head of the Provincial Government. The General Assembly consisted of the Governor, of a Legislative Council of not less than ten members nominated by the Crown for life and of a House of Representatives of not fewer that 24 nor more than 42 members. Thirty seven men, known as Members of the House of Representatives (M.H.R.) were elected to the first General Assembly. While the constitution was a unitary one with the General Assembly supreme, in practice, especially in the 1850s and early 1860s, opinion and convenience supported a federal interpretation and the Provincial Councils dealt with a wide field of legislation.

A man could be a representative at both provincial and national level. The first General Assembly included two Superintendents and the most prominent members of the Provincial Councils. Superintendents, if not members of the House, were usually called to the Legislative Council. They and their supporters were powerful in the House. The franchise was given to all men over the age of 21 who possessed the property qualification. A man might vote in any electoral district in which he possessed a qualification.[1]

By their contemporary standards the New Zealand European settlers had a rather open francise but it was essentially non-democratic. All women were excluded. And in practice, because of inability to show individual title to land, the Maori male population was also excluded. A combination of the franchise restrictions and the allowance of plural voting gave effective control to the well-to-do. For almost forty years, until the advent of the Liberal Government in 1891, political power was to remain indisputably the preserve of men of property.

In the 1853 elections the leaders of the various Settlers' Constitutional Associations were to the fore among those winning the positions in the

---

1  Possession for six months past of a freehold of the clear value of £50 or a leasehold the lease being one of not less than three years of the clear annual value of £10, or who occupied a tenement of the annual value of £10 within the limits of a town or £5 elsewhere.

## The Early Provincial Period

new system of Government. The Settlers' Constitutional Associations had, during the Crown Colony Government period, been accepted by the settlers as their advocates and this acceptance became a major influence at the first elections. Writing specifically of the Otago Settlers' Association, McLintock has argued that when "the Constitutional Act became operative, the Association's selection of candidates for the General Assembly and the Provincial Council conferred on them a semi-official status which was a just tribute to the widespread nature of its activities".[2] Such a statement is applicable to the other settlements, all but Auckland, that had Settlers' Constitutional Associations. In each of them the political positions subject to election were won mainly by those who had been leaders in the agitation for self-government. This was of considerable consequence to the New Zealand newspapers. The Settlers' Constitutional Association leaders had also been dominant in journalism. Their gaining of the new official positions was also a process whereby those prominent in journalism now also became prominent elected office holders.

### New Zealand Newspapers and the 1853 Elections

The election results were to place the New Zealand newspapers in the remarkable position of having many of their prominent people simultaneously prominent in elected political life. Of the seven newspapers in publication at the time of the elections, only the Wellington based *New Zealand Spectator* was to be without electoral success.

With the exception of Auckland the first elections were not marked by deep divisions. For years the dominant issue had been that of self-government. Having won self-government nothing else had yet surfaced to become a major issue. The role of the newspapers in the various provinces at the first elections was largely that of a gentlemanly refereeing of a contest among allies. Broad's statement concerning the Nelson elections that "the question was mainly a personal one there being as yet no Provincial political parties, and no burning public questions",[3] is generally applicable to all the provinces but Auckland. In each settlement the resident landowners were the most powerful group and the elections were to choose which of them should become the settlement representatives. It was within this group that considerable

---

2 McLintock (1949). pp.286-87.
3 Broad (1892) p.115.

## The Making of the New Zealand Press

success was gained by those who had been prominent in the newspaper agitation against the Crown Colony Government.

In Otago, William Cutten, the proprietor and editor of the *Witness*, was elected both to the Provincial Council and the General Assembly. Added to this the Superintendency was gained by William Cargill, the father-in-law of Cutten and leader of the Otago settlement since its inception. Election to both the Provincial Council and General Assembly was also gained by James Macandrew, a merchant and landowner, who had been prominent both in the Otago Settlers' Association and in his work on the *Witness*.

In Canterbury the most prominent politician after the elections was J.E. FitzGerald, the manager and editor of the *Lyttelton Times*. He was elected to the General Assembly as well as being elected Superintendent. When the General Assembly was finally called together FitzGerald became leader of the first Administration. Charles Bowen, John Hall, W.S. Moorhouse and H.J. Tancred were all regular contributors to the *Lyttelton Times* during the agitation for self-government. They were among those elected to the Provincial Council. Moorhouse was also elected to the General Assembly.

The dominant political power in Nelson was the group of original resident land purchasers, known to themselves as the Nelson Supper Party. Less respectful members of the Nelson community dubbed them the Forty Thieves. Charles Elliott, the *Examiner* proprietor, was from this group and was himself elected to the Provincial Council. Edward Stafford, a landowner and prominent contributor to the *Examiner*, had been nominated for the Superintendency by Elliott and was the successful candidate for the position.

In Wellington, Robert Stokes, proprietor and editor of the *Spectator*, was in subsequent years to gain political office. But in 1853 the *Spectator*'s support of Governor Grey was to deny electoral success to its personnel. None of the printer-proprietors of the *Independent* were to seek political office but Isaac Featherston, leader of the Settlers' Constitutional Association and long-time editor of the *Independent*, was elected unopposed as Superintendent. He was also elected to the General Assembly as was Samuel Revans, the proprietor of the first settlement newspaper. Revans also became a member of the Provincial Council.

New Plymouth was the settlement long without a newspaper. Not until 1852, eleven years after the first settlers arrived, when an Albion press was obtained from John Williamson in Auckland, transported by bullock dray to the Manakau, and shipped to New Plymouth, did the *Taranaki Herald* make its first appearance. The paper was owned by William Collins, a recent immigrant who had been a printer in London on the *Morning Post,* and Garland Woon, who in 1852 had recently finished an apprenticeship on the *New Zealander.* Collins and Woon both had the aim of beginning a viable printing business and the *Herald* had no favourite candidate in the first elections. The initial Superintendency election was a three way contest between resident landowners, all of whom had been contributors to the paper. They were J.T. Wicksteed, one time editor of the *Wellington Gazette,* Resident Agent for the New Zealand Company in New Plymouth 1842-47, and the real inaugural editor, as opposed to nominal editor Woon, of the *Herald;* William Halse, a pro-Grey candidate who had been Resident Agent, 1848-52; and the successful candidate, Charles Brown. After the election the *Herald* became a supporter of Brown.

Only Auckland experienced rancour at the first elections. Auckland, then the New Zealand capital, came to self-government with its community "divided into two major factions: a settler group led by the merchants; and a pro official group composed of civil officers of the government, and the military, and their clients and supporters".[4] These factions had been there before self government when the two Auckland newspapers had divided their allegiance between them; the *Southern Cross* championing the settler group with William Brown, the paper's proprietor, becoming the group's most prominent member, while the *New Zealander* gave its support to Grey and the official group.

These loyalties were carried into the provincial period to be displayed at the initial Superintendency elections. William Brown and Lieutenant-Colonel R.H. Wynyard, who had been the Lieutenant Governor of New Ulster and was Commander of the troops in New Zealand, were the rival candidates. Wynyard, who took no personal part in the contest, had his campaign primarily run by Williamson in the columns of the latter's *New Zealander.* Brown naturally received the enthusiastic support of his newspaper with this support owing much to the *Southern Cross's* editor, Hugh Carleton. Carleton was a landowner who had been engaged in journalism since his arrival in Auckland in 1845. He was a contributor to the *New Zealander* and its editor for a period prior to 1848

---

4 Stone, (1980a), p.157.

when he commenced and edited the *Anglo-Maori Warder*. Williamson and Wilson were the proprietors of the *Anglo-Maori Warder* and stopped the paper after six months on account of Carleton's criticisms of Governor Grey's policies. Carleton's allegiance from this point was given to the settler group. He became editor of the *Southern Cross* in 1849 and held the position through the 1850s.

Those elected to the General Assembly from Auckland included William Brown and Hugh Carleton of the *Southern Cross* and Thomas Forsaith, a regular contributor to and past editor of the *New Zealander*. John Williamson was elected to the Provincial Council. The election for Superintendent was won by Wynyard giving supporters of Governor Grey their only victory in the various provincial superintendency elections.

It was the Auckland Superintendency election that gave the first taste in New Zealand of a vitriolic journalism that was to become widespread throughout the country. It was what could be expected when political conflict was coupled with personal involvement. The prospective merits of the candidates were strongly contested in the two newspapers. Neither side was free of invective. The intensity of feeling can be gauged from a series of attacks on Brown, published during the campaign, which became the subject of later legal action.[5]

The following are representative:

> Sale of Horses! Mr Gammon has been favoured with instructions to sell by public auction, at the "Squib Inn", the under-mentioned horses: Malice This famous steeplechaser by Mr Tom Paine's Infidelity, out of Egotism: has frequently been known to clear the turnpike gates of Decency, Truth and Fair Play, indeed nothing is too high for him; he has entered for the "Superintendency" steeplechase, or, rather, he has entered himself a circumstance never recorded of any other horse, but accounted for by the usual development of his organ of self esteem.
> (*New Zealander,* 23 April 1853)
> ... And supposing he did reach it, (the Superintendency) on what book would he be sworn into office? A correspondent of the New Zealander states, "when the census was taken, Mr Brown

---

5 Williamson and Wilson were found guilty of libel, the jury however, awarding Brown only 20s of the £1000 damages sought. See *New Zealander,* 10 September 1853.

## The Early Provincial Period

did not classify himself under any sect or denomination of Christians"; at least so I understand the letter signed Spectator. If this be the case what oath will bind him?
(*New Zealander*, 14 May 1853)

After the 1853 elections the New Zealand General Assembly and the various Provincial Councils included a large number of men who had been active in journalism prior to self-government. Many had been involved not because of a desire to be journalists. In the absence of self-government the New Zealand newspapers had been a major aspect of the colonists' political agitation and for many participants journalism had been a substitute and *de facto* political involvement. Others, whose orientation had been primarily to journalism, found that in New Zealand their occupation gave them a political prominence.

### Newspapers and Provincialism

After the elections the involvement of politicians in journalism was to continue. The advantages of the personal prominence and political support given by newspaper backing were to be recognized by all New Zealand politicians. And newspaper backing was most likely to be received by those who were personally connected with the newspaper concerned.

After the elections, however, the relationship between journalism and politics was to take a new turn. The overwhelming approval won by those who had led the agitation for self-government was not to continue. In their new role as elected politicians the new officials were the participants in the political divisions that soon surfaced in the General Assembly and Provincial Councils. The divisions were also to involve the various newspapers which soon became partisan advocates within the ongoing debates of political life. The connections between individual politicians and individual newspapers that had been forged during the agitation for self-government were now to be used to further individual political careers. Newspapers became recognized participants and forces in the political system.

While not part of the official political system as defined in the Constitution Act, newspapers were accepted as partisan supporters and each was to be recognized as the mouthpiece of a particular politician. It was this personal advocacy for a politician that was to be a major feature of the political advocacy of the newspapers in the early provincial period. Before the development of party politics either provincially or nationally, each newspaper's political linkages were usually with individual politicians. A common pattern was for a newspaper to be the advocate for a prominent politician who was simultaneously that newspaper's proprietor. During the first years of the provincial period there developed in each province a pattern of newspaper support and opposition which corresponded to, and helped publicly define, each province's major political divisions. Some newspapers had both, but all had either patterns of ownership or day to day management and control which linked them with a particular segment of the developing political divisions. During these years partisan political advocacy was every newspaper's major orientation. There were few attempts to found newspapers with a different orientation and these attempts all failed to meet with long term success.

The contemporary journalist, Richard Wakelin, has argued that the implementation of the Constitution Act brought consequent changes to the orientation of the New Zealand newspapers. Describing the Crown Colony Government period as a time when the newspapers were "bound together by common opinions, common ties and common interests" he states

> The division of the Colony into Provinces, and the official positions most of the writers for the press then acquired, put an end to all this, and from that date there were no longer any Colonial newspapers, all public questions, generally speaking, being viewed and discussed from a mere Provincial standpoint.[6]

The provincial emphasis of self-government in New Zealand ensured, as Wakelin observed, that newspaper advocacy would be from a provincial rather than national perspective, but their partisanship went beyond this. Within each province the newspapers became involved in one or other side of the provincial political conflicts. Once those with newspaper connections gained political office the newspapers acted, and were recognized in such terms, as their partisan advocates.

## Auckland

In Auckland the partisan political activity of the newspapers remained unchanged during the 1850s. There were few attempts to start newspapers in that decade and, of those that were attempted, none to offer a serious challenge to the *Southern Cross* or *New Zealander*. The

---

6   Wakelin (1877) p.92.

## The Early Provincial Period

political success of the province's newspaper personnel was notable. Wynyard, the Superintendent, was forced to resign the office in January 1855 after the Secretary of State found it incompatible with another he held, that of Acting-Governorship. For the next eight years the Superintendency rotated among the city's newspaper proprietors. Brown won the election in March 1855 but left the country later in the year and was succeeded by his partner, J. Logan Campbell, until he resigned in September 1856, also to leave New Zealand. Williamson, of the *New Zealander,* then won the election and held office until October 1862.

This journalistic prominence was also a feature at the national level. Williamson became a M.H.R. at the 1855 elections, remaining in the General Assembly until his death in 1877. Carleton, editor of the *Southern Cross* remained in the General Assembly until 1870. J. Logan Campbell, as well as succeeding his partner to the Superintendency, was also elected to succeed Brown in the General Assembly. He was there in 1855, 1856 and 1860. Thomas Forsaith, ex-editor of the *New Zealander,* was in the General Assembly of 1853-55 and 1858 60, and was the leader of the short-lived second Administration, that of 1854.

The *New Zealander* and the *Southern Cross* were integral to the political process in Auckland. Factions gathered around the rival newspapers and political attacks and defences were conducted through the pages of the two newspapers. Political support was not restricted to those, such as proprietors and editors, who had personal connections with the newspapers. All aspects of the political divisions in Auckland were within the newspapers' ambit. Thus Frederick Whitaker, Brown's opponent in the 1855 election for Superintendent, was not personally connected with the *New Zealander* but John Williamson acted as his campaign manager and the *New Zealander* as his advocate.

The emphasis the Auckland newspapers placed on partisan political activity remained supreme during the 1850s. There were attempts in that decade to bring a new focus to journalism, particularly to political journalism, and it is instructive to review these attempts.

The main attempt at innovation in Auckland was the *Auckland Examiner* which began publication in December 1856. The *Examiner's* management quarrelled both with newspaper political allegiance and the emphasis on provincialism. Its inaugural issue challenged the existing newspapers on these issues.

> A newspaper devoted exclusively to the interests, material and moral, of this colony, has long been called for by every class of

Auckland politician. What they demand, and what we aim at establishing is an organ untramelled by party ties, while thoroughly imbued with the sentiment that our Colony is ripe for a radical change in the administration of its affairs.
(*Auckland Examiner*, 11 December 1856)

The newspaper requirements of Auckland had, however, been read incorrectly and, although the *Examiner* lasted for four yours, it was due more to the perserverance of its proprietor than to any significant public support.[7] The successful new newspapers of this period are those which began, not as independent entities, but as the voices of political opponents to the faction supported by the existing paper.

In Auckland two further attempts to start newspapers were made, both in 1859. They were the *Telegraph* in September and the *Independent* in October. They survived five and three months respectively. A full run of the *Independent* is in existence but no copies of the *Telegraph* remain. Judging from the welcome extended to the *Telegraph* by the *Independent*, the two were allied publications.

The *Independent* was owned, printed and probably edited by John Moore. Moore, one of the more colourful figures in New Zealand journalism, was first in Auckland in 1841 when he became the printer for the Auckland Newspaper and General Printing Company. He had thus been the printer for the first five newspapers in Auckland. During this time he had been convicted of assaulting a rival printer and tried but acquitted on a charge of theft of type. Moore had left Auckland but returned to found the *Independent*. The *Independent* was published bi-weekly and, like the *Examiner*, aimed to be independent of political affiliation. It was accused, mainly by the *Examiner*, of being started to advance Roman Catholicism, but this was always denied.

> The principle that we advocated at our advent has been scrupulously adhered to. Neither party in politics or sect in religion has been endorsed by our advocacy.
> (*Auckland Independent*, 29 December 1859)

The paper came to a sudden close on January 2, 1860. No hint was given of its ending, in fact a statement in the final issue indicated the paper was a living concern.

---

7   Charles Southwell, the proprietor, was no stranger to negative reactions to his journalistic endeavours, having been imprisoned in England for a blasphemy he published there. Southwell died in August 1860. His paper lived for five more months.

*The Early Provincial Period*

> We have been guilty of the presumption of quaking twice a week, for 14 weeks, and yet we still survive the growls of our neighbours who kindly advised us to be quiet, that there was no room for an *Independent*. We have made room, and we have no reason to be dissatisfied with our accommodation from the public.
>
> (*Auckland Independent*, 2 January 1860)

One suspects that the sudden end of the *Independent* would have much to do with articles published in the *Examiner* that accused Moore of being the J.J. Moore who had the previous year decamped from Melbourne with some six or seven hundred pounds worth of stolen type.

None of the attempts in Auckland to begin new newspapers were successful. The two that lasted through the decade, the *New Zealander* and the *Southern Cross*, were those that had been closely linked with political factions in Auckland and which did not pretend to any political independence.

**Taranaki**

In Taranaki two main political factions were to emerge and they were each to be supported by a newspaper. After the 1853 elections the *Taranaki Herald*, which during the campaign had not favoured any one of the three Superintendency candidates, gave its support to the winner, Charles Brown. In the campaign for the second Superintendency elections in 1857, however, the support of the *Herald* was withdrawn from Brown and given to his opponent, George Cutfield, who won the election. Charles Brown made plans to begin an opposition paper and the first issue of the *Taranaki News*, of which Brown was the principal proprietor, appeared on 14 May 1857. The editor, Richard Pheney, was the ex-editor of the Herald who had resigned in protest at the *Herald's* policy change prior to the 1856 elections. With the support of his *News*, Brown ran successfully for Superintendent at the next election, which was in 1861, and held the post to 1865.

The editorial comments of the *Herald* on the occasion of Pheney's resignation are of interest:

> It has always been our desire that our paper should be the organ of public opinion: that it has not been so has been to us a matter of unfeigned regret. Finding that the *Herald* would

soon degenerate into literally an official paper, we have resolved to seek other literary assistance to ensure an impartial and honest discussion of public affairs.[8]

The fear that the *Herald* was becoming "an official paper", a mouthpiece for the Superintendent and his party, is a pertinent observation. But it is a statement that can be made in general of the New Zealand papers during the 1850s. They all, within their provinces, were advocates for one or other of the political factions. The *Herald*'s editorial comments are somewhat misleading in that rather than aiming for "an impartial... discussion of public affairs" it is more correct to see that paper as changing allegiance from one provincial faction to another. Both of the Taranaki papers were political advocates.

The establishment of the *Taranaki News*, the second New Plymouth newspaper, is an instance of a pattern that was to occur in all the other provinces that had only one newspaper. In all of them second newspapers were started by political opponents of the politicians supported by the existing newspaper. In each province press advocacy and opposition became an integral and powerful component of the political system.

**Wellington**

Wellington, like Auckland, came to self-government with two established newspapers, one of which, the *Spectator,* supported Governor Grey, while the *Independent* was among his most effective critics. Wellington, like Auckland, was divided into two political camps, with the opposing views having been in existence since soon after the formation of the settlement. While the proprietors of the two newspapers were never themselves leading political personalities, their newspapers clearly stood as mouthpieces for the rival groups. The first elections had resulted in an overwhelming victory for the Constitutionalists, those who had agitated for self-government. This group was led by Isaac Featherston and the *Independent* championed Featherston during his long tenure of the Superintendency. Prior to self-government the *Spectator* had been the voice of the Wellington pro-official group which had supported the Crown Colony Government. After self-government this group formed the Wellington party under the leadership of Edward Jerningham Wakefield. The *Spectator* became their advocate. While Featherston was not to be ousted from the Superintendency, the

---

8 Quoted in Scholefield, (1958), p.130.

## The Early Provincial Period

Wellington party was not without success and, in the 1857 election was to win a majority on the Provincial Council. The deadlock thus created between Featherston and his Executive on the one hand and the Provincial Council on the other was not settled until 1861 when Featherston and his allies were successful in that year's election.

As the political trials became closely contested so did the newspaper advocacy for the opposing camps became more strident. The two newspapers were to show progressive disregard for both electoral niceties and the canons of taste. This first became apparent in 1856 when the election of Samuel Skey, an opponent of Featherston, to the Provincial Council in 1856 prompted the *Independent* to publish the names of all who voted for Skey. The *Spectator* in spite of branding this practice an attempt "to intimidate voters from exercising their electoral franchise according to their conscience and judgement, by the threat of publicity...", followed suit by publishing, in the form of a letter from E.J. Wakefield, the names of those who had voted for Skey's opponent.[9]

The debate between the two factions, the Rowdies and the Feather-my-nest party as they insultingly labelled each other, was bitter and unrelieved. The condemnation of them by Puseley, a contemporary visitor to New Zealand, is not without justification. "The local (Wellington) press, which comprises a couple of newspapers, may be pronounced the worst conducted in the colony. Indeed the press and the acrimony of the people are typical of each other, while both are as bad as anything in a civilised country can be."[10] Puseley, however, had merely struck Wellington at a time of particular political conflict. The other centres were equally capable of invective.

In Wellington no competitors challenged the *Spectator* and *Independent* from 1845 to 1859. In that year began a new type of newspaper, one that was to be given away but was designed to gain its revenue from advertising. This paper was the *New Zealand Advertiser*, whose proprietors were Joseph and Edward Bull and Charles and Edward Roe. Joseph Bull, the printer, had arrived from Dublin, where he had practised his trade. Edward Roe, who was editor, was the man who had worked on the *Gazette,* eventually becoming its printer, and who had been the first printer and a co-proprietor of the *Independent*. No price was to be charged. It was to be published bi-weekly with a guaranteed circulation of 2000 per week. Presumably 1000 copies of

9   *New Zealand Spectator and Cook's Straits Guardian,* 25 October 1856.
10  Puseley (1858), p.317.

each issue were printed. The advertising rates were 3d per line for the first, and 1d per line for subsequent insertions. The paper promised to be largely an advertising sheet with no intention of entering the weightier arena inhabited by the *Spectator* and *Independent*.

The *Advertiser* represents the first appearance in New Zealand journalism of the ethos of commerce for its own sake. While others had been hopeful of profit, the Bull and Roe brothers are the first to advance it as the *raison d'être* for a newspaper. However, their sincerity can be doubted for their newspaper was soon to lose its revolutionary approach. Within the first month of publication they had begun editorializing.

> It is not our metier to take part in the politics of this place, we therefore trust that the following observations will be attributed to our regard for the prosperity of Wellington, and not to any desire of imputing blame to the powers that be or those who differ from them.... Can nothing be done to establish a Banking Company for New Zealand, which, shall be entirely independent of Australian speculation?
> 
> (*New Zealand Advertiser*, 23 April 1859)

After 58 issues they dropped their byline guaranteeing a 2000 circulation and began charging 3d per issue or 20s per year subscription. The advertising rates remained unchanged. The paper changed to assume both the usual format and the political advocacy of the New Zealand journals of the time. It began as a 4-page, often a 6-page, advertising sheet with a little light reading thrown in on page 3. But this format was so short-lived it is probable the Bull and Roe brothers were using the *gratis* distribution format as a means of building circulation and gaining wide public attention. Certainly the amount of advertising in the early issues is such as to count against economic arguments for changing the format.

The paper rapidly developed a political policy which made it, like the other newspapers, a partisan advocate within Wellington. It concentrated on local affairs and gave its support to the Council, thus working against Superintendent Featherston.

> The Superintendent and his Executive are responsible for the present distress of the labouring classes because the Council will not submit to be deprived of their right, as the people's representatives, to enquire into and sanction the expenditure of the public money. This is the true posture of political affairs

*The Early Provincial Period*

here, and the real reason of the complaints of the Government party. The Council is acting on behalf of the People. The Superintendent is striving for the aggrandisement of himself and his friends.
(*New Zealand Advertiser*, 16 November 1859)

The *Advertiser*, then, came out in clear opposition to the *Independent*, though, operating from the other end of the social scale to the *Spectator*, it was not generally allied with that paper. The Bull and Roe brothers continued the *Advertiser* until 1867. It was in financial difficulty when they sold the property and the paper ceased publication on 31 May 1868.

**Nelson**

Nelson, which had an amicable first election in 1853, fought subsequent elections keenly. In 1857 the second Superintendency election was conducted on party lines with a coherent opposition being formed against the resident landowners' group. John Perry Robinson was the opposition candidate for Superintendent. Dr David Munro was the landowners' candidate to succeed Stafford. Alfred Domett, M.H.R. for Nelson, was the most able of the past editors of the *Examiner* and was recalled to the post so as to champion Munroe. Robinson narrowly won the Superintendency.

The second Nelson newspaper, the *Colonist*, arose in opposition to the *Examiner*'s identification with the views of the larger landowners. It was originally intended to start the paper in time for the 1857 provincial election where the *Colonist* opposed the policy of land aggregation. The paper missed this deadline but was active in political affairs from its inauguration where it was recognized as "the organ of the working men's Superintendent, Mr Robinson and his party".[11]

The *Colonist* is the first example in the southern settlements of a newspaper begun by settlers who, in the New Zealand Company classification, were emigrants rather than colonists. Robinson, referred to by his supporter Saunders as "a working mechanic and a poor man", had arrived in Nelson in 1842 and had shared in the early years of hardship experienced in that settlement, including a period when "for want of more congenial employment (he had) been obliged to work on the roads for the New Zealand Company".[12] Robinson, however, was an

---

11 Broad (1892) pp. 122-3.
12 Saunders (1896) Vol.1. p.332.

ex-committeeman of the Birmingham Mechanics Institute and a man of considerable self education. He opened and ran a school in Nelson, then was for four years in Auckland. On returning to Nelson he commenced farming, became a member of the Provincial Council and was establishing a business as a sawmiller when he was persuaded by William Wilkie to stand as a candidate for Superintendent.

William Wilkie, the co-proprietor of the *Colonist,* was the man who found most of the money necessary for that enterprise. Described by Saunders as "a hard headed Scotchman ... long known as the most independent and uncompromising Liberal, and the most consistent public economist in Nelson,"[13] he had also been in Nelson since 1842, having arrived from New South Wales. He had begun a business as a storekeeper and had been successful. References to Wilkie and Robinson as "mechanics" are references to their social origins rather than their mid 1850s occupations. Practically all settlers aspired to land ownership. Wilkie and Robinson were following a common pattern of upward social mobility and Robinson's political success plus the commencement of the *Colonist* are important stages in this mobility. The *Colonist*, which from its inception until its closure in 1920, was one of the main liberal papers, should not be regarded as an example of a New Zealand working class press. While it had working class origins its political advocacy was also to climb the social scale.

Wilkie's co-proprietor of the *Colonist* was William Nation, the printer of the paper. Nation, who had been printing in Sydney, was induced by Wilkie to move with his plant to Nelson.

The group organized around the *Colonist* rapidly achieved political dominance in Nelson. Robinson held the office of Superintendent until his death in 1865, increasing his majority at each election. His allies who were elected to the Provincial Council included Emanuel Eban, the first editor, and Alfred Saunders who was a leader writer for the newspaper. Saunders, in 1865, succeeded Robinson as Superintendent.

The *Examiner's* political influence declined as that of the *Colonist* grew. This decline was most notable from 1860 when the runholders, who were established in the Wairau area of Nelson province and whose interests were supported by the *Examiner,* separated themselves from both Nelson and the *Examiner* by seceding and starting the province of Marlborough.

---

13 Ibid.

## The Early Provincial Period

That the management of both the *Colonist* and the *Examiner* saw themselves in ideological conflict may be gauged from the *Colonist*'s opening statement and the *Examiner*'s reply. While much of the *Colonist*'s rationale for existence rested on Nelson's growth, it also clearly saw itself at odds with the province's existing paper.

> ...and is it not time that an engine so mighty for good or evil as the Press, should no longer be under the entire control of any single firm, or of any single party, but be placed within the reach of all, and be made available for the exposure of every abuse and the promulgation of every salutary truth?There are few individuals in Nelson, who have not at some time regretted the absence of a publication by which they might oppose the particular tenets that may for the time being be supported by the only newspaper in the province.
> (*Colonist*, 23 October 1857)

The *Examiner*, in a general welcome to its opposition, accepted that the two papers would be at odds.

> We have to welcome today into the arena of our little provincial conflicts a new champion, in the shape of the first number of the *Colonist* newspaper
> ....We have nothing to do but congratulate him and the community on the soundness of his view of the duties of an expositor of public opinion, and assure him we cordially reciprocate his intentions, and trust that whatever editorial differences of opinion may arise between us at all times be expressed in a spirit of courtesy and goodwill corresponding to his own.
> (*Nelson Examiner and New Zealand Chronicle*, 24 October 1857)

The call for courtesy and goodwill, which was generally followed in subsequent debates between the two newspapers, reflects the ambivalent position faced by the proprietors of the *Examiner*. Robinson and his group had won election success even before the *Colonist* began. The landowners group were experiencing a political decline that led, in 1860, to their secession from Nelson and the formation of the separate province of Marlborough. Elliott and the landowners were increasingly conscious that their own political power was, at best, threatened. Their case was far from one in which confrontation could be successful.

## Canterbury

In Canterbury a distinguishing feature of the *Lyttelton Times* was the strength of FitzGerald's early efforts to remain open to differing opinions. He promised and to his credit maintained the position, that the *Lyttelton Times* would not be a partisan press while it remained the sole newspaper in the settlement.

> As long as there is but one public journal in a colony, we hold it to be the duty of the editor to avoid above all things making it exclusively the organ of any particular party. He ought so far to consult the public good as to make his journal a means for enabling parties or individuals to lay their views before their fellow countrymen, and his columns ought to be equally and liberally open to all.
> 
> (*Lyttelton Times*, 11 January 1851)

FitzGerald was not attempting to develop an identity for the press independent of political divisions in Canterbury. While maintaining a newspaper open to all opinions he saw this as a temporary measure forced by the fact that the *Lyttelton Times* was the only newspaper in the settlement. He saw his stand as unusual and was to reverse it as soon as possible.

The settlement's second newspaper was the *Canterbury Advertiser*, launched by Charles J. Rea in time for the first elections. Rae was not well known in Canterbury and the paper had little influence. It lasted three months before ceasing with only 20 of its promised 200 subscriptions being paid.

FitzGerald welcomed the new paper, declaring he would now be able to express openly his own convictions.[14] He also took the occasion to signal a policy change for the *Lyttelton Times*.

> We have received a long letter from Mr Brittan which we will publish, if possible, next week. There being, however, another organ of public opinion in the settlement, we take this opportunity of saying that we no longer consider ourselves bound to place our columns at the disposal of those who may

---

14 *Lyttelton Times*, 24 April 1852.

wish to criticise our remarks. We faithfully kept the pledge we gave so long as we stood alone; but now we stand in the position of any journal in England, or elsewhere, and shall adopt the usual role.
(*Lyttelton Times*, 15 June 1852)

The Mr Brittan referred to is Joseph Brittan, later the proprietor and editor of the third Canterbury Newspaper, the *Canterbury Standard*, which first appeared on 3 June 1854 and ran for 12 years, to 23 April 1866, when it was purchased and closed by *The Press*. The differences with Brittan were also to be discussed by FitzGerald in a letter to Henry Selfe, administrator of the Canterbury Association. "We have lately had our first political division here. Brittan has come out a snob after all. He has managed to disgust all classes. The gentlemen by a cocky snobbish manner which is inevitable to men of low birth who have been elevated, and the rest of the community by his having showed strong symptoms of changing his political creed and going over to the Government."[15]

Brittan's low birth was of consequence to FitzGerald, the grandson of a baronet, and appears to have coloured his understanding of Brittan's allegiance to the settlers. There is no other evidence to suggest Brittan was a supporter of the Crown Colony Government. Sir William Fox lists him, along with FitzGerald, as one of the Canterbury leaders in the agitation for self-government.[16]

During the agitation Brittan had been a frequent and welcome contributor to the FitzGerald-controlled *Lyttelton Times*. Nor were his subsequent politics substantially at odds with those of FitzGerald. At the 1857 Superintendency election when he was the unsuccessful candidate in opposition to W.S. Moorhouse, Brittan was regarded as a FitzGerald man. Although unsuccessful in his bid to become Superintendent, Brittan did achieve some political success and the *Standard* acted as a political vehicle for him. Brittan was in the Provincial Council from 1855-57 and 1861-62. He was the leader of the Executive in 1855 and was Provincial Secretary under Tancred in 1855-57.

With both papers advocating a conservative, pro-runholder position, there was more consensus than conflict between the *Standard* and the

---

15 FitzGerald to Selfe, 6 August 1852.
16 Fox (1890), p.11.

*Lyttelton Times* for the first two years of the *Standard*'s life. But in 1856 the *Lyttelton Times* changed hands. Ingram Shrimpton, the paper's original owner, had arrived in Canterbury in 1854 when he began managing the paper. However, after the death of his son in 1856 he sold the control of the paper to Charles Bowen and Crosbie Ward. This partnership continued for three years when Bowen was bought out in 1859 by William Reeves. There were two other minor partners. Bowen and Ward were Moorhouse associates and supporters and, thus, from 1856 the "cheap land party" held the paper. Political support was transferred to Moorhouse who won the 1857 Superintendency elections and held the post to 1863. Moorhouse edited the paper in 1856-57 relinquishing the post prior to his election. Crosbie Ward then became editor until his death in 1867. Both Bowen and Ward were personally politically prominent.

*The Press*, the final Canterbury paper of this period, was launched in 1861 as a political journal and as a counter to the *Lyttelton Times*. The major early personality, as with the *Lyttelton Times*, was again J.E. FitzGerald who, after sailing to England in 1857, returned to the colony in 1861. It would appear that FitzGerald was financed into *The Press* by the Canterbury runholders in order to oppose Superintendent Moorhouse's programme of public expenditure, to keep the conservative voice alive, and to give FitzGerald a political platform. FitzGerald wrote of the inauguration of the paper in the following terms:

> Sitting after dinner in Ilam about a month ago I said I saw no hope for a better state of public policy here unless there was a new newspaper started which could tell the truth without fear or favour. In five minutes the thing was settled. If I would undertake the management of it it was to be started and £500 was put down on the spot. It was soon found that there was a little press and some types to be bought... The first number appeared nearly three weeks after the conversation referred to[17]

It is not known how many were at the dinner at Ilam referred to but, by Ilam, FitzGerald means the home of John Charles Watts Russell, then a leading Canterbury pastoralist. A five member syndicate was formed to publish *The Press* with J.E. FitzGerald as manager. As well as Russell, the syndicate comprised H.P. Lance, H.R. Tancred, R.J.S.

---

17  O'Neill (1963) p.22

Harman and the Rev. J. Raven. All were wealthy men and were the financial backers of *The Press*. The Rev. Raven was also of considerable practical aid to the new newspaper. He performed the organizational tasks, such as finding premises for *The Press*. Most importantly he persuaded George Watson, owner of the only available press, to sell it to them and work as the paper's printer.

Accepting FitzGerald's account that the Ilam meeting took place prior to the date of the first issue of *The Press*, it would appear that the impetus prompting both the Ilam meeting and the formation of the syndicate was FitzGerald's long letter in the *Lyttelton Times* of April 20 1861 castigating the policies of Moorhouse and their support by the *Lyttelton Times*. *The Press*, then, as with other New Zealand papers of the period, became an active part of its local political arena. It put into words, for readers, the values pertinent to alternative policies. With its backing FitzGerald resumed the political career he had interrupted in 1857.

**Otago**

In Dunedin, the *Otago Witness* was the only paper in publication when provincialism began. Cutten, the proprietor and editor, gave his support to his father-in-law, William Cargill, the leader of the settlement who became the first Superintendent. As with the other provinces, the paper's political advocacy aroused opposition and when, in 1856, another paper was started the *Witness* found itself described in less than flattering terms.

> No publication of the *Otago Witness* has for a considerable time appeared without being sullied by the grossest misrepresentations the frequency of which proves them to have been made wilfully and deliberately.
> (*Otago Colonist*, 26 December 1856)

The role of the *Witness* as an ongoing participant in Otago affairs was one followed by its opposition, the *Otago Colonist and Invercargill Advertiser*. The *Colonist* was printed and published by William Lambert but the major backer was James Macandrew for whom the *Colonist* acted as a political support. William Lambert, an English non-conformist, had worked as a printer on the *Chronicle* and the *Morning Post* in London and on the *Sydney Morning Herald* before coming to New Zealand. Lambert, after the commencement of the *Colonist*, began a short career in Otago provincial politics. But, of the two, Macandrew was the major political figure. James Macandrew was an Otago merchant who arrived from Britain in his own schooner in 1851. He had been prominent in the agitation for self-government and had been a frequent contributor to the *Witness*. He was a member of the Otago Provincial Council from 1853 to 1859 and Superintendent of Otago from 1859 to 1861 and 1867 to 1876. He was a member of the General Assembly from 1853 to 1860 and again from 1865 to his death in 1887.

The *Witness* was quick to point out that, while it was perhaps less than impartial, no more could be said of the *Colonist*.

> ... we did hope, as we have been "the one-sided press!" there would have been less of the t'other-sided press in our contemporary. Two papers will be of great advantage to the public if they can be supported; but if one is to fail, we doubt much if the public would be better represented by the Colonist than they have been by the *Witness*.
>
> (*Otago Witness*, 27 December 1856)

The politics of the two Otago papers were, however, more complicated than a respective backing of two factions, one headed by Cargill, the other by Macandrew. Until late 1854, Cargill and Macandrew were allies. At this time, Cutten began to oppose Macandrew and fell out of favour with both of the dominant Otago politicians. The disagreement was over the Provincial Executive's policy for the appropriation of the revenue for 1855. It was exacerbated both by personal antagonism between Cutten and Macandrew and by the opposition of Cutten, an Englishman and an Anglican, to the Provincial Executive's wish to maintain the Scottish and Presbyterian biased immigration policy. According to Lambert both Cargill and Macandrew in 1856 requested him to begin a newspaper "as the only one then in existence had opposed itself to the best interests of the Province". Unlike Macandrew, Cargill did not sign an agreement with Lambert, stating "it would appear ungracious in him to sign a document having for its express acknowledged object decided opposition to his daughter's husband".[18] Not until June 1857 were Cutten and Cargill reconciled and in opposition to Macandrew. Only at this point did the *Colonist* become Macandrew's support vehicle and the *Witness* Cargill's.

---

18 From a supplement to the *Otago Colonist* printed to defend the newspaper in the form of a letter from the editor. 26 August 1857.

## The Provincial Press and Political Advocacy

Partisan political advocacy was a matter the management of the various newspapers considered normal and proper. The practice had developed in New Zealand prior to self-government. The last years, especially, of that period had been a time of intense political agitation, coordinated through the colony's newspapers, in pursuit of self-government. But in the provincial period, this political agitation in pursuit of the common goal of self-government became partisan political advocacy on behalf of particular politicians. Such political advocacy was seldom conducted according to standards of decorum or fair play. Their political conduct was a trait of the New Zealand newspapers which was commented on, usually negatively, by contemporary observers. Puseley's "unfavourable opinion of colonial periodicals" included the view that "the New Zealand newspapers represent all those petty jealousies and political animosities with which so many of the inhabitants are infected. ... Whatever is said or done by one party, or the leaders of a party, is sure to be disapproved or condemned by another".[19]

Such a pattern of newspaper belligerency was not, however, peculiar to either the press or New Zealand. In his well-known condemnation, Edward Gibbon Wakefield was to indicate that it was a general characteristic of colonial politics. "Colonial party-politics ... are remarkable for the factiousness and violence of politicians, the prevalence of demogoguism, the roughness and even brutality of the newspapers, the practice in carrying on public differences of making war to the knife, and always striking at the heart".[20] While not all would have had so negative a view the point to be taken is that the New Zealand newspapers were primarily political advocates. Each population centre had two newspapers which were linked, respectively, with that province's major political groups. Newspaper ownership and journalistic involvement were common among leading politicians and newspapers were publicly recognised, not as impartial observers, but as impassioned participants in the political process.

While the fact of partisan political advocacy was common for the nineteenth century press, its nature in New Zealand was intensified by

---

19 Puseley (1858) pp.245-6.
20 Wakefield (1914) p.185.

the peculiarities of the New Zealand situation. Prior to self-government the conduct of political activity through the colony's newspapers had given political experience to journalists and journalistic experience to would-be politicians. Thus a majority of the major elected officials had close connections with New Zealand newspapers. Their connections varied from actual ownership to a period of intermittent contributions to a newspaper. But in all cases there were personal connections between politicians and newspapers. Press political advocacy was not usually advocacy for a political party, these were as yet generally undeveloped but personal advocacy for a particular politician. In the majority of cases the pattern was one of advocacy on behalf of the newspaper's proprietor, who was also a prominent politician. In Auckland this applies to both of the newspapers. Brown and then Logan Campbell were successfully supported by the *Southern Cross* until the routing of their group in 1856. Williamson's period of political supremacy, which followed, was championed by his *New Zealander*. In Taranaki, the second newspaper, the *News*, was owned by, and offered support for, Charles Brown. In Canterbury, Brittan's newspaper, the *Standard*, supported his political ambitions and the *Lyttelton Times*, which for its first few years had a non-resident proprietor, supported after its sale, the political ambitions of its new proprietors, Ward, Bowen and Reeves. In Otago the two newspapers were also seen as political advocates for their principal proprietors, Cutten and Macandrew.

In those cases in which the newspaper proprietor was not politically prominent the newspapers were still linked into the pattern of partisan political advocacy. In Taranaki the first newspaper, the *Herald*, changed its favoured Superintendency candidate before the second elections but the fact of political advocacy was continuous. In Wellington the *Independent* was always the advocate for Featherston. Stokes of the *Spectator* did have a minor political career but the paper's major advocacy was for E.J. Wakefield and his associates. In Nelson, Elliott had some personal political success but the two newspapers' political advocacy was oriented, respectively, towards the two major political groupings in the province.

Whether or not a newspaper's proprietor was personally involved in political life, the political connections were inherent in the press. Politically partisan journalism was the only journalism in New Zealand. Judging from the lack of success of the few alternative newspapers, the public understanding was such as to consider political partisanship a

## The Early Provincial Period

proper and necessary aspect of journalism. So too did politicians consider press advocacy to be necessary for the public acceptance and electoral success of themselves and their policies. It was possible, as Robinson demonstrated in the 1857 Superintendency elections in Nelson, to win an election without a supporting newspaper. But in practice, as the subsequent foundation of the *Nelson Colonist* indicates, few cared to fight elections without the backing of a newspaper. The press was considered vital for the extension to the public of a general political orientation or of any particular interpretation of political events. As a consequence newspapers were supported not only by those who were standing at elections but also by those who stood to benefit from their success. Thus prominent Canterbury pastoralists established *The Press* not merely to support J.E. FitzGerald but so that their conservative political orientation would receive a public presentation. In the years in which a new political order was being established in New Zealand, newspaper backing was considered necessary for any individual's success in a political career. But also it was seen as essential to the public presentation and consequent electoral success of any interpretation of the political nature and proper direction of New Zealand society.

The predominance of politically partisan journalism in New Zealand was aided by the conditions which prevailed in the colony. Regular and fast communication between settlements and from other countries was not possible until the advent in the 1860s of the telegraph and of regular mail ships. The isolation which had, during the Crown Colony Government period, given newspapers little choice but to be political discussion forums continued and press concentration remained on local politics. The European population also remained small. While the European population had increased five-fold from 1842 to 1858 it still totalled less than 60,000. The twelve newspapers in the six major settlements were still operating with a population base insufficient for proprietors to gain a financial return from their newspapers. In the circumstances the newspapers, throughout these years were not operated for financial profit. With no possibility of successfully pursuing financial profits from newspaper publication, they were published for other reasons. It was the motive of political rather than financial gain that lay behind the New Zealand newspapers during these years.

The same motivation was felt by those who were journalists in the 1850s. As will be discussed, there was during this period the first appearance of professional journalism. But, while the manual staff were, as before, paid for their activity, editorial involvement was still largely restricted to those whose efforts were rewarded politically rather than financially. This applies to those who had been active in journalism prior to self-government and who carried on the tradition of un-remunerated journalistic activity for the political gains to be made both for their allies and personally. Thus, Hugh Carleton, engaged in Auckland journalism since the mid 1840s and, after self government, a long term member of both the General Assembly and the Auckland Provincial Council was the long-term editor of the *Southern Cross*. Journalistic involvement for political rather than financial gain also became the practice among the new newspapers. Thus, Emanuel Eban, Robinson's ally and himself a member of the Nelson Provincial Council, became editor of the *Nelson Colonist*.

The general unavailability of economic success for journalistic ventures meant that political considerations had been the dominant force behind the New Zealand press. During the early provincial period newspaper growth in the various provinces had followed and also helped define the local political divisions. It was in the 1860s that financial success first became a realistic possibility, and thus a new motivation, for newspaper proprietors. I now turn to the newspapers of the 1860s and to the interplay of newspaper proprietors' political and financial concerns.

# 6. The Start of the Daily Press in New Zealand

In the week in May 1861 when FitzGerald first published *The Press*, further south, in inland Otago, Gabriel Read was prospecting in the Tuapeka where he discovered gold shining "like the stars in Orion on a dark frosty night".[1] The discovery of gold was followed by a population increase and business growth that, among other matters, transformed the press.

In the 1860s the New Zealand newspapers experienced a commercial growth that considerably affected their political activity. There developed new operating conditions whereby existing owners were obliged to accept an end to their dual positions as prominent politicians and newspaper proprietors. The changing conditions also provided new commercial opportunities which led to the entry of a new group of newspaper proprietors whose orientation was primarily that of the business entrepreneur rather than the established one of political activist. The changes were first felt in Otago.

**Julius Vogel and the Daily Press in Otago**

After the Tuapeka gold strike, Otago was rapidly to become the most heavily populated of the New Zealand provinces. The possibility of a commercially profitable newspaper had suddenly appeared in Otago and was to be quickly exploited. New Zealand's first daily, the *Otago Daily Times*, soon began publication. The paper started, and continued, as an allied publication of the *Witness*, one of Otago's two existing weekly newspapers.

The major impetus for the *Otago Daily Times* was Julius Vogel. Vogel, a 26 year-old journalist resident in Victoria when Gabriel Read made his gold strike in May 1861, was also a gold assayer. He must have realized there were opportunities awaiting in Otago and rushed to the scene for he arrived there in the spring of 1861. He immediately found employment on the staff of the *Colonist*, James Macandrew's newspaper. His stay there, however, was to be measured in weeks for he was to find with Cutten of the *Witness* not just employment but a business partner. The start of their partnership is sketched by Gillon:

> Mr Cutten, the proprietor and editor of the *Witness*, although a brilliant and witty writer, had a constitutional distaste for

---

1   Gabriel Read's Narrative, p.127-8. Quoted in McLintock, (1949), p.451.

the work, and between his official duties, his duties in the Council, and his editing, his hands were more than full. It was soon noticed that he was becoming intimate with Mr Vogel, and one day I learned that Mr Vogel had joined Mr Cutten in partnership and that there were going to be some changes in the paper...soon it became known that the *Otago Daily Times* was to appear, with Messrs Cutten and Vogel as proprietors, Mr Vogel as editor, and Mr B.L. Farjeon as manager. Most people thought the venture a mad one, and predicted an early collapse; but Mr Vogel was full of enterprise and energy, and laughed at these dismal prognostications. The prospectus was issued and preparations pushed vigorously forward.[2]

15 November 1861 saw the start of New Zealand's first daily. The *Otago Daily Times* was the first newspaper to indicate the circulation possible in the 1860s. It was also the first to use industrial age printing technology. When the paper was started, the printing press used for the *Witness* was replaced by a hand-worked cylinder printing machine brought over from Melbourne. At this point the circulation of the *Otago Daily Times* was 2750. This was an enormous increase on previous rates; the *Witness* in late 1855, for example, was recorded as having 210 subscriptions. A steam-driven two-cylinder machine was imported from Britain and was in service in August 1862. At the time of introduction of this technology the paper's circulation topped 7000. While the *Otago Daily Times* remained during this period the paper with the highest circulation, this type of growth did become a general feature of the press.

Vogel's entry into New Zealand journalism and the commencement of the *Otago Daily Times* represents the turning point in a process of commercialization for the New Zealand press. A desire for commercial profit had long been present among the country's newspaper proprietors. But not until the advent of the *Otago Daily Times* was commercial profit a realistic expectation for newspaper concerns. The *Otago Daily Times* was immediately a profitable newspaper. It began with a price of 3d but doubled that in August 1862, the same time as the new steam-driven printing machinery enabled them to double the size of the paper. The return they received enabled Cutten and Vogel to meet the management

---

2   *Otago Daily Times*, (1924), p.12.

demands of a daily paper. These were quite different from those of a more leisurely weekly. The staff engaged in the manual work of newspaper production had to be increased and their wages had to be high, double that of their Melbourne confreres, so as to keep them away from the gold diggings.[3] B.L. Farjeon was employed as business manager and Daniel Campbell, the printer of the *Witness*, managed the mechanical side of the enterprise. A salaried reporting and editorial staff had to be found. No longer were the efforts of an editor/proprietor sufficient. The original literary staff of the *Otago Daily Times* was Vogel, E.T. Gillon and W.H. Harrison. Gillon and Harrison were both to have distinguished careers in New Zealand journalism. This staff was soon increased by a sub-editor and another reporter. Vogel was himself editor of both the *Witness* and the *Otago Daily Times* and also functioned as the entrepreneur of the new commercial enterprise.

Vogel, in his opening editorial, pointed to a new journalistic path for his paper.

> From this day we aspire to be the historical mirror of all that occurs in Otago of all that in anyway affects its history....
>
> The *Times* is designed to supply the want now generally felt of a daily journal, containing an account of all passing news of interest, and full commercial intelligence. We do not desire to reflect on or come into collision with the two weekly papers already existing. Our sphere and theirs will be widely different.
> (*Otago Daily Times*, 15 November 1861)

The existing weeklies, however, were greatly affected by the advent of the daily press. The *Witness*, also jointly owned by Vogel and Cutten, rapidly became the minor and less influential of the allied publications. The *Witness* remained as the partnership's weekly publication and gradually became a weekly digest containing both original material as well as reprints from issues of the *Otago Daily Times* of the previous week. It became oriented not towards Dunedin city readers but towards country subscribers who were unable to receive newspapers daily. This combination of daily and weekly was to be the normal organizational structure for the major newspapers until twentieth century transport increased the reach of the dailies, making the weeklies obsolete.

The other publication, the *Colonist*, was at least equally affected by the *Otago Daily Times*. Once the *Otago Daily Times* was established

---

3   On one occasion though, all but one of the composing staff had "fled to the fields."

*The Making of the New Zealand Press*

Macandrew and Lambert, the *Colonist* proprietors, attempted to keep pace with their rival. The frequency of the *Colonist* was increased to daily publication in July 1862. At the start of the next year Macandrew and Lambert reorganized their holdings by beginning the *Daily Telegraph,* which incorporated the *Colonist,* and by starting the *Weekly Colonist* as the weekly associate of the *Telegraph.* As with the *Witness* and the *Otago Daily Times,* the *Weekly Colonist* had a lesser status than the *Daily Telegraph.* Dunedin was thus the first city both to have a daily paper and to have opposing dailies.

Vogel held that the *Otago Daily Times* was to be "the historical mirror of all that occurs in Otago". This notion was not specified any more clearly but can be read as a desire not only to report the events of the province but to do so in a neutral manner. Such an interpretation is reinforced by the stated desire not to "come into collision with the two weekly papers already existing", both of which were recognized as partisan advocates within the community. Even if such was Vogel's intention it does not describe his subsequent actions. Vogel's intention to report "all that in anyway affects (Otago's) history" did not exclude his making that history. He brought to Otago journalism a sense of growth and destiny that both could and should be monitored daily. The more leisurely pace of the weeklies was no longer sufficient. But he did not propose or implement any change to the established press policy of partisan advocacy. Vogel edited both the *Otago Daily Times* and the *Witness.* The political policy of the two publications was naturally identical and, importantly, the partisan advocacy was present in both publications.

Vogel, as was the standard practice, used his papers to found and support a personal political career. He likely had political as well as journalistic ambitions from his arrival in Otago. His years in Victoria had combined the two. Certainly his New Zealand political career began quickly. The Otago Provincial Council in December 1862 passed the Otago Representation Ordinance which divided the province into 18 electoral districts and increased the number of members from 21 to 35. Vogel was one of the aspirants brought forward by the wider representation. He was elected the member for Waikouaiti in June 1863. In September of the same year he was elected, if only fortuitously, to the General Assembly. The manner of his election indicates how difficult it was to attract able candidates for general elections and also offers a reason new arrivals, such as Vogel, could so rapidly achieve political prominence. It was during the performance of his journalistic duties that Vogel took the opportunity to join the, then less than sought after, House of Representatives.

In his role of journalist, Vogel was present on the spot where the nomination was to take place, but on arriving, he found that a people intent on the search for gold to the exclusion of all else, had declined to send a single representative to attend the ceremony. There was no candidate, no proposer, no public only himself and the returning officer. Seeing his opportunity, Vogel, at once went out and got two men to propose and second him. When he returned with them two or three more people had arrived on the scene. Their motive appears to have been curiosity rather than deep political conviction, for they stood by, passively assenting, while the newly-found candidate was being proposed, seconded, and declared elected. [4]

The *Otago Daily Times* became, and was seen to be, as much a partisan press as any of its predecessors. In this regard the opening comments of its rival, the *Daily Telegraph,* even allowing for inaugural hyperbole, are instructive. The *Daily Telegraph* called the *Otago Daily Times*:

...the thick-and-thin advocate of the land monopolist and speculator, whose schemes are death to the working classes. ...The welfare of the Province is not safe in his (ODT editor's) keeping. It is absolutely imperative to the progress of society that there should be a second daily paper, whose aim and object shall be not only to encourage and circulate truth, but to dispell error  not only to counsel wisely, but to keep in check and destroy the evil tendency of the *Daily Times*.
(*Daily Telegraph,* 3 January 1863)

## Daily Journalism, Political Advocacy and the Press in Otago

Later in the 1860s the demands of daily journalism were to modify the nature of the press's political participation. But, at least initially, the newspaper proprietors did not see the daily press as demanding any major change to the political advocacy performed by the earlier newspapers. The daily press took over and continued the roles of political supporter and mouthpiece for leading politicians. Change,

---

4    Burdon (1948) p.23.

however, was to come and was to take place despite the wishes of the existing proprietors.

The financial and managerial needs of the daily newspapers were to conflict with the desire of newspaper proprietors for political advocacy and support. This showed first in Dunedin with the collapse of Macandrew's and Lambert's papers. The early 1860s, the years in which Macandrew and Lambert began the *Daily Telegraph* and the *Weekly Colonist*, was also a period when Lambert's short political career had just ended and Macandrew's was in tatters. Macandrew had been dismissed from the Superintendency in March 1861 and did not regain the post for six years. He had also left the House of Representatives with the dissolution of the Second Parliament in November 1860 and was not re-elected until July 1865.

With their newspapers beginning during Macandrew's period of political obscurity, Macandrew and Lambert experienced considerable difficulty in increasing circulation rates for the *Daily Telegraph* and *Weekly Colonist*. Soon both papers raised their prices and this exacerbated their circulation difficulties. The *Weekly Colonist* raised its price to 6d a copy while the *Daily Telegraph,* which started at 1 ½d, doubled that to 3d the same as the *Otago Daily Times,* which had come down from 6d when the *Daily Telegraph* began. In April 1864 both the *Daily Telegraph* and *Weekly Colonist* were purchased by their rival and closed down.

Lambert and Macandrew kept a daily paper going for almost two years but were not able to establish it successfully. It is noteworthy that the unsuccessful attempt coincided with Macandrew's period of political misfortune. His political unpopularity contributed to their papers' lack of success but, most importantly, it was now becoming apparent that the financial demands of the press were too great to allow any single politician to continue an uneconomic paper so as to maintain that paper's political support. This was the case in the 1850s and Macandrew had himself been one of the practitioners of the art. A wealthy proprietor/politician could maintain an uneconomic weekly newspaper with a circulation in the hundreds. Such uneconomic newspapers could be supported by profitable allied enterprises, such as a printing establishment. But the daily press required a larger, paid staff and a more elaborate and expensive technology. It also began in Otago in a time of rising costs generally. With the appearance of a daily press the level of finance needed to maintain a newspaper was such that the continuation of an unprofitable newspaper was generally well beyond the means of any single individual. The situation was to be exacerbated in the following years as the sale price of copies of daily newspapers was lowered. This also put a greater reliance on advertising, the continuation of which was itself dependent on circulation levels remaining high.

Business and political considerations were also to clash on the *Otago Daily Times* where economic demands were generated that precluded Vogel, or anyone else, from using the paper in a manner that ran counter to them. To follow this it is necessary to outline first the changes in the early ownership structure of the *Otago Daily Times* and *Witness* newspapers. Cutten was the first to go. He appears to have disliked the business,[5] and took, as an opportune time to leave, a £500 damages verdict awarded against the paper in an 1864 libel case brought by the N.Z. Banking Corporation. The paper then came under the control of J. Vogel and Co., Vogel taking B.L. Farjeon,[6] the paper's business manager, into the partnership. As with nearly all the New Zealand papers, the early records of the *Otago Daily Times* have been destroyed but it is apparent that the need for investment capital to finance his expanding business forced Vogel to include others as controllers of the enterprise. In 1866 a limited liability company entitled the Otago Daily Times and Witness Newspapers Co. Ltd was formed under the provisions of the 1860 Companies Act. Vogel remained as editor. He was also a director, but control was shared with Mr John Bathgate (afterwards Judge Bathgate), Mr F.C. Simmons (Rector of the Otago Boys High School), and Mr James Rattray (merchant). The expansion of the *Otago Daily Times* was financed by the issue of £6000 worth of debentures at 10% interest. Presumably Bathgate, Simons and Rattray were major debenture holders or agents for such holders.

In 1868 matters came to a crisis. The rapid Otago growth of the early 1860s, which had provided the *Otago Daily Times* prosperity, was at an end. The goldrush had moved to the West Coast and 1867-68 were years of commercial depression in Dunedin. The depression was keenly felt by the paper's management. In March 1868 the company had three

---

5 "Mr Cutten was of an easy-going disposition, and constitutionally disinclined to shoulder the worries and anxieties of daily journalism. It did not require a great deal of persuasion, therefore, to induce him to part with his share in the paper". *Otago Daily Times*, (1924), p.18.

6 Farjeon was not to remain long in journalism. Receiving kindly criticism of his first novel from no less a person than Charles Dickens, he severed his business connections and moved, in 1867, to England to pursue a literary career.

directors Vogel, Rattray and Mr W.D. Murison. Vogel's co-directors, faced with the need at least to gain sufficient return from the newspaper to pay the interest on the debentures, argued that Vogel's editorial advocacy of his personal political beliefs was exacerbating the paper's financial difficulties and, in April, moved to fire him. Vogel's major political platform at the time was a championing of the separation of the North and Middle (now South) Islands, and the weight of the *Otago Daily Times* was thrown behind this. In 1868 the high point of the support for separation was passed. The telegraph, by this time, had placed the two islands in constant communication thus removing some of the logic of isolation from the separation argument. Also, attitudes within provinces tended to become more centralised as a province's financial status worsened. It is not unreasonable during a time of depression in Otago to expect a growing opposition to Vogel's separation proposals. Both Murison, one of the co-directors, and Bathgate, in 1868 the company secretary, were political representatives. It is possible that political differences with his co-directors at least added to Vogel's problems. Vogel attempted to counter his co-directors by offering to lease the property of the Company. At a July general meeting this move was soundly defeated by the shareholders in a 96-to-nil vote and Vogel was ousted from the paper he had founded. Vogel then started, on 16 November 1868, another morning daily, the *New Zealand Sun,* in opposition to the *Otago Daily Times.* This paper, however, folded within a few months[7] and Vogel's day to-day connections with Otago journalism ceased.

His need for additional capital for business expansion had led Vogel to include those who brought such capital, or at least their representatives, as directors of the *Otago Daily Times.* While the additional capital did allow the expansion of the business, the addition of further directors made vulnerable Vogel's domination of the *Otago Daily Times* and eventually cost him his newspaper. Additional directors ensured control of Vogel both as a businessman and as an editor. The immediate reason for Vogel's ousting was the unpopularity, as perceived by his co-directors, of his political advocacy but it was the financial needs of his daily newspaper which had led him, in the first place, to accept co-directors.

In Otago both Vogel and Macandrew were politicians who owned and operated newspapers which they used in the service of their respective

---

7   The latest copy remaining is dated 11 March 1869.

political ideas and careers. But they also saw their newspapers as more than their political servants. For both of them their newspapers were business enterprises which, in the burgeoning early 1860s, they viewed as potentially profitable. In both cases, however, there was to be conflict between their commercial and political aspirations. With the high running costs associated with daily newspapers it was no longer possible for out of favour politicians to continue their unpopular newspapers for the sake of their newspapers' political advocacy. Macandrew lost his *Daily Telegraph* when, during his period of political disfavour, the paper was unable to attract a circulation high enough to cover expenses. Vogel faced another problem but one which, while it did not mean the end of the *Otago Daily Times,* did also lead to his loss of the newspaper. The sound commercial reasoning leading to the reorganization of the *Otago Daily Times* as a limited liability company made problematic Vogel's personal control of the newspaper. When Vogel's political advocacy was perceived as in conflict with the commercial strength of the company, the commercial needs were regarded by the other directors and shareholders as the more important and Vogel was removed.

## Commercial Growth, Political Advocacy and the Canterbury Press

In Canterbury the commercial possibilities of the press in the 1860s were soon apparent.

During its first year FitzGerald became, rather mysteriously, sole proprietor of *The Press.* This should not be seen as a non-profitable and troublesome concern being gladly given away, as was the case, for example, when Cutten acquired the *Witness* in Dunedin in 1853. The possibility of a profitable business was early apparent. Yet, for some reason, the original partnership was dissolved and, at the end of June 1862, the paper was handed over to FitzGerald. He became the sole proprietor of *The Press*. The only surviving reference to the transaction is in a letter from FitzGerald.

> ... (the paper) is the only thing I see out of which to make a living. I cannot speak in sufficient terms of the proprietors whose liberality has enabled me to take it up. I intend to make it the best paper in the Southern Hemisphere.[8]

---

8   FitzGerald to Selfe. Quoted in O'Neill, (1963), p.39.

## The Making of the New Zealand Press

Through the 1860s, due to FitzGerald's efforts and his increasing level of borrowed capital,*The Press* became a more and more substantial newspaper organisation. In 1862 he began the *Commercial Advertiser*, a weekly eight-page publication which sold for 3d. *The Press* had been from the start a six-page paper selling for 6d. The *Commercial Advertiser* consisted of advertising only. It ran for 21 issues which would have taken it to February 1863. It may have received insufficient support but also FitzGerald may have closed it so as to reserve advertising *The Press* for, on St. Patricks Day 1863, he began issuing *The Press* daily. The paper now had four pages and sold for 3d. At this stage it had a weekly circulation of 5000.

Then a bi-weekly, the *Lyttelton Times,* although being gradually overtaken by its rival, declined to take the risk and meet the challenge.

> The *Times* has no present intention of coming out daily. In the opinion of the Proprietors, the time has not arrived for taking such an extreme step. Neither the amount nor character of the population warrant them in thinking that the Province can support a daily paper. From close observation and experience they are satisfied that the public are fully supplied with the means of advertising, and that any further extension of those means would be unnecessary. They think that the foreign mail services are not sufficiently frequent to afford news for a daily journal, and if they were, that the inland postal communication would not enable them to distribute it. For these and other reasons they are not prepared to increase the number of their issues. To be ready for emergencies they have prepared the plant and premises requisite for a daily paper. Should a payable gold-field be discovered in the Province they are ready to take the field at once. If no such sudden stimulus should arise, it will require considerable increase in population to induce them to enter upon such an enterprise.
> (*Lyttelton Times,* 20 March 1863)

The *Lyttelton Times* had a correct understanding of the contemporary commercial situation in the province. It was, however, a short-sighted view. FitzGerald was, on other occasions, as well as this able to score unchallenged against the *Lyttelton Times*. He took *The Press* to equality with its rival and, in the long term it was *The Press* that survived.

## The Start of the Daily Press

FitzGerald's innovativeness was further shown on 5 September 1863, when a lithographed map of the Waikato was issued as a supplement to illustrate reports of the land wars. With the exception of Wellington's single issue *Victoria Times* in 1841, this was New Zealand's first news illustration.

On 5 February 1864, FitzGerald attempted the introduction of a daily evening paper. *Theatre* was a 1d sheet which contained the night's play-bill at the Princess Theatre as well as advertisements and any important news that had come in since the morning edition of *The Press*. It was discontinued within the month in favour of another daily, the *Evening Post*. The evening daily was considered of lesser importance than its morning stablemate.

> It is with great pleasure that we place before the public our first issue of this little paper. We do not pretend any great things, but shall endeavour to give every evening the local news of the day, telegraph of shipping arrived in port, and such commercial intelligence as may be of importance. Politics we shall entirely leave in the hands of our more important contemporaries as more suitable to them. We trust to be deserving of that support from the public of Christchurch which our small enterprise shall require.
> (*Evening Post*, 27 February 1864)[9]

A year later, on 18 February 1865, FitzGerald started a further publication, the *Weekly Press*, a 16-page collection of material which, in the main, had first appeared in the parent daily. It sold for 6d and was a success, especially in the back-country areas where, due to the infrequent mail deliveries, it competed well against the *Lyttelton Times'* three issues per week.

By this stage the combined circulations of FitzGerald's papers were close to that of his rival. The competition between the two concerns became even more intense in July 1865 with new moves being made by both sides. On 1 July 1865, the *Lyttelton Times* followed FitzGerald's lead and brought out its weekly, the *Canterbury Times*. Later in the

---

9  Some doubt shrouds the existence of this paper. Scholefield, (1958), who is unsure whether the paper was the *Evening Post* or *Evening Mail*, holds it "was heralded in 1864 but did not materialise" (p.22). O'Neill, (1963) p.45, offers the above quote but fails to state where the paper can be sighted.

same month FitzGerald introduced the *Monthly Summary,* an extract from the previous four weeks issues of *The Press,* of its leading articles, news stories, political reports and correspondence. The *Monthly Summary* sold for 1s and was published the day before the scheduled departures of the mail ships for England. Copies of the *Lyttelton Times* had been sent regularly to England since 1851. With one effort FitzGerald took his English circulation above that of the *Lyttelton Times.*

In the same month, however, the *Lyttelton Times* had also begun daily publication, thus finally removing FitzGerald's advantage. To counter this, in the following month he increased the sheet size of *The Press,* making the two Christchurch morning dailies equal in format.

The variety of publications begun by FitzGerald from 1862 to 1865 were not political advocates but are instances of a new sense of commercialism. FitzGerald had continued to operate *The Press* as a political newspaper in support of his own political ideas and career. But with the other publications he was trying out new saleable commodities and was researching and aiming to meet a new market. He was successful in building a substantial business enterprise but that very success was eventually to cost him his ownership of the enterprise. To follow this it is necessary to outline his relationship with the firm of Harman and Stevens, a partnership which specialized in managing the affairs of absentee landowners. As individuals Harman and FitzGerald had been among the opposition to Moorhouse, and Harman was a member of the original syndicate which formed *The Press.* FitzGerald's business activity required an increased staff at both the manual and editorial levels as well as an increase in printing and ancillary machinery plus larger buildings in which to house the enterprise. Such a newspaper concern required considerable capital, both for expansion and for running expenses. FitzGerald stated it as follows:

> I have paid my way, including wages now never less that £100 every Monday morning. I have bought large quantities of plant, have built largely, and have now £4000 of debts on the books.[10]

FitzGerald's debts were in the main to Harman and Stevens to whom, in October 1863, FitzGerald had given the power of attorney to manage the business. This authority was an acknowledgement, initially, of FitzGerald's practical rather than financial indebtedness to Harman

---

10   FitzGerald to Selfe, 22 May 1864.

and Stevens. FitzGerald, who had resigned from the House of Representatives in 1857, was re-elected to it in June 1862. His political involvement, especially his absences from Canterbury, often precluded him from having day-to-day control of *The Press*, and Stevens had begun to act for him as the business manager of the enterprise. The practical demands of political position and of newspaper proprietorship were in conflict for FitzGerald in the 1860s in a way that had not occurred in the 1850s. In the 1860s the business concerns of the increasingly commercial press required a day-to-day administration and control that had not been needed a decade earlier. It became progressively more difficult for the one individual effectively to be both an elected political representative and a newspaper controller. An increased division of labour was needed and Harman and Stevens's control of *The Press* began as agents for an owner absent because of political duties.

FitzGerald, after giving the power of attorney to Harman and Stevens, began borrowing heavily from them to finance the expansion of his newspaper concerns. A year later, in October 1864, he was in debt to them for £3987. Late in 1866 the debt had increased to £8836 and it was at this stage that Harman and Stevens began to oust FitzGerald from the business. When, in March 1867, FitzGerald was appointed Comptroller-General of the Colony and moved to Wellington, his home until his death, *The Press* was under the total control of its two principal creditors.

The end for FitzGerald probably came in 1865 when the *Lyttelton Times* had finally removed his advantage by itself coming out daily. It was not a year of business growth in Canterbury and, rather than holding still or beginning to repay his debt, FitzGerald continued the attack and, increasing his debt, purchased new plant so as to equal the format of the older paper. FitzGerald, however, displayed considerable business acumen in developing the paper and the money he put into it was always wisely spent. Although at the cost of his personal control of *The Press*, he did put it on a sure footing at the scale necessary to take advantage of the population increase of the 1860s and 1870s. It was due to his initial daring and skill that *The Press* became a viable concern alongside its established rival and Christchurch was for so long able to enjoy that rarity in New Zealand cities: competing morning dailies.

As a final point in regard to FitzGerald's removal from *The Press*, one can only agree with O'Neill's conclusion that the firm of Harman and

Stevens, while interested in keeping *The Press* profitable, did not have FitzGerald's own interests at heart.

> ... it is difficult to resist the conclusion that Harman and Stevens viewed with equanimity, even if they did not actively hasten the train of events that lead to their taking over *The Press*. Harman's interest in the proprietorship had been made clear many years earlier; and it is certainly improbable that he and his partner, who were among the shrewdest financial brains in Christchurch in their day, would have allowed *The Press* to run away with so much of their capital if they had not contemplated the possibility indeed almost the certainty of taking over the business themselves.[11]

Sometime in the late 1860s the business was formed into a company and the paper's ownership widened. O'Neill, speaking of the 1870 shareholders states, "Little remains.... to represent the formerly dominant interest of the 'Church Party', the landed gentry, the settlement leaders. It is mainly a group of business-men, perhaps more interested in steady dividends than in literary prestige or even political influence."[12] This change was exemplified during the 1870s by the dominance of Charles Alexander Pritchard in The Press Company. Pritchard, resident in Dunedin since 1863, had conducted a timber and shipping business until a combination of competition from Tasmanian timber exports, the increasing age and declining utility of his sailing ships, and his insufficient capital to purchase steamers, forced him to look for a new business. He began buying shares in The Press Company in 1871. It is difficult to determine when he took overall control of the company. In 1879 when the total capital was £30,000 he had shares with a face value of £16,800. But he was managing director from 1872. O'Neill, however, exaggerates the nature of the changes to the policy of *The Press*. It was not a matter of financial profit replacing political influence as the motivation of the newspaper's proprietors. Both were sought. Pritchard had no personal political career but *The Press* remained as a firm political advocate. In particular in the 1870s its opposition to Grey's Ministry was as strong as any political stance taken by FitzGerald during his years of ownership of the paper.

The combination of direct political involvement and journalistic

---

11  O'Neill (1963) p 86.
12  Ibid p 92.

## The Start of the Daily Press

endeavour ceased for FitzGerald, as it had for Vogel, when the need for additional capital made vulnerable his control of his papers. In Vogel's case loss of control had come with incorporation, while for FitzGerald his personal indebtedness had given Harman and Stevens control of *The Press*. In both cases the investment needs of an increasingly commercial newspaper concern had led to changed circumstances and the removal of proprietors who were also political representatives from the newspapers that had acted as their political advocates. While it was in no sense a removal of political advocacy from New Zealand newspapers, both cases are instances of a change to the previous majority pattern, that of newspaper advocacy on behalf of the newspaper's proprietor who was also a prominent politician.

Even when the possibility of takeover was not present, the growing economic needs of the New Zealand press in the 1860s was to put pressure on those who combined newspaper ownership with a political career. This is most noticeable in the decisions made by William Reeves of the *Lyttelton Times* in the years from 1867. The *Lyttelton Times* had had a political and business division of labour apportioned between Reeves and Crosbie Ward, the two major owners, but in 1867 Ward died at the age of 35 whereupon Reeves contested and won his deceased partner's seat. Reeves, however, was to resign the seat in the following year. Newspaper management was not the part-time occupation of previous decades and, with his partner dead, Reeves found himself forced to devote full attention to his business. The specific reason for his return as full-time business manager of the paper was an act of retrenchment on Harman and Stevens's part. They controlled Reeves's rival, *The Press*. Faced with a continuing depression they, from April 1868, ceased daily publication and *The Press* became a tri-weekly. Reeves seized the opportunity to gain overall control of the Canterbury newspaper field and moved to bring out another daily paper. Accordingly he resigned his seat in Parliament on 2 May 1868 and on 14 May 1868 the *Lyttelton Times* brought out an evening daily, the *Star*, which is now, along with *The Press*, one of the two surviving Christchurch papers.

Reeves intended his sacrifice of a political career to be temporary and he stood for election in 1871 becoming M.H.R. for Selwyn until Parliament's dissolution in December 1875. Higher office was possible for him as Vogel twice offered him a portfolio. On both occasions, however, Reeves decided his newspaper commitments prevented him from accepting. "Somewhat later he was offered the Chairmanship of Committees in the House of Representatives, but refused that also, as he had decided to devote his life to the direction of his newspaper."[13]

Reeves' political sacrifice did pay dividends for his business as he gained the initiative in his competition with *The Press*. His major success was the establishment of his evening paper, the *Star*. He was unsuccessful in what would have been another aim, that of killing off his rival while it was in a weakened state. Harman and Stevens's decision to revert to tri-weekly publication had been a mistake. Sales and revenue continued to decline. In December 1868, under FitzGerald's persuasion (he still held 80 shares of £25 each),[14] they returned to daily publication and also lowered the price to 1d. This saved the paper but the eight months of tri-weekly publication had given the *Star* the time necessary to build up a circulation. Not until six years later, in 1874, did The Press Company retaliate against the *Star* by sponsoring another evening daily, the *Globe*. At this point the two newspaper concerns returned to parity and the situation was to remain largely unchanged for sixty years, until the newspaper war of the 1930s.

**Newspaper Proprietors as Entrepreneurs**

The commercial potential of newspapers became clear in the 1860s. It led not only to the replacement or to changes in the behaviour of the existing proprietors but became the impetus for the launching of a number of new newspapers by new proprietors. These new proprietors were differentiated from the old by their lack of concern with personal political involvement and their concentration on managing their new newspapers as sound and profitable businesses. Both the Cook Strait settlements were to host newspapers of this type and, in both cases, the newspapers were to become established and successful.

In Nelson the new paper, the *Evening Mail,* was begun on 5 March 1866 by Robert Lucas, a Somerset printer, who had arrived in the city in 1859 or 1860 and started a printing establishment. After two unsuccessful attempts to establish a newspaper in his first year in Nelson, he waited until 1866, judging that conditions were finally favourable.[15] The *Evening Mail* was unlike the other two Nelson papers

---

13 *Christchurch Times* Souvenir Supplement, 29 June 1935.

14 Harman and Stevens reformed the ownership structure of *The Press* on 1 December 1868 as The Press Company Ltd. It had a capital of £4000 in £25 shares. FitzGerald was allotted half the shares but they were secured to Harman and Stevens.

in that business rather than political involvement was the primary reason it was started. By the time of the *Evening Mail* Nelson's population was over 10,000 strong. It was 2560 in 1842 when the *Examiner* began. The greater population meant that a paper as a profit-making enterprise was possible and the *Evening Mail* was begun to exploit this opportunity. The first editorial immediately disavowed the role of political advocate as had been followed by the *Examiner,* and the *Colonist.*

> We desire expressly to state that this journal has not been started in opposition to those at present existing; nor at the desire of any particular sect or party; but mainly to supply an evident requirement of the whole community. We think that this city has arrived at such a stage of prosperity and importance, that only a daily paper can properly express its varied requirements.
> (*Evening Mail,* 5 March 1866)

This new orientation received a fuller treatment on the front page, the paper's first advertising page.

> No expense will be spared by the Proprietors in obtaining for this Journal the most complete and reliable mercantile intelligence from the chief commercial centres of New Zealand, Australia, etc. Authentic accounts from the various goldfields of the West Coast and other parts of the Colony; the earliest intelligence of all matters of local interest, of the progress of events in the North Island; the English and colonial news, on the arrival of each mail steamer; and of all matters likely to be of interest to the inhabitants of this City.... in fact no pains will be spared to render the *Evening Mail* a first class Merchantile Journal.

Lucas' term "Merchantile Journal" refers to a new type of daily press in New Zealand. The term "Merchantile Journal" does not refer to a specialized publication for the business community. On the contrary the low price of the new paper, the *Evening Mail* being Nelson's first penny paper, was calculated to give the paper a wide circulation. The links with the business community can be seen in this fact for a penny paper,

---

15  The *Nelson Advertiser and Family Paper* lasted for almost seven months. The other, the *Nelson Intelligence and Day of the Golden Isle* had a shorter life.

by virtue of its low price, both gains a wider circulation, thus making itself more attractive to advertisers, and becomes dependent on advertising to make up the deficit caused by its lower selling price. Apart from its price, the novel item offered by the *Evening Mail* was news, as is clear in the above quotation. The increased frequency of publication of a daily meant the news could be printed as soon as it was available. The other vital link in the news chain was the telegraph, a device which gave a flow of news sufficient to feed a daily publication. From the *Evening Mail*'s first edition it can be seen that the paper's inauguration was timed, albeit unsuccessfully, to coincide with the arrival of the telegraph.

> We are sorry to be unable to announce that the telegraph line is opened in time for our first publication. The contract for fixing the posts and wires was to have been completed on Saturday last ...

Although the *Evening Mail* did not appear at the behest of "any particular sect or party", it was not the province of a newspaper to divorce itself from political matters, a fact the *Colonist* was quick to point out.

> The *Mail* announces that it does "not pretend to be in any respect a political paper", yet, in only its second and third issues, as if to prove the impossibility of creating a non-political colonial journal, it touches on political topics, refers to the increased taxation of this colony, and warns us to remove its causes.
>
> (*Colonist,* 9 March 1866)

The point made by the *Colonist,* however, was gained only by means of an incomplete and misleading quotation from the *Evening Mail.* The complete relevant paragraph is:

> The *Evening Mail* will not pretend to be in any respect a Political Paper; yet as occasion may offer, when it will be necessary to express an opinion upon such matters, the proprietors desire to state that it will be a thoroughly independent Journal, attached to no party, devoted to no faction, seeking only to advance the interests of this Province, and the property of the entire Colony.

## The Start of the Daily Press

The *Evening Mail* recognized the necessity to report and discuss political matters. It aimed to do so, however, without losing its independence, without itself becoming embroiled in political affairs. Such a desire was a departure from the established political role of the various New Zealand newspapers; that of recognized linkages with, and support for, a particular political group. This new orientation, as represented by the *Evening Mail*, was both a new understanding of the political process in New Zealand and a statement that the press was not classifiable within the orbit of political allegiance.

A further specification of the nature of newspaper political independence was to be given in the North Island. In both the major centres, the social and political changes that accompanied the land wars were to become the occasion for a change of newspapers.

In Wellington, the original strong rivalry between the *Spectator* and the *Independent* had become muted over the years and, by the late 1850s, the pair had settled into a stable sharing of the market. The advent of the *New Zealand Advertiser* with its early adoption of the normal newspaper format and pricing structure disturbed the Wellington press equilibrium. Of the two established Wellington newspapers, the *Spectator* was the more hurt by the advent of the *Advertiser* and, from this time on, it experienced a decline that culminated, ironically, in its closure on 5 August 1865 by means of its purchase and incorporation into its undesired offspring, the *Independent*. New competition, coupled with its own increasingly unacceptable editorial policy, led to the *Spectator*'s downfall. The "aristocratic" *Spectator,* as Hocken terms it,[16] began and continued as a support and discussion medium for the higher status members of the Wellington community. Its alliance with this group and, especially, its eventual support of the British Colonial office and of Grey and his policies had meant that the paper had adopted, among other measures, a peaceful policy towards the Maori. It was this policy, coupled with its opposition to land confiscation, which in the bellicose 1860s exacerbated the *Spectator*'s difficulties.

The final blow for the *Spectator* was the presence in Wellington of yet another newspaper, the *Evening Post*, which, early in 1865, meant there were four newspapers operating in the city. The *Evening Post*, the only Wellington paper of this period which still continues, is, like the *Nelson Evening Mail*, an example of a commercial rather than a political paper. It was begun as a penny daily to take advantage of the incipient

---

16   Hocken (1901) p. 104.

economic opportunities present in journalism. Though it was to have political views and allegiances it was not begun to promote any specific political group or policy. There were no recognized political figures among its proprietors or backers and, like the *Nelson Evening Mail*, it was to quarrel with the established doctrine that newspapers were political advocates attached to recognized political groups.

The first issue of the *Evening Post* was on 8 February 1865. It was begun by Henry Blundell and David Curle. The partners soon realized there was not a living for both of them in the venture and the notice of dissolution of the partnership is in the *Evening Post* of 8 July 1865. Blundell continued the paper as sole proprietor.

Blundell and Curle were both professional newspapermen who wished to gain a viable journalistic concern and were prepared to reside wherever necessary to further this aim. Blundell was a printer who had worked for 27 years in Dublin on the *Evening Mail* ending as manager of the paper. Emigrating to Melbourne in 1860, he was in New Zealand for a period in 1861 before settling permanently in 1863. He worked for the *Lyttelton Times* and the *Otago Daily Times* before, in 1864, moving to Marlborough and starting the *Havelock Mail* to serve the Wakamarina diggings. Curle was in association with Blundell by this stage. Noting that the Marlborough goldfields were already failing, they considered a North Island site for their paper. Rejecting Wanganui because of its proximity to the fighting, they decided to take the opportunity, three years after a daily had been established in New Zealand, of starting the first daily in Wellington.

The paper opened with an unpretentious statement which attempted to place it on a different level from that of the existing journals.

> From the success attending the issue of family Evening Papers in the other Provinces of New Zealand and in the sister colonies the proprietors of the *Evening Post* are lead to hope that the inhabitants of Wellington will hail with pleasure the appearance of a journal devoted to their interests.
> (*Evening Post*, 8 February 1865)

But in the next few weeks it was obvious that the paper was not without opinions many of which were political in content. On the major question of the war, it was to state its case early and was to be firmly on the side of majority opinion.

... we are convinced it is owing in a great measure to the philo-anglo-mania that this war (if it can be called war) has been so protracted and unsuccessful, and it is high time we put aside all ultra-philanthropic doctrines, allow of no ecclesiastical interference, and exert every measure to strike terror into the hearts of the cowardly murderers of our fellow-countrymen. (*Evening Post*, 15 February 1865)

Blundell, like Lucas in Nelson, recognized that his paper would, by virtue of being a newspaper, both report on political matters and state political opinions. Like Lucas, however, he de-emphasized the role of the press as a political forum as hitherto practised. Blundell's policy was always to decline to be associated with political partners or to stand for any public office for fear of compromising his paper's independence. It was this policy which distinguished him from previous proprietors and it was this policy which was advanced as a mark of newspaper independence and objectivity.

Major changes occurred among the Auckland newspapers, as in those of the rest of the colony, in the 1860s. As in Wellington and Nelson, Auckland was to have, with the *New Zealand Herald,* a newspaper founded primarily for financial, rather than political, profit. But, before it appeared, both of the existing newspapers were to follow the lead of the *Otago Daily Times* and change to daily publication.

The first to change was the *Southern Cross,* which became a daily on 20 May 1862. The Auckland population had grown from 2795 in 1842 to 24,420 in 1861. This was not much less than Otago's mining-swollen 1861 population of 27,163 and the Auckland increase had been, by far, the more steady. The 1858 figures, for example, had been 18,177 in Auckland, while that for Otago and Southland combined was 6944. It would not be long before Vogel's lead was followed in Auckland and New Zealand's second daily started. The major figure in the *Southern Cross* in the 1860s was Robert Creighton. William Brown, the proprietor, had left Auckland for Scotland in 1855 never to return. He retained, however, his business interests and, in 1861, had employed Creighton in England to go to Auckland and take over the *Southern Cross.* Creighton became manager and editor on the day the paper started as a daily.[17] The price was reduced from 6d to 3d, the same price as Vogel's *Otago Daily Times.*

## The Making of the New Zealand Press

In 1863 the *New Zealander,* owned by William Wilson and John Williamson, followed its rival into daily publication. However, the *New Zealander* had outrun its period of influence and was in a time of decline that ran to its closure in 1866. The *New Zealander* had long been one of the few papers in the country with a pronounced sympathy for the Maori. This attitude, which dated back beyond the paper's long support for Grey and his policies to its original linkage with the Wesleyan Mission in New Zealand, cost it public support in the 1860s. Late in 1863 Williamson and Wilson were to dissolve their partnership. Main, who then became printer and publisher of the paper, describes the termination of the partnership as "owing to a difference of opinion over the policy to be advocated by the paper in the Taranaki and Waikato wars (Williamson) being for the philo-Maori party, and (Wilson) in favour of what was then known as 'the vigorous prosecution' policy, and compelling the natives to submit to the supremacy of the law and of the Queen".[18] While there is no questioning the sincerity of either man's beliefs, one cannot but suspect that Wilson, who had been the practical manager of the *New Zealander,* was applying a pragmatic newspaperman's appreciation to the political realities of the day. Wilson had long been happy to concur with Williamson's philosophy, but in the jingoistic atmosphere of the 1860s, pro-Maori sentiment met with little white support.

With Wilson gone, Williamson became sole proprietor of a declining paper. The financial difficulties of the paper grew and, when in May 1866 the *New Zealander*'s office burnt down, the paper was not revived.

On leaving the *New Zealander* Wilson immediately made plans to begin another newspaper and printing business, and on 13 November 1863 the *New Zealand Herald* was first issued. Wilson's partner on this

---

17 Creighton was later to advance some rather tortuous logic in pursuit of a claim that his was New Zealand's first daily: "... six years ago, in the present month, we published the first daily newspaper printed in the North Island, we had almost said in the Colony, because the *Otago Daily Times* preceded us by a few weeks only, and it ought to be remembered that that paper was the first political fruit of the newly discovered goldfields, which have worked such a marvellous transformation on the Middle Island. The influx of the mining population and trades of Victoria revolutionized Otago, politically as well as socially; and the *Daily Times* was really, at the start, a Victorian, and not a New Zealand paper. Therefore, we hold, that the first purely New Zealand newspaper which appeared daily was published in Auckland." (*Auckland Free Press,* 11 May 1868.)

18 Main (1891) p 2.

## The Start of the Daily Press

venture was David Burns from the staff of the *New Zealander*, who became the first *Herald* editor. Burns left the partnership within the first year of operation, leaving Wilson sole proprietor.

The *New Zealand Herald* began with decided views on the two major political questions of the day, the future relationship of the North and South Islands, and the New Zealand wars. For the first it wanted continual union and, for the second, a strong military approach.

> ... The native rebellion, though the most prominent and not the least important, is not the only question that agitates New Zealand... There is another and vital question... which the government are seeking to set at rest, dealing with it in the most considerate and conciliatory spirit. That question is the better government of the Middle Island, on which an animated and adjoined debate in the House of Representatives has already taken place. In the course of the arguments employed, allusions to the removal of the seat of government from Auckland, of possible separation of the Northern and Southern Islands, were made... thoughtful discrimination will be necessary to constitute a form of legislature such as, without injustice to Auckland, shall prove satisfactory to the Middle Island... even with such distracting questions as the seat of Government, and possible separation, there is an evident and an honourable anxiety on the part of representatives, both of North and South, to inculcate the old and wholesome precept, 'Union is strength'.
> 
> ... But how are the rebels to be called to account? Their best friends are free to confess that a crushing defeat would be the truest mercy to them ... The rebels should be energetically dealt with. The war has been one of their own compelling. They commenced it with cold-blooded, deliberate assassinations. They are following it up with stealthy murders of defenceless women and children. The fruits of a life of industry are the sacrifices of their vengence. Agriculture perishes. Commerce languishes. Enterprise stands still. And a great and glorious country runs to ruinous waste until the murderer and marauder shall be imperatively taught that life and property must be preserved and Law and Order maintained inviolate.
> (*New Zealand Herald*, 13 November 1863)

The Herald thus supported the Government on the constitutional question of representation for the two islands. In regard to race relations the *Herald,* in Main's words, "advocated a 'vigorous prosecution' policy",[19] but it is also pertinent to quote Scholefield's assessment. He sees Wilson as starting "a paper which would be more in sympathy with public opinion" and cites the *Herald* as "a striking example of a newspaper founded as a business rather than a political organ".[20] This is not to say that the *New Zealand Herald* was, or is, an apolitical journal. The paper's opening statement and its subsequent actions have shown this is far from the case. More to the point is to say that, as with the later *Evening Post, Nelson Evening Mail* and other similar papers, the *Herald* was not founded as, and did not become, a springboard for personal political careers for its owners. It was this point that, the proprietors argued, gave them political independence. As their prospectus, republished in the first issue, put it:

> (The proprietors are) so entirely free from political, personal or party bias that they can point to their abstinence upon every occasion of entering into any competition for place or office, whether in the General or Provincial Legislatures, or in any other branch of the public services. This, they believe, may be regarded as one material guarantee for political independence. (*New Zealand Herald,* 13 November 1863)

**Political Advocacy and Political Independence**

The new commercial journalism led to a significant change in the political role of the press. Prior to self-government, newspapers had acted as political discussion forums with participation in these forums being largely confined to the higher-status settlers in the various settlements. After self-government, this practice continued but was contained within a framework of partisan advocacy within each separate province. In the economically unattractive climate that existed for newspapers prior to the 1860s, such a political role became the major orientation in New Zealand journalism. With the new commercial journalism, however, the role of political advocate as hitherto practised had to take account of and become compatible with the new role of the newspaper as a profit-oriented business enterprise. There was also the

---

19  Ibid p. 3.
20  Scholefield (1958) p. 83.

appearance of new proprietors who eschewed the role of personal political involvement. In practice the role of political advocacy did not end but declined in importance against the advertising and news giving functions. There was, however, a specification of the political views that could be advocated. This became apparent with Vogel's dismissal from the *Otago Daily Times*. It was not that an editor or owner could no longer use a paper to advocate political beliefs. Both the *New Zealand Herald* and the *Evening Post,* two major examples of the new commercial journalism, had by this time strongly advocated decided political views. Political advocacy *per se* was not the problem. When political advocacy and commercial activity could both be successfully conducted then all went well. But when political advocacy entailed commercial failure, or unacceptable commercial risk as perceived by a proprietor's monetary allies, then political advocacy had to give way. The new state was that financial survival, with its demand for profit, took precedence over other requirements. The point was politely but firmly made to FitzGerald of *The Press* by his creditor Harman.

> Your position here as a leading politician has sometimes, I think, acted to your prejudice as a newspaper proprietor. With all deference to your judgment and knowledge of the business, which I admit to be far greater than that professed by our firm in such matters, I believe it would be better for you that we should conduct any negotiations which may be thought desirable with the *Lyttelton Times* or any other office. Papers are in the habit of hitting each other pretty hard at times; and in the small circle of provincial politics it is impossible to prevent the idea which will inevitably rise in the heat of party conflicts that AB (of *The Press*), who is perfectly well known, has been using rather strong language against CD (of the *Lyttelton Times*) whose individuality is equally well ascertained; and thus, feelings of hostility arise, which are not conducive to friendly knowledge of facts when I say that such is the case: and I propose that, for the future, we should be the exponents of your proposals, or even that you will allow us, as the commercial agents of the paper, to make proposals which would not be entertained from yourself.[21]

---

21  Harman to FitzGerald. Quoted in O'Neill, pp.80-81.

An editor or owner could still use a paper as a political platform and it was also to become apparent that the new business orientation was itself a political statement. However, any political advocacy now had to command sufficient support so as not to endanger the paper financially. Especially in times which were less than financially buoyant, the advocacy of unpopular political beliefs was not permitted. Business imperatives were now paramount.

The shareholding system that became the method of control of such newspapers as the *Otago Daily Times* and *The Press* ended the personal dominance of a single proprietor. As a result, the practice whereby a newspaper was the political mouthpiece for its proprietor, who was also a prominent politician, became less common. As the experience of Reeves of the *Lyttelton Times* indicated, even when newspapers remained under the control of a single proprietor, the demands of a daily newspaper forced a proprietor to choose between a political career and continuing day-to-day control of his newspaper. Newspaper proprietors were less able to have a prominent personal involvement in Provincial Councils or in the General Assembly. This change received support from the new newspapers where there was a new ideology whereby personal political involvement was seen as inappropriate for proprietors. This was a major change and, as was argued by the proprietors of the *New Zealand Herald*, this change was seen as an indication of the political independence of newspapers.

However, the assertion of political independence must be seen as distinct from political neutrality. While personal political advocacy became less common and, at least for the new newspapers, began to be seen as improper, the espousal of decided political views remained. While many newspapers no longer had an irrevocable commitment to the political views and careers of their proprietors, newspapers remained as political advocates. As before, there was within each province, and increasingly over the whole country, a pattern of newspaper support and opposition which articulated and helped define the major political divisions. As before, newspaper managements considered it their professional right and duty actively to support and promote politicians of their choice. Only too often the ending of personal political involvement by newspaper proprietors served as a justifying and obfuscating argument for the political neutrality of the New Zealand press whereas the fact of political allegiance remained.

# 7. Politics and Profit: Main Centre Daily Newspapers 1860-1879

My intention in this chapter is to examine the political and economic motivations behind the established and the attempted daily newspapers in the two decades from 1860 to 1879. I restrict myself to the main centres of Auckland, Dunedin and Wellington. Christchurch will not be discussed here. The two main newspaper concerns there, *The Press* and the *Lyttelton Times,* also began and controlled the other important newspaper ventures in that city. These have already been examined. In the three cities to be discussed both the political and economic concerns of newspaper controllers were important. Economic success was aimed for, and was accompanied by, a decline in the previous pattern of newspapers acting as personal political advocates. But this did not entail the end of partisan political advocacy. This remained as normal newspaper policy.

In the two decades from 1860-1879 the rate of foundation for newspapers in New Zealand was higher than at any other time, before or after, in the country's history. A country which in 1859 supported 15 newspapers saw a further 181 founded in the following 20 years. In these 20 years these foundations were offset by 87 cessations. Thus there were 109 newspapers publishing in New Zealand in 1879.

This rate of foundation reflected considerable optimism among would-be newspaper proprietors. Nor was this optimism without justification. The gold discoveries and the population growth of the 1860s and 1870s,the success of the *Otago Daily Times* and other early daily newspapers, and the economic growth attendant on the borrowing policy of the 1870s all made founding a newspaper appear a worthwhile business risk. For some decades a large number of the newspapers in the country were to receive both public support and financial success. 1910 was the year in which the number of newspapers reached its height. There were, in that year, 193 newspapers publishing of which 67 were dailies. After 1910 improvements in road and rail transportation increased the reach of the larger dailies and there began a decline in the number of newspapers. Not only did smaller center publications fold under the competition from their city counterparts but also the larger newspaper concerns gradually ceased publishing weekly stablemates to their dailies.

This process of decline in the number of newspapers emphasizes the importance of the 1860s and 1870s in the long-term newspaper history of New Zealand. Of the current newspapers in daily publication all but two were founded by the end of the 1870s. The exceptions to this pattern of newspaper foundation are the Wellington morning daily, the *Dominion,* which was started in 1907 and the *National Business Review* which began daily publication in 1987.

## Auckland

After the foundation of the *New Zealand Herald* at least eight separate attempts were made in the 1860s and 1870s to start further daily papers in Auckland. What was to become known as the *Auckland Star,* which is still publishing, gained supremacy in the evening field. There were to be no serious challenges to the *New Zealand Herald*'s and *SouthernCross*'s hold over the market for a morning paper.

The first competitor was the *Auckland Evening Post* which was started on 28 November 1864 by two otherwise unknown would-be proprietors, Michael Wood and J. Donchaise. Only the one copy of one issue, the first, survives. How long the paper continued is unknown. The paper's opening statement is representative of all but one of the attempted dailies over this period. The political role of the earlier papers, the desire to be an advocate and participant in local and national affairs, was pushed into the background, and the self-image of an independent information-giver reigned supreme.

> Respecting politics we have at present no opinions to express, we enter upon our course independent of all party feeling ....
> The principal topic to which we shall render our most earnest attention will be that of the commercial interest. A complete resume of the day's shipping in connexion with the state of the markets, auction sales, etc, etc, will be found in our columns. All other matters of local interest appertaining both to town and country will be duly sought after, such as Police news, town and country improvements, amusement, and other subjects of alike character, not of course forgetting the most important of all, viz: to furnish our readers with every scrap of intelligence that may come to hand respecting the all important question of public interest at this present time Is it to be peace or war?
> (*Auckland Evening Post,* 28 November 1864)

The *Auckland Evening Post* failed to become established. Its difficulties and its failure were those of most would-be daily newspapers of those or subsequent years. It had, as did all intending dailies, the need to attract a high circulation so as to offset the high costs of daily publication. It also, again along with all intending dailies, faced the problem of attracting a mass rather than a specific readership. Previous New Zealand newspapers had usually been oriented towards politically defined specific audiences. At least in theory this should give room for as many newspapers as there are political groupings. It also follows that newspapers would not attempt to attract readers by changing the newspapers' policy. Political newspapers attracted new readers by educating and converting readers of other political persuasions, not by changing the newspaper policy to give it a wider appeal. The new daily newspapers, however, were oriented to a mass rather than a specific audience. While this gave them the widest possible potential readership it left them in a position of considerable vulnerability in regards to any established daily newspaper. The existing newspaper also was oriented to the same mass audience. Would-be challengers did not have a specific untapped readership to attract. Nor, being forced to have a general appeal, could they offer much that was different to the presentations of the existing dailies. Would-be challengers could offer little that was novel.

The major variation that could be offered by daily newspapers was time of publication. In practice, the pattern that emerged was one where two time-slots, morning and evening, were distributed among the competing dailies. The process of competition was one where, eventually, in the main centers, two dailies remained, one in each time slot. In the case of Christchurch this point was not reached until the 1930s. It does not represent an end point. Dunedin has in recent years lost its evening newspaper. Further closures are conceivable.

The *Auckland Evening Post* was the first attempt in that city to fill the vacant evening time-slot. It was unsuccessful. Not until 1870 when the *Star* was established was the evening position won. While the dailies of the 1860s were appealing to a mass audience they were also in a process of anticipating the arrival of such an audience. It was some years before either the readership or the newspapers were established. The early years were, for many newspapers, years of anticipating a readership and survival was precarious. The position was more difficult for the evening than the morning newspapers. The morning dailies also needed and sought a mass readership. But, in their quest for a growing circulation they began with an established, although small, readership. The evening dailies sought from the start the newly literate.

The *Post* was followed, on 9 July 1867, by another attempt at an evening paper, the *Evening News*. It was started by James Allen, junior, who had worked for the *Southern Cross*. The paper ran until 7 December 1871 but suffered declining fortunes from 1870 after the death of Allen. His father, James Allen, senior, took over the paper and lost much support because of his opposition to Vogel and his policies. This opposition to Vogel indicates the nature of the political motivation of the new commercial newspapers. The *Evening News*, like the other commercial newspapers, stated that it was politically independent. But like them it meant by this that its management were not personally seeking political office. It did, however, have political allegiances. As with the other contemporary newspapers the *Evening News* followed a policy of political advocacy. Unhappily its opposition to Vogel, at the time of Vogel's national political ascendency, was incompatible with public acceptance of the newspaper. A morning edition, the *Morning News*, was attempted in 1870 but at the end of 1871 the whole concern was purchased by the *Star* for £430 and closed down.

In 1868 there began the *Auckland Free Press*, a penny daily. With the end of the war, its editor foresaw a period of prosperity for Auckland, and so there was to be, but not immediately and not for the *Free Press*. There was first a time of depression occasioned by the withdrawal of the troops. It was not an opportune time to oppose the *Herald* and *Southern Cross* and the *Free Press* was to survive only six weeks.

A political daily followed in 1869. This was a political newspaper in the old style; one established not for commercial gain but begun deliberately to promote the political career of a favoured individual. The candidates for the Superintendency election of that year were John Williamson and Judge Gillies. It was Gillies's supporters who began a paper in his interest. It was the *Auckland Daily News* and ran from 4 November to 9 December, which was one week after the announcement of Gillies's election.

The paper started with the usual affirmations of independence.

> The projectors of *The Auckland Daily News* have been for some time impressed with the necessity that was growing up in this province for a thoroughly efficient and independent journal,

whose chief aim shall be to lead and expound public opinion uninfluenced by party ties.
(*Auckland Daily News,* 4 November 1869)

But its colours were immediately obvious.

> The question is not, as assumed, one of Centralism against Provincialism, but of reform against abuse and chronic misrule: honesty and economy against jobbery and extravagence: a straightforward and impartial administration of the affairs of the province against a corrupt system of petty patronage, the most odious and intolerable, and which not only is wasting the substance of the people but demoralising them at the same time. Even in years gone by a bad pre-eminence in this respect almost invariably attachs to Mr Williamson's rule.
> (*Auckland Daily News,* 4 November 1869)

During the campaign few chances were missed to attack Williamson. An example is the following:

> The charge of "violent assault" against Patrick Bonfield—a notorious partizan of the ex-Superintendent, was heard before the bench at Shortland on Tuesday, and resulted in the sentence of a fortnight's imprisonment.
> (*Auckland Daily News,* 16 November 1869)

The management of the newspaper succeeded in their political aims. Their candidate did win office. But it was not possible to keep the newspaper going so as to continue support for Gillies. The *Daily News* was a newspaper that was part of Gillies's electoral campaign. It was against the trend of change which was seeing the demise of newspapers as personal political advocates. The short life of the *Daily News* was an indication of the temporary nature of any attempt to revive the older journalism.

1869 was also the year in which a change of ownership took place with the *Southern Cross*. The *Southern Cross* continued through the 1860s and well into the 1870s, but in spite of the fact that it had the advantage of precedence over the *New Zealand Herald,* it was financially the less flourishing of the two major Auckland dailies. Its disadvantage was the absence of guiding leadership. Nor was it again to receive strong management. In 1862 when the *Southern Cross* began daily publication,

## The Making of the New Zealand Press

Robert Creighton had been appointed by William Brown to edit and manage the newspaper. Creighton stayed with the paper until 1865 when he was elected to parliament and resigned as editor. But for much of this time he had been in the field as a war correspondent and thus was out of day-to-day contact with his charge. The paper continued with various editors until 1869 when Julius Vogel acquired control. After being ousted from the *Otago Daily Times*, and running the short-lived *New Zealand Sun*, Vogel went north to Auckland in 1869 presumably in search of a new political power base.

The contradictions between the political and commercial desires of newspaper proprietors are most clearly seen with Julius Vogel. Vogel, in being the principal figure in the early years of the *Otago Daily Times*, is the individual most singly responsible for indicating New Zealand newspapers could achieve commercial success. His removal from that newspaper also made him, with his Otago-based political career, an early casualty of the commercial demands of the daily press. Yet he remained desirous of having a newspaper which was both a commercially successful daily and a political advocate for him personally. He formed a company which took over the *Southern Cross* property for £12,000. Vogel acquired a controlling interest with a personal investment of £4600. Vogel edited the paper and Charles Williamson was manager. However, almost immediately on completion of these changes, Stafford's government fell, Fox became Premier, and Vogel was summoned to Wellington as Colonial Treasurer. The paper was thus again under the control of an absentee owner and continued as a losing concern. Vogel became Premier in April 1873 and, in May, he sold his interest in the *Southern Cross*, moving his newspaper attention to Wellington. The new owners failed to revive the *Southern Cross*. It was to be closed down in 1876.

The next paper was the *Auckland and Thames Leader* which started on 4 December 1869 and may have lasted into 1870. It was followed, on 4 January 1870, by the *Morning Advertiser*, which also had only a short life. Both papers were run by J. Harnett and Co. who, in the first issue of the *Morning Advertiser* (copies of only the first two issues survive) list their newspaper experience. It is an instructive chronicle of the nomadic character of the times. In their sixteen years of experience they had been Proprietors, Printers and Publishers of:

## Main Centre Daily Newspapers 1860-1879

Victoria. 1. *The Age* 2. *The Weekly Age* 3. *The Leader* 4. *Der Kosmopolit* 5. *My Note Book* 6. *The Wesleyan Chronicle* New South Wales 7. *The Twofold Bay Times* New Zealand. Southland 8. *The Southland Times* 9. *The Weekly Despatch* Marlborough 10. *The Marlborough Times* West Coast 11. *The Evening News* 12. *The West Coast Times* 13. *The Evening Despatch* 14. *The Leader*. 15. *The Ross Guardian* 16. *The Waimea Chronicle* The Thames District 17. *The Times* 18. *The Evening Star* 19. *The Auckland and Thames Leader* Auckland 20. *The Morning Advertiser*.

The *Auckland Star,* which continues as Auckland's sole evening daily, began as the *Evening Star* on 8 January 1870.[1] The initial impetus for the paper came from William Tyrone Ferrar.[2] Ferrar presumably saw, with the death of Allen of the *Evening News,* a chance for another evening paper and he enlisted as a partner George McCullogh Reed, newly arrived from Victoria, who became editor of the paper. The paper was first printed by the *Southern Cross* but, in March 1870, Henry Brett, a printer with the *New Zealand Herald,* bought a third interest in the paper and the printing was transferred to the Herald's office. Henry Brett learnt the printing trade in Sussex and came to New Zealand in 1862. He was a reporter for the *Southern Cross* to 1865 then moved to the *New Zealand Herald*. Brett's entry into the *Star* was partly because of Ferrar and Reed's realisation that they needed both experienced collaboration and more capital. It was also to forestall Brett's negotiations to purchase their rival, the *Evening News*. In 1871 Ferrar sold out to his partners and left for New South Wales. By the end of 1871 the *Evening News* had been purchased and incorporated in the *Star,* and Brett and Reed had begun issuing their paper from their own press. The *Star* had a circulation of 2700 in 1872 and 4700 in 1875.

The *Auckland Star* developed a strong political advocacy in opposition to that of its main morning rival, the *New Zealand Herald*. The *Star* was later to become an advocate for the Liberal party and, in the years prior to the rise of that party, was a major supporter of the developing liberal perspective. Reed, who had been a member of the Australian Parliament

---

1  It was titled the *Evening Star* to 8 March 1879 when it became the *Auckland Evening Star*. Its third and present title was first used on 13 April 1887.

2  Little information is available as to Ferrar. Scholefield describes him as "a young man on the commercial staff of another paper in Auckland".(1958), p.87.

in 1866 and 1867, did have some personal political ambitions for he was a member of the Auckland Provincial Council from November 1873 to October 1876. But, in keeping with the changed political strategy of newspaper proprietors he was more important as a political supporter than as a public politician. Particularly, he was influential in aiding Sir George Grey in 1875, to enter the House of Representatives. Reed left the *Star* early in 1876. He sold his interest in the business to Brett for £4000 and left for Dunedin where he purchased the *Otago Guardian*. Brett was then sole proprietor of the *Star*. He appointed as editor Thomson Wilson Leys, who had earlier joined the staff after serving an apprenticeship on the *Southern Cross*. Leys was to be a long-serving editor and in 1889 was to become Brett's partner in the business.

With the successful establishment of the *Star* there were two dominant newspapers in Auckland, the *New Zealand Herald*, the morning daily, and the *Auckland Star*, the evening counterpart. They were not the only newspapers. The *Southern Cross* was the longest lasting newspaper in Auckland but was in decline and was soon to be closed. All the other papers were short-lived and never achieved commercial success. There were also to be future challenges but a similar lack of fortune awaited them.

The main competitor to the *Star* in the 1870s was the *Echo*, the fate of which was to be typical of challenges to established daily newspapers. The *Echo* began publication on 9 November 1874. It gave the usual promises of concentration on news and non-partisanship in politics and also saw a second evening daily as necessary for Auckland.

> We propose, then, to supply a want which is felt by many and should have been long since felt by all the want of another evening paper in this city.
> (*Echo*, 9 November 1874)

However, this want was not considered to exist by the public and, after a year of operation during which it lost £3000, the *Echo* was purchased by the *Star* and closed down.

A major change in the Auckland newspapers in the 1870s was to be to the ownership of the *New Zealand Herald* when Alfred George Horton became a partner. Horton purchased the ailing *Southern Cross* in 1876. Because of new roading plans in Auckland, the directors of the *Southern Cross* were forced to erect new premises. They opted instead to sell and found a purchaser in Horton. Horton immediately entered into negotiations with Wilson's two sons, who had taken over the *Herald* on the death of their father, and at the end of 1876 the two properties were amalgamated. The *Southern Cross*'s final issue was on 28 December 1876. The weeklies were also amalgamated with the *Southern Cross*'s weekly, the *Weekly News*, being the title that prevailed.

The two main Auckland newspapers long remained under the control of their founders or their decendants. The *Star* did not become a public company until 1920, the *New Zealand Herald* not until 1925. Even then the original control remained. Brett and Leys incorporated their partnership in 1920 with a public issue of £100,000 in shares. They themselves retained £150,000 of the total £250,000 capital. When the *New Zealand Herald* was made into a company, the business had a capital of £650,000. All directors were members of the Wilson and Horton families.

The daily newspaper press of Auckland, by the middle of the 1870s, was dominated by the *Herald* in the morning and the *Star* in the evening. There were to be further attempts to begin daily newspapers but none were to meet with any success. One determined attempt was from the *Evening Bell*, which published from 12 May 1885 to 12 May 1888. It never exceeded a circulation of 500 and lost its promoters some £10,000. The next major challenge, again to the *Star*, was that by the *Sun* from 1927 to 1930. Now well into their second century, the *Herald* and the *Star* remain dominant.

The nature of the daily press, with its attempt to appeal to a general rather than a specific audience, meant would-be dailies had to compete directly with the established newspapers. Yet the high circulation and established advertising revenue of the existing newspapers gave them a security of tenure which foiled all attempts to oust them. Thus the 1860s and 1870s, which saw the start of the daily press, also saw two concerns obtain long-lasting positions.

The nature of the political advocacy of the *Herald* and *Star* was not to be followed by all New Zealand newspapers but did typify the usual behaviour. The management of both newspapers accepted that political advocacy and partisan political support were normal and proper for the press. They did not, however, feel that they themselves should follow political careers nor did they consider they should irrevocably offer their support to any politician or political group. There was no understanding that the two newspapers would always support opposing sides and thus maintain a political opposition to one another. The two newspapers were politically united notably during Grey's Ministry from 1877-1879 when both papers supported the Government, and in the twentieth century after the decline of the Liberal party, when both papers opposed the rising Labour party. But generally, until the decline of liberalism, the two newspapers were in opposition, with the *Star* being the liberal advocate and the *Herald* being a voice, first for the established continuous ministry, and then for the conservative opposition to the Liberal party.

## Dunedin

Having had only three newspapers prior to 1860, Dunedin was to have a great variety of them in the following two decades. With the *Otago Daily Times* showing that financial success was possible in the now populous Otago, competition soon arose. Otago was the most populated province and Dunedin became the city in which journalistic enterprise was highest. The following listing gives an indication of the range of publications started in Dunedin in that 20-year period. Initial and final publication dates, where known, are shown.[3]

| | |
|---|---|
| *Otago Police Gazette* | 28 October 1861-? |
| *Otago Daily Times* | 15 November 1861 |
| *Dunedin Advertiser and Business Directory* | 19 April 1862-? |
| *Evening News* | 20 November 1862-? |
| *Daily Telegraph* | 3 January 1863-April 9, 1864. |
| *Evening Star* | 1 May 1863 - 1979. |
| *Dunedin Leader* | 17 October 1863-1867. |
| *Saturday Review of Politics, Literature, Philosophy, Science and Art* | 20 February 1864-3 June 1871. |

---

3  This listing is adapted from Paul (1924) and from Scholefield (1958).

## Main Centre Daily Newspapers 1860-1879

| | |
|---|---|
| *The Monthly Review by Mr J.G.S. Grant and the SaturdayReview* | 16 April 1864-? |
| *Otago Christian Reformer* | July 1864-? |
| *Otago Daily Mail* | 2 July 1864-? |
| *Dunedin Punch* | 27 May 1865-? |
| *Otago Newsletter* | 1866 ?-? |
| *Illustrated New Zealander* | November 1866-? |
| *Illustrated New Zealand Herald* | March 1868-August1883. |
| *New Zealand Sun* | 16 November 1868-1869. |
| *The Guiding Star* | 16 November 1868-? |
| *Evening Independent* | 22 January 1869-June 1869 |
| *Otago and Southland Mining Journal and GoldfieldsAdvertiser* | 8 November 1869-? |
| *Observer* | 1869-1869. |
| *Echo* | 27 November 1869-17 November 1883. Suspended: 8 March 1873-28 February 1880. |
| *Daily Advertiser and Southern League* | 3 July-10 November 1871. |
| *Morning Star* | 1 December 1872-22 July 1873. |
| *New Zealand Tablet* | 3 May 1873 |
| *Otago Guardian* | 23 July 1873-6 October 1877. |
| *Otago Christian Record* | 20 September 1873-? |
| *Southern Mercury* | 3 January 1874-6 October 1877. |

*The Making of the New Zealand Press*

| | |
|---|---|
| Saturday Advertiser, Time Table and New Zealand Public Opinion | 17 July 1875 19 September 1893. |
| *New Zealand Magazine* | January 1876-October 1877. |
| *New Zealand Press News and Typographical Circular* | 1 March 1876-c.1879. |
| *Liberator* | 11 March 1876-? |
| *Licensed Victuallers' Gazette* | 22 March 1876-? |
| *Sandfly* | 25 August 1876-? |
| *Independent Review* | 9 December 1876-? |
| *New Zealand Christian Record* | 1877-? |
| *Morning Herald* | 3 December 1877-2 September 1890 |
| *Dunedin Evening Tribune* | 1878-December 1879. |
| *Temperance Herald and Good Templar Record* | 9 March 1878-1881. |
| *New Zealand Presbyterian* | 1 July 1879-1893. |
| *Evening Omnibus and Tramway* | 23 July 1879-? |
| *Penny Post and General Advertiser* | September? 1879-? |
| *Sunshine* | 5 December 1879-9 January 1880. |
| *New Zealand Freemason* | 6 January 1880-? |
| *North-East Valley Weekly Advertiser* | 15 November 1880-31 October 1881. |

Apart from the sheer increase in the number of publications after 1860, the years are notable for the appearance of specialized publications and for the general lack of long-term success. The 44 publications listed are close to evenly divided between would-be general newspapers and specialized publications. It is not possible to be exact on this point for some are of nebulous title and have no surviving copies. But it appears that as the daily newspaper press with its intended general appeal began, so also began another range of publications oriented towards specifically defined groups. Most of the publications met with little success. Most of the publications of unknown duration, judging from the dates of copies still available, ceased within a few months at most. Seven of the listed publications published continuously for more than five years. Only three were to continue into the twentieth century. These are the *Otago Daily Times*, the *Evening Star* and the *New Zealand Tablet*. Little is known about many of the listed publications apart from their titles. Newspapers with which Vogel had an association, the *Witness*, the *Otago Daily Times* and the *New Zealand Sun*, have already been discussed, as also have James Macandrew's newspapers, the *Daily Telegraph* and the *Weekly Colonist*.

Twelve weeks after the *Daily Telegraph* closed in April 1864 another morning daily, the *Otago Daily Mail*, took its place as the rival of the *Otago Daily Times*. The closing date of the *Otago Daily Mail* is uncertain but it did not compete well against the *Otago Daily Times*. No issues beyond April 1865 survive. The *Otago Daily Mail*, as had Vogel and Macandrew with their newspapers, attempted to combine commercial success with political support for the proprietor, Frederick Joseph Moss. He was a member of the Otago Provincial Council from 1863 to the beginning of 1867, spending most of the time on the Executive Council.

Evening dailies, not so directly in competition with the *Otago Daily Times*, also appeared early in the 1860s. The first, the *Evening News*, further removed itself from competition by adopting a less prestigious role than the morning paper and by eschewing any political involvement. The paper aimed at presenting commercial news, press telegrams which had arrived too late for the morning papers, plus

> interesting local events, and paragraphs of such light reading that may be generally palatable in the half hours during relaxation of business, or in those devoted to amusement.
> ....our unpretentious Journal will not have leading articles to dispose of, and most of our stock will be second-hand commodities, which we propose selecting with our most judicious discrimination.

(*Evening News*, 20 November 1862)

## The Making of the New Zealand Press

The *Evening News* began without leading articles but, in Dunedin as elsewhere, they were to become a normal feature of the evening newspapers. Copies of the *Evening News* only to January 1863 survive. How long the paper continued is unknown.

Another *Evening News*, started in 1867, was publishing the following year. That this newspaper existed is known from records of a libel case. Issue 187 of 28 March 1868 attacked two Dunedin citizens for their action in appealing for funds to assist the wives and families of Irish prisoners. The paper had no sympathy with the appeal and included the following.

> ..As the Fenian bride makes her bed so on it she must lie — those who lie down with dogs must not expect to be free from fleas ... The men who formed a procession on St Patricks Day were either silly fools, or else Fenian knaves. If the former, they should be conveyed to either the Benevolent or Lunatic Asylum, and if the latter, Dunedin gaol would be their proper place[4]

At least in 1868 the *Evening News* had leading articles, even if of dubious quality.

Stability came to evening newspapers when George Bell entered the arena. He started the *Evening Independent* but, on the bankruptcy of the *Evening Star*'s owners, bought that paper for £675 and incorporated his *Independent* in it. The paper closed in 1979. The Evening Star Co (Ltd) was incorporated in 1895 but the paper was always controlled by Bell and his descendents. As well as being proprietor, Bell edited the paper until his retirement in 1895. Bell followed what was becoming the common policy of the newspaper proprietors of the 1860s; that of no personal political involvement coupled with a strong political advocacy. Bell was a political liberal and the *Evening Star* became an Otago supporter of this developing New Zealand perspective.

The newspapers that began in Dunedin in the 1870s faced the difficulty of beginning against established competition. As in other centres the position of strength enjoyed by an established newspaper was generally such as to make each newcomer a temporary problem rather than a serious threat.

---

4    Quoted in Paul (1924) p.106, who also records the proprietor of the *Evening News* as being acquitted.

Bell's evening daily, the *Evening Star,* after the passing of the *Evening News,* was without competition for six years. In 1876 another *Evening News* was started. It lasted for two years before folding, to be followed a few months later by the *Evening Age,* subsequently called the *Evening Tribune,* which lasted a little over a year. The *Evening Tribune,* when offered for sale in 1879 was passed in at £400, an indication of the minor status of the enterprise.

The most important of the dailies begun in Dunedin in the 1870s was the *Otago Guardian*. Its proprietors eventually purchased the *Otago Daily Times* and amalgamated the two properties. The manner in which this took place was also a process whereby a major change in the political advocacy of the *Otago Daily Times* occured. A morning daily, the *Otago Guardian,* the major competitor of the *Otago Daily Times,* appeared in 1873, edited and managed by R.J. Creighton. Creighton, at the time M.H.R. for Eden, had been prominent in Auckland journalism since 1861. The *Guardian* was owned by shareholders rather than any single individual.

> As a guarantee to the public that the *Guardian* will not be governed by a clique, we have simply to refer to the fact that its proprietory is larger than that of any other newspaper in New Zealand, and that it includes men of all ranks and of every shade of opinion in this community.
> (*Otago Guardian,* 23 July 1873)

The Guardian Printing Company (Limited) took over from 19 June 1874, the *Southern Mercury* , which then became its weekly associate. In 1875 George Fenwick, who from this point until his death in 1929 was the dominant figure in Otago journalism, became manager of the *Guardian*. The *Guardian* sold for 2d and the competition hurt the *Otago Daily Times* which increased its size and reduced its price to 3d. Fenwick realised the *Guardian* could not continue against the *Otago Daily Times* and advised the directors to sell or close down. This advice was followed and in April 1876 G.M. Reed, previously co-proprietor of the *Auckland Star,* "paid £3,000 for the two papers upon which various owners had lost £10,000 since the beginning of 1873".[5] Fenwick, however, failed to heed his own advice and remained with the *Guardian*,

---

5   Scholefield, (1958), p.177.

first continuing as manager but very soon as co-proprietor with Reed. A mutually ruinous competition between the two morning papers remained until October 1877 when Fenwick and Reed pulled off a major coup by purchasing for around £30,000 the *Witness* and the *Otago Daily Times*.

The negotiator on behalf of Fenwick and Reed in the transaction was William Hunter Reynolds who is referred to by the *Otago Daily Times* as a "confidential intermediary".[6] In view of Fenwick and Reed's need to borrow most of the capital required, and of Reynolds subsequent position in the *Otago Daily Times*, it is likely that Reynolds also had a personal interest in the purchase. Reynolds was an old Dunedin identity who had arrived in Otago in 1851 as a member of James Macandrew's party of migrants on board Macandrew's schooner. Reynolds had a major political career and was a member of the successive Waterhouse, Fox, Vogel and Pollen Ministries. He was subsequently also in the Stout-Vogel Ministry.

The two properties were merged in October 1877 with Fenwick and Reed becoming co-proprietors. The financial dictates that prevented a continuation of press competition, however desirable, were ably presented in the *Guardian*'s final editorial.

... For upwards of four years the trial has been made as to whether it was possible to sustain in Otago two papers of the class of the *Times* and *Guardian*, resulting in the conviction that it is not possible. A large amount of capital, amounting in the aggregate to some fifteen thousand pounds, has been sunk in the effort to maintain a position in opposition to a long established journal ......... We are aware that many people are inclined to say that there should be two morning papers in every centre of population, so as to have what is called a representation of the two sides of every question. If those who desire such luxury had proved their estimate of its importance during the past four or five years, it is not improbable that such desire might have continued to be realised in the case of the metropolis of Otago.

(*Otago Guardian*, 6 October 1877)

---

6   *Otago Daily Times*, (1924), p.25.

This, however, was not to be the end of competition. Nor was the co-proprietorship of Fenwick and Reed to be long lasting. The *Otago Daily Times* staff displaced in the merger retaliated by starting the *Morning Herald*. They also received the support of the old *Otago Daily Times* directorate. The *Herald*, which started on 3 December 1877, was a penny daily and the *Otago Daily Times* circulation fell as a result of the new paper's appeal. The price of the *Otago Daily Times* remained at 3d. Reed and Fenwick took the prudent course and protected themselves by turning their business into a limited liability company. The capital was £40,000 in 4,000 shares of £10 each, of which £7.10s per share was called up. The prospectus was issued in April 1878 and directors elected at a first meeting of shareholders on 10 June 1878. The directors included W.H. Reynolds, who was appointed Chairman of the Board, and George Fenwick, who became Managing Director. G.M. Reed was not among the directors. He had been editor of the *Guardian* and, on the amalgamation of the two properties, had become editor of the *Otago Daily Times*. He was not to remain with the paper. Whether he was ousted or removed himself willingly is unknown, but by the end of 1878 he had left Dunedin and New Zealand.

Fenwick wished to meet the competition of the *Herald* by also reducing the *Otago Daily Times* price to 1d. He first suggested this to the Board of Directors in November 1878 but was not successful until February 1881, by which time a further £2 per share had been called on. After the price reduction the paper's circulation, according to the *Otago Daily Times*, doubled in a fortnight and trebled within six weeks.[7] The consequent increased advertising revenue removed the *Otago Daily Times*'s financial problems and it was now the *Herald*'s turn to falter. In May 1884 it removed itself from competition with the *Otago Daily Times* by becoming the *Evening Herald* and struggled through the decade. In 1890 it was merged into the *Globe*, a liberal paper launched under the impetus of the maritime strike. The *Globe* ceased in 1893.

The political stance of the *Otago Daily Times* changed with the change of ownership. It had been, after the ousting of Vogel, an antagonist of his policies and had thus been an anti-government paper from 1869 to 1876. Nor had it been an advocate for Sir George Grey, whose 1877 to 1879 Ministry began in the month the *Otago Daily Times*

---

7   Ibid, p.28.

changed hands. But the change of ownership led to a political advocacy on behalf of Grey's Ministry. W.H. Reynolds, the Chairman of the Board, was an ally of Vogel and later an ally of Grey. He had resigned from the House of Representatives in March 1878 and the following month, the month Fenwick and Reed turned their partnership into a limited liability company, had been made a member of the Legislative Council.

After the ending of Provincial Government in 1876 there was a realigning of political allegiances among those who had previously been divided on the issues of provincialism and centralism. Reynolds was reconciled with the important Otago politicians, James Macandrew and Robert Stout, and all three became allied with Sir George Grey. Macandrew was a member of Grey's Ministry throughout Grey's two-year term as Premier. Stout was also a minister being appointed Attorney-General by Grey in March 1878.[8]

The political advocacy of the *Otago Daily Times* thus turned to be one of support for Grey. With this change a further development in the nature of newspaper political advocacy took place. Here again a substantial measure of control over a newspaper was exerted by political figures. The new situation was not a return to personal advocacy for the newspaper's proprietors. George Fenwick, as Managing-Director and later as editor, had no personal political career. William Reynolds, the Chairman of Directors, had finished the major part of his political career and was now merely a member of the Legislative Council. The advocacy was not for him personally. But the advocacy was for Grey's Ministry and had become so because of the change of ownership of the paper.

The stance of the *Otago Daily Times* was to change again in the 1880s, but the type of control arrived at in 1878 was to remain and was to occur in other newspapers. It was a company control with a directorship which included men of partisan political loyalty and influence. This control saw the political stance of the newspaper of as much importance as its economic profitability. The new proprietors of the 1860s had placed profitability paramount and had ended the practice of personal political advocacy. But newspapers had remained as powerful political advocates. The dominant shareholders of the *Otago Daily Times* of 1878

---

8   Stout was also a shareholder in the *Otago Daily Times* and, although not eventually elected a director, was named among the provisional directors in the prospectus issued in April 1878.

had no quarrel with profitability and realized the need for financial success if the paper were to continue. But equally they secured the newspaper to ensure that its political advocacy was for the people and policies they supported. It was not a return to ownership by, and advocacy for, prominent politicans. It was a manifestation of a more general political division in which shareholders accepted their well-being was linked with the success of a political group and oriented their newspaper so as to further a political view.

**Wellington:**

In Wellington there were, after the establishment of the *Evening Post* and the closure of the *Spectator,* three newspapers in publication. The *Independent,* then in its third decade, was the only financially secure concern. The *Evening Post's* first few years were financially difficult. David Curle, Henry Blundell's original partner, withdrew from the newspaper because of the inability of the concern to provide a living for them both. Blundell, unable to afford staff, ran the newspaper as a family concern. He and his three sons did all the reporting, editing and printing of the newspaper. It was some years before Blundell was able to engage salaried staff. But by 1874 he was able to afford a visit back to Dublin. It was either here, or four years later at his death, that the paper began to employ an editor.

The contrasting careers of Henry Blundell and David Curle illustrate the advantages enjoyed by those who were able to found a newspaper in the 1860s and survive the difficult first years. By the end of the 1860s the Blundells were prospering and had developed a newspaper concern that has been prominent in New Zealand journalism ever since. Curle retained his newspaper ambitions and appeared as proprietor or co-proprietor of various publications but was never to found a lasting or successful concern. In 1868 he founded the *Hokitika Daily News.* The paper ended some time in 1869. At some time in the early 1870s, Curle bought the *Ross Guardian,* a weekly. It lasted until 1879 but he had sold it before then for he was in Fielding in 1878 where he was co-founder of the *Fielding Guardian.* He soon left the paper for he had ambitions in the capital. In Wellington in May 1878 he became co-proprietor of the *Evening Chronicle,* a daily which lasted until 1880. In 1880 he returned to Hokitika where he managed the *Evening Star* and in 1881 began the *Hokitika Guardian.* In 1884 he purchased the *Evening Star* and combined

*The Making of the New Zealand Press*

the two papers as the *Hokitika Guardian and Star*. It became a daily in 1888 but the once vibrant mining town now had too small a population for newspaper success. In 1893 Curle sold out and moved to Dannevirke where he bought the *Dannevirke Advocate*. He ran the paper for eight years before selling it in 1901. He does not feature in newspaper records again and presumably, at this point, at the age of 64, retired. He died in 1917.

The third Wellington newspaper, the *New Zealand Advertiser,* was in the worst position of the three. Two years after the start of the *Evening Post* it was in such financial difficulties as to necessitate the sale of the enterprise. The name was changed to the *New Zealand Times* and the proprietory was at pains to indicate it was an entirely new journal.

> ... the *New Zealand Times* is a new journal. It has ... a new name, never before adopted by a newspaper in the country and we fear of a somewhat ambitious sound. It has a new proprietory, to some extent a new staff, and is printed and published in new premises, and that every morning instead of only three days in the week. The only condition wanting to effect the decease of the one journal and to launch the other into an absolutely new life was supplied by the non-issue of the *Advertiser* on its usual day of publication. Thus a break occurred, which completely serves any continuous thread that might still have connected the two journals, and our announcement is justified by the facts as they actually exist.
> (*New Zealand Times*, 16 September, 1867)

The first issue contains the notice of dissolution of Joseph and Edward Bulls' partnership and business. They, along with the Roe brothers had begun the *Advertiser*. The Roe brothers had left some time previously. The new proprietor was named as Richard Pearson. However Pearson, a stamp department clerk, was a nominal owner obscuring the identity of the real proprietor, John Martin. Apart from his eventual membership of the Legislative Council, Martin never had a personal political career. But his intentions for the *New Zealand Times* were not primarily commercial. The newspaper had a short life but began with a strong support for the Government rather than with protestations as to the newspaper's political independence.

... We believe no other Government to be possible at the present time, not only because the extraordinary state of parties at present entirely forbids the chance of the compact organisation of a powerful opposition prepared to take the reins of State, but because the complete disintegration of parties and the absolute confusion which has fallen on the Assembly, makes it a necessity to the country that the *personnel* of the present Administration should not be altered, as containing the only men, willing to act together, who are capable of shaping into such form as will give a tolerably consistent result to the legislation of the Houses of Assembly as they are at this moment composed.
(*New Zealand Times*, 16 September, 1867)

By offering its support to Stafford's ministry, the *New Zealand Times* was in opposition to the *Wellington Independent*. This opposition also took place in Wellington provincial politics where the *New Zealand Times* opposed Featherston, who was championed by the *Independent*. The paper was due for a quick collapse. It started as a 2d daily and was the first of the Wellington morning papers to try daily appearance. Five weeks later the following appeared in its columns.

From this date the *New Zealand Times* will appear as a tri-weekly journal, and in making this change it is with a conviction, on practical grounds, that this Province is not yet prepared to support the enterprise of a daily newspaper. At some not distant period possibly the want may become sufficiently great to warrant its establishment but without the concurrence of business men, to whom a newspaper is as much a necessity as their support is to its success we cannot pretend to supply it.
(*New Zealand Times*, 21 October 1867)

The paper just saw out the month as a tri-weekly and the final issue was on 1 November 1867. Martin's attempt and failure is a further indication of the financial difficulties to be experienced, from the 1860s on, by anyone who wished to begin a newspaper. The self-made Martin was a man of sufficient means to have carried, for its political value, a newspaper of the type present before the 1860s. But a daily newspaper was beyond him. The political advocacy of the *New Zealand Times* was not unpopular. Nor was it an advocacy already followed by an existing

Wellington newspaper. But the paper gained neither sufficient circulation nor advertising for Martin to be able to carry on.
The year 1868 saw three papers started in Wellington. None was to have a long life. Edward Bull attempted to revive the *New Zealand Advertiser*. In this appearance it ran from 31 May 1868 to, probably, some time in early 1869. The last issue available is that of 10 February 1869 and this may have been the final issue. Henry Blundell regarded a paper run by the Bulls as a serious threat and moved to discourage it by publishing a further paper himself. This was a morning edition of the *Evening Post*.

The third paper for 1868 was Richard Wakelin's *Wellington Journal*. This was a tri-weekly morning newspaper selling for 1d per issue. Wakelin had founded the *Wairarapa Journal* on 1 January 1868 but was unable to obtain the necessary extra printing work to make his business pay. So he moved to Wellington in March 1868 and started the *Wellington Journal*. Wakelin was aiming for more than a profitable newspaper. He had no personal political career but had strong liberal political leanings and used his newspaper assiduously to advocate his political preferences. The following editorial extract illustrates his policies and his style.

> ... in this country at least there is no class, family, or party, which has the slightest claim, and what is more important, the slightest power to have its interests considered in preference to those of the people as a whole. We are essentially a democratic community, not only in reference to direct political power, but still more so with regard to our social state, and that as a consequence those liberal principles most characteristic of democracies are sure to prevail...
> (*Wellington Journal*, 8 May 1868)

Wakelin's newspaper was not to become established successfully. The last copy available is that of 22 July 1868 but the paper may have lasted longer for the plant, including an Albion double demy press, was not sold until 25 November 1868 when it was purchased by the proprietors of the *Wairarapa Mercury* for £200.

In 1870 there was a further attempt to revive the *Advertiser*. This time its title was the *Daily Advertiser and Wellington Register*. Its proprietors were Joseph Bull and William Mahony. They returned to the initial format of the *New Zealand Advertiser* and published the

## Main Centre Daily Newspapers 1860-1879

*Daily Advertiser* as a *gratis* sheet. It had four pages of which at least three were advertising. This appearance of the *Advertiser* was to last almost two years. It ended on 7 November 1871.

Throughout these years and in spite of the various challenges to its position, the *Independent* remained as the leading morning newspaper in Wellington. Its political advocacy was consistent. Always a partisan supporter in local politics of Featherston it was, in national politics, linked always with William Fox and, on his ascendency, with Fox's ally, Julius Vogel. The political advocacy of the *Independent* had never been a personal one for the proprietors. As the *Independent* gained commercial stature, its political advocacy remained largely unchanged. It included a partisan reporting and an initial raising of issues. Newspapers and their management, as in the 1850s, remained as important actors within the political process. A striking illustration of this is the 1865 aid shown to Fox in publishing his letter discussing the causes leading to the resignation of his Ministry. Unable to discuss the matter in the House, Fox's strong Opposition view of the peace settlement and land confiscation was published in full and given the following accompaniment.

> Mr. Fox occupies so prominent a position in the political world that his letter, which we publish today, is not likely to pass unnoticed .... Mr Fox has given so complete a history of all that took place during his term of office, that it is quite needless to supplement it by any comments of our own. A bold outline by the hand of a master gives a better idea of the object, than a more elaborate picture by an inferior artist, or one less acquainted with the subject. We can, however, testify to its correctness.
> (*Wellington Independent*, 7 January 1865)

A long-expected change in Wellington journalism was the increase in publication rate by the *Independent* to daily frequency. The *Evening Post* began in 1865 as a daily, the year in which Thomas McKenzie became sole proprietor of the *Independent*. In spite of the example of the *Evening Post* and other shorter-lived rivals, McKenzie was slow to move to a daily format. Only in 1871 did he feel a change was warranted.

> Today is the first issue of the *Independent* as a "daily" ... The recent extension of telegraphic communication, the progress of settlement in the interior of the province, and the exigencies of

## The Making of the New Zealand Press

> the commercial community, have rendered a "tri-weekly" no longer adequate to the needs of our readers and subscribers.
>
> (*Wellington Independent,* 14 January 1871)

The change was accompanied by a decrease in size (from six to four pages) and price (from 3d to 2d). At the same time he announced a new weekly newspaper, the *New Zealand Mail,* to complement the *Independent*.

> On Saturday we intend publishing a "weekly", containing all the news of the week and a great amount of matter, original and selected, specially interesting to country settlers. Our first weekly will appear next Saturday.
>
> (*Wellington Independent,* 14 January 1871)

The *Mail* was a 20-page paper. It was soon enlarged to 24 pages, and sold for a 5s per quarter subscription or for 6d per issue.

1872 saw the first evening newspaper rival to the *Post*. This was the *Evening Telegraph*. It was short-lived and no copies of it remain.

The next Wellington evening paper, which started on 25 February 1874, was William Hutchinson's *Tribune*, another attempt to combine personal political support with commercial journalism. Hutchinson, an ex-editor and co-proprietor of the *Wanganui Chronicle,* had used that paper as an advocate for his political ambitions and this had not aided the paper financially. Moving his operations to Wellington he was to repeat that experience.

The *Tribune, A Daily Chronicle and Advertiser of Colonial Commerce, Agriculture and Politics* was a 1d daily and was accompanied by a *Weekly Tribune,* published every Thursday. Hutchinson ran a paper with a clear programme of advocacy for the Government and agitation for the abolition of provinces, which was imminent.

> The programme of Public Works and Immigration has been accepted by the country, and whatever differences of opinion may have existed or may still exist on the subject, there can properly be no standing still midway.... The native policy of the present Government has been an eminent success... Provincialism, as involving double government and, still more and worse, diverse legislation, leads to weakness and circumlocution. It should be set aside ...
>
> (*Tribune,* 25 February 1874)

## Main Centre Daily Newspapers 1860-1879

> One of the good effects of Mr Vogel's policy one of the best, indeed, although the least noted is its effect upon the people. In finding abundant work and good wages for the working classes, incentive and temptation to crime have been largely removed.
> (*Tribune*, 9 April 1874)

The *Tribune* was to be the longest lasting of the evening newspapers set up against the *Post*, but even so it was to last only six years and only under a variety of proprietors and titles. The first major change came late in 1875 when the following was published.

> Certain commercial changes in connection with the *Tribune* lead to a change in the editorial department as well, and the gentleman who has had charge of the latter, since the commencement, ceases his connection with it today.
> (*Tribune*, 4 December 1875)

The *Tribune* had not achieved financial stability in its first two years and Hutchinson had been forced to sell the paper. It was purchased by a group of three, headed by E.T. Gillon. Gillon had been editor of the *Evening Post* but had resigned shortly before in order to contest, unsuccessfully, a seat in Parliament. The name was changed to the *Evening Argus and Tribune* but, apart from support offered to Gillon's electoral campaign, little else differed. The paper continued as a liberal publication with a strong emphasis on abolition of the provinces. Even Hutchinson remained for he served as editor for a time during the *Argus*'s life. Financial success was equally unobtainable for the *Argus* and, at the end of March 1878, it ended. But again it was a continuation under another guise for the paper had been purchased by Thomas Gardiner[9] who, from the same office, the next day, published the *Evening Chronicle* with the next serial number. The paper continued as a liberal publication and, again, failed to prosper. David Curle, Blundell's original partner, came in as co-proprietor on 16 May 1878. Gardiner left the paper, and the country, within the year in order to evade a libel suit brought by the *Evening Post*. Curle continued and took in Alan Anderson as co-proprietor. The paper was kept as a four-page

---

9  Little is known of Thomas Gardiner. Scholefield, who seems sceptical about the matter, records him as having spent 24 years in journalism and as having owned a Sacremento newspaper. (1958),p.37.

penny daily and, by late 1880, the proprietors were attempting to sell it. They were unsuccessful and the final issue was announced by the following.

> No satisfactory tender having been received for the purchase of the Plant, Stock and Goodwill of the *Evening Chronicle* the trustees have decided to stop the publication of the paper from this date.
> (*Evening Chronicle*, 16 December 1880)

During the *Tribune's* various lives, two major and two minor changes occurred in Wellington journalism. The minor two were the beginning of the *Daily Telegraph* in 1875 and the *Weekly Mercury* in 1879. The major changes were the starting of the *New Zealand Times* in 1874 and the *New Zealander* in 1878.

The *Daily Telegraph* was a further attempt to begin a morning paper. The proprietor, William Mahoney, was from the family who had been co-proprietors of the *Daily Advertiser*, the last of the papers attempted by the Bull's. It began on 7 December 1875 and only one copy of one issue, the first, survives. It is not clear how long the paper survived but it must have been only for a short period.

The other minor Wellington paper for this period is the *Wellington Weekly Mercury*. Only one copy of one issue, the first, survives. And, from that copy, the imprint is torn! Probably there was only the one issue. It offered something for which there was, as yet, no market; an avoidance of political matters and a concentration on entertainment.

> On ordinary political questions we do not intend to express any opinions ... We believe that under either party the Colony cannot suffer much and that the difference between the administration of "Tweedledum" and "Tweedledee" is a very slight thing indeed. Avoiding controversy it will be our aim to lead our readers into the shady houses of Art, Literature and Science, where they may enjoy at their leisure the song of the poet, the wisdom of the sage, and the fancy of the novelist.
> (*Wellington Weekly Mercury*, 31 October 1879)

In spite of the number of newspapers started in Wellington in the 1860s and early 1870s the capital city was to have just two dominant newspapers, the established *Wellington Independent* owned by Thomas

## Main Centre Daily Newspapers 1860-1879

McKenzie and the new evening paper, Henry Blundell's *Evening Post*, which by the late 1860s was also established and well able to fend off competition. Both owners saw partisan political advocacy as a normal and proper function for their newspapers. In national politics they had diverged with the rise of Vogel, with the *Wellington Independent* becoming a supporter and the *Evening Post* an opponent of the continuous ministry. But neither of the proprietors had a personal political career. Both these owners were primarily oriented towards the financial success of their newspapers. In the mid and late 1870s there were to be two significant challenges to this orientation. In both cases, the change of ownership of the *Independent* and the commencement of the *New Zealander*, the newspaper management was to be closely connected with the governing Ministry. Discussion of these two newspapers will be considered below within the context of the relationship between the press and the government which grew with the development and use of the telegraph.

# 8. New Zealand Journalism and the Daily Press

The advent of the daily press was accompanied by far-reaching changes in the nature of journalism. Prior to 1853 the New Zealand press was a few newspapers which were mainly advocates for the resident landowners and through which was coordinated the agitation for self-government. It was a colonial press united by its attempt to replace the Crown Colony Government with local government. From 1853 to the start of the commercial press, which can be dated as beginning with the *Otago Daily Times* in 1861, the New Zealand press remained a small number of newspapers. They shared a dominant concern with being partisan political discussion forums within each province. No longer with the shared task of winning self-government to unite them, the management of the various newspapers did not maintain the contact of pre-independence days. But a similarity of size of circulation, of upper class-biased readership, and of concentration on provincial political affairs remained. The provincial focus of newspapers was not total. All newspapers were also interested in the national political arena. Many provincial debates were conducted on the national stage. All newspapers had orientations towards the status and policies of the General Government which were largely dictated by provincial considerations. The various newspapers' various positions in regard to national politics were by no means the same but all newspapers, although taking different debating positions, were at the debate. They showed a similarity of concern and interest, if not of policy.

In the 1860s this similarity lessened. The sheer increase in the number of publications made dissimilarity more likely. But the increase was also accompanied by an increase in the types of publication. Many of the new publications were not general newspapers but were journals oriented to specific audiences. Religious and temperance publications were the first of this type but they were followed by others. Even the newspaper press became a diverse group. Many of the new newspapers, particularly those away from the main centres, were small circulation weekly publications printed on the iron-framed fixed presses of the type used in the 1840s and 1850s. The main centre newspapers, at the other extreme, were rapidly becoming large scale businesses. Differences of circulation, technology, capital investment, staff and revenue quickly grew.

## Journalism as a Profession

It was among the large daily newspapers that, in the 1860s, professional journalism began to be a major aspect of newspaper life in New Zealand. Professional journalism refers to the employment of people to contribute to or edit newspapers, who were to receive a salary for their services, who were to regard journalism as their major source of income, and who were appointed for their journalistic competence rather than for their political loyalty and prominence. This was an application to journalism of the new bureaucratic organization of work. It appeared in newspapers in England and the United States early in the nineteenth century. The press throughout the eighteenth century was at pains to provide a variety of versions of unproven material for the benefit of ideological factions. The same concerns occupied the New Zealand newspapers at least into the 1860s. Running an early newspaper was an intensely personal matter. At times the one man was owner, editor, reporter, printer and business manager. Commonly in New Zealand assistance was given voluntarily to a newspaper proprietor by men who saw their efforts as a form of public and political service.

Professional journalism had been present in New Zealand before the 1860s but had not been dominant. The first notable instance is that of Richard Wakelin, who arrived in Wellington in 1850. Experienced as a contributor and editor in England, he was initially unable to gain employment with either of the Wellington newspapers. The *Independent* did later publish a series of unsolicited letters from him on education. Impressed with his ability, it was at the end of the Crown Colony Government period that McKenzie, the proprietor, first engaged him, temporarily in 1851, to report the proceedings of the General Legislative Council, then about to sit in Wellington. Shortly after this he was appointed permanently to the *Independent* "as general and shipping reporter, sub-editor, etc".[1] He later, on Featherston's retirement, replaced him as editor. Unlike Featherston, he was a salaried editor. Wakelin, as editor, championed Featherston but received no personal political reward for doing so. His own political views were, in fact, quite different from Featherston's and when, in later years, he was proprietor

---

1 Wakelin, (1877) p. 19.

of his own newspaper, Wakelin was regarded as one of the more able advocates for a liberal position. His editorship of the *Independent*, however, is the initial instance in New Zealand of a journalist engaged for his professional expertise and expected to advocate his employing newspaper's political stance regardless of his own personal views.

This type of professional appointment was, however, a rarity in New Zealand in the 1850s. The newspapers were partisan political advocates and, generally, the most important trait for journalists was a personal political commitment that made them not only political advocates but also active politicians in their own right. Where appointments were made for reasons of professional competence rather than political belief, the nature of the appointment was such as not to interfere with the dominant political role of the newspaper. This is well illustrated by the case of G.S. Sale who was appointed as founding editor of *The Press* in Christchurch. Although editor, Sale accepted that his position was not that of controlling functionary of the newspaper. The political role of the newspaper was all-important, and its political controller the dominant personality. As Sale expressed it,

> I saw at once that I had no right whatever to pronounce an opinion on the burning question of the day,[2] and I recognised that I had been appointed editor mainly because of my supposed literary qualifications... I therefore decided to confine myself to the duty of 'getting up' the paper and to writing on general subjects or on European events... The life and soul of the paper was always Mr FitzGerald. He was the main author of its existence and its politics were his politics.[3]

*The Press* was founded in 1861 but prior to the announcement of the Otago gold discoveries and prior to the commencement of the daily press. It was with the start of a daily press that a professional staff became a normal feature of New Zealand journalism. Not only did the higher frequency of appearance place the work required beyond the tolerance level of the previous voluntary labour, but the profit-seeking and achieving nature of the daily press rendered voluntary labour inapplicable. Not all newspapers immediately changed to a full-time

---

2 Moorhouse's Lyttelton railway and tunnel scheme and the attendent borrowing policy.
3 Quoted in O'Neill, (1963), pp. 20-1.

*Journalism and the Daily Press*

salaried staff, nor did all new newspapers immediately begin with such a staff. As is indicated by Blundell's *Evening Post,* many were unable initially to afford a staff and began as family concerns. But the rapid trend was for newspapers to employ full-time staff. During the 1860s the occupation of journalism and its constituent divisions from reporter to editor appeared as facets of the country's employment structure.

Professional employment in journalism became a stepping stone for some who went on to become newspaper proprietors in their own right. The Otago Daily Times and Witness Newspaper Company in Dunedin was the first concern to produce a daily newspaper and the first to be a substantial employer of a full-time salaried staff. It attracted many men to its staff who had ambitions and saw the opportunities to begin their own newspapers. The three who were the most successful eventually were George Bell, Henry Blundell and George Fenwick.

Bell, who arrived in New Zealand in 1863, both reported for the *Otago Daily Times* and, from 1863 to 1869, edited the *Otago Witness*. In 1869 he began his own *Evening Independent* but soon purchased the long lasting *Evening Star*.

Blundell, the founder of the Wellington *Evening Post,* settled in New Zealand in 1863 and began working for Vogel in the *Otago Daily Times*. He left the following year to begin his first New Zealand newspaper, the *Havelock Mail*.

George Fenwick was perhaps the most successful of the three eventually acquiring the *Otago Daily Times* itself. In 1859, at the age of twelve, he was apprenticed to the *Otago Witness*. He finished his apprenticeship six years later. His apprenticeship thus coincided with the foundation and first years of the *Otago Daily Times* and covered the years of most rapid change in New Zealand journalism. In 1867 and 1868 Fenwick was co-proprietor of the *Tuapeka Press and Goldfields Gazette*. In 1869 he co-founded the *Cromwell Argus*. He sold in 1875 and returned to Dunedin where in 1876 he was proprietor of the short-lived *Evening News*. As has been discussed, he became manager and later co-proprietor of the *Otago Guardian*. He, with his co-proprietor, purchased the *Otago Daily Times* and *Otago Witness* and amalgamated the *Guardian* with the *Witness*. In a long and distinguished career Fenwick became the first president of the Newspaper Proprietors Association and was eventually knighted for his services to journalism.

The status of journalism was high in New Zealand. This was by no means usual. In the England whose newspapers New Zealand editors recognized as home journals, journalists of the working class press were vilified by established public opinion. Even in regard to the established and acceptable newspapers there was doubt if journalism was a profession. With little remuneration or tenure of position and no practice of monopoly privilege, it had few of the generally accepted hallmarks of a profession. John Stuart Mill, writing in 1829, was in no doubt of the status of English journalists.

> You know in how low a state the newspaper press of this country is. In France the best thinkers and writers of the nation write in the journals and direct public opinion; but our daily and weekly writers are the lowest hacks of literature, which when it is a trade, is the vilest and most degrading of all trades, because more of affectation and hypocrisy, and more subservience to the baser feelings of others, are necessary for carrying it on, than for any other trade, from that of a brothel keeper upwards....[4]

In New Zealand it was different. While the occupation of journalism eventually was to be of similar standing in both countries, in New Zealand it descended from a loftier regard. Journalism in New Zealand began as a voluntary service for their community and their class performed largely by well educated, capable and generally well regarded male members of the colony's elite; the small group of aristocratic and upper middle class migrants who became the New Zealand ruling class. Journalists in the successful struggle for self-government and in the subsequent legislatures gained publicly recognised political influence and power. Particular newspapers and the press generally were frequently criticized. But with a record of power, influence, and association with the gentry, journalism in New Zealand was a respected profession.

The status of journalism as a profession was not a problem in New Zealand. In England the nature of a profession itself was under change and much of the odium that fell on journalism, a profession unrecognized by the state, was symptomatic of a wider disdain and directed at one of its more visible illustrations.

While accepted as a profession in New Zealand, journalism, as in England, was to become one of the lower professions. With no educational

---

4   Mineka, (1963) pp.38-39.

qualifications or formal entry requirements it was to differ from other professions. It was also hampered by the practice of anonymity. Anonymity made it impossible for an individual journalist to gain any public recognition as superior in his occupation. It thus denied him much bargaining power against an employer. Anonymity meant depressing the price journalists could get for their work as much as stifling their individuality.

The New Zealand press began as and largely remained an anonymous press. However, prior to the 1860s, when communities and newspaper circulations were small enough for newspaper managements to have a face-to-face relationship with their subscribers, anonymity was formal rather than actual. Various writers at times wrote under pen names which soon became well enough known to acknowledge rather than conceal their identity. But there was no argument with the understanding that journalism should be anonymous and, from the 1860s, there was an actual anonymity to the great majority of newspaper writing.

The rationale for journalistic anonymity was presented by *The Press* on the occasion of a lapse by the *Lyttelton Times*.

> A statement appeared a week ago in the *Lyttelton Times* to the effect that *The Press* was under the management of Mr. FitzGerald. No one knows better than the Editor of the *Lyttleton Times* that there is an impropriety and discourtesy in invading the privacy in which time and well-established custom has concealed the names of those connected with the anonymous press .... The sole value and object of an anonymous press is, that the opinions it promulgates may go before the public solely for what they are worth; entirely free either from the influence on the one hand, or the unpopularity on the other, which may attach to their author. This is the great safeguard of a perfectly free press, and by this principle we abide.
> (*The Press*, 1 June 1861)

The *Lyttelton Times* accepted the scolding.

> We desire to offer an ample apology for a mistake committed by us last Wednesday week with reference to *The Press*, a mistake which that paper has very properly pointed out.
> (*Lyttelton Times*, 5 June 1861)

Journalistic anonymity was, of course, the English practice. This fact itself gave it acceptability in New Zealand. But the English, and New Zealand, pattern was by no means universal. Especially in France little attention was paid to anonymity and from 1861 the situation there was one which required signatures for all political articles. The French situation is relevant to New Zealand for there were marked similarities between the practice of journalism, particularly political journalism, in the two countries. In both countries the practice of journalism, unlike in England, received status and respect. In both countries there was close association between journalism and politics. Newspapers were identified with political groups and acted as partisan advocates. Writing for newspapers was regarded as a political act and a normal step in a political career. To be a journalist was an accepted method of attempting to gain political office. The requirement in France for signatures on political articles ensured that the avenue from journalistic recognition to electoral success remained open. It was an avenue that was to close in New Zealand but not completely until the extension of the franchise. While the franchise remained select, journalists could maintain a face-to-face relationship with a significant portion of the electorate and continue to gain public recognition.

One of the more interesting features of the change to professional journalism was the manner in which it combined with the political activism that had always been a feature of New Zealand journalism. Even though many proprietors considered their own personal involvement in political life would prejudice their papers' independence, they did not require their staff to also refrain from personal political involvement. Nor did the public's understanding that political activism was a proper feature of the New Zealand press suddenly disappear in the 1860s with the arrival of the daily newspapers. Thus, numbers of professional journalists stood for election to the House of Representatives.

David Mitchell Luckie is one example of a professional journalist of this type. An emigrant from Scotland, he had considerable journalistic experience there before he emigrated to New Zealand in 1863 and settled in Nelson. He immediately found employment with the *Colonist* and soon became its editor and then co-proprietor. He remained as editor and co-proprietor until he left Nelson in 1873. This was his only period of newspaper ownership. Luckie represented Nelson City in the Provincial Council from 1869 to 1872, and first stood for the House of

Representatives in 1866. He argued during the campaign that his occupation made him especially fitted to be a public representative.

Inclination and early training, together with the peculiar nature of my business, make my interests and the public interests one.
(*Colonist*, 12 January 1866.)

The willingness of Luckie and other New Zealand journalists, when political candidates, to acknowledge their occupation is a further indication of the higher status journalism enjoyed in New Zealand as compared with England. English journalists were reluctant so to identify themselves because of the strong feeling against their occupation. Luckie was unsuccessful in a rugged campaign.[5] He was eventually successful and was M.H.R. for Nelson from 1872 to 1875. After he became a parliamentary representative he left the *Colonist* and Nelson and became, in Auckland, editor of the *Southern Cross*. When in 1876 the *Southern Cross* was purchased by A.G. Horton and closed down, Luckie became leader writer for the Auckland morning rival of the *Southern Cross*, the *New Zealand Herald*. He was there to 1878 when he moved to Wellington and became editor of the *Evening Post*. In 1879 he became Commissioner of the Government Insurance Department.

Robert James Creighton is another instance of a professional journalist with parliamentary ambitions. Like Luckie an experienced Scottish journalist, he was appointed in 1861 to move to Auckland and take control of the *Southern Cross*. He first entered the House of Representatives in April 1865 at a by-election. His first term was only for nine months but he was later M.H.R. from 1869 to 1875, first for Newton and then for Eden. On first entering the House he ceased editing but continued as manager of the *Southern Cross*. In 1868 he made a brief attempt to become a newspaper proprietor. He started the *Auckland Free Press* which, beginning during a business depression, lasted only six weeks. Sometime after this he became editor of the *New Zealand Herald*. How long he held the post is uncertain but in 1873 he

---

5 The campaign included accusations in the *Colonist* that the firm of Curtis Bros (Oswald Curtis being Luckie's electoral rival) were conniving at and encouraging smuggling by their employees and were persecuting the Nelson acting Collector of Customs. See the letter from Honesty in the *Colonist* of 20 February 1866 and the reports of the inconclusive libel action in the *Colonist* of 30 November 1866 and 4 December 1866.

*The Making of the New Zealand Press*

was the inaugural editor and manager in Dunedin of the *Otago Guardian*. He left that position in 1874 or 1875 to edit in Wellington the successor to the *Independent*, Vogel's *New Zealand Times*. In early 1876 he left New Zealand for San Francisco and his parliamentary and New Zealand journalistic career ended.

The *Southern Cross*, the *Otago Guardian*, the *New Zealand Times* and the *New Zealand Herald* were similar newspapers in that the editorial policy of all four was in support of the landed interests who were the political power in the country. Creighton was not being asked, by working for these different newspapers, to make large changes to his own political beliefs. Luckie, however, was so required. The *Nelson Colonist* was one of the earliest newspapers in New Zealand to regard itself as liberal and to advocate policies consistently at odds with those followed in New Zealand.[6] Luckie was elected to Parliament while co-proprietor and editor of the *Colonist*. But he served most of his term in the House while editor of the *Southern Cross* with an editorial policy far removed from that of the *Colonist*.

Payment for parliamentarians was not introduced until 1884. There was nothing unusual in members of the House being in paid employment whilst also being representatives. Creighton began his parliamentary career while working for the *Southern Cross*. Luckie was editor of the *Southern Cross* for most of his term in Parliament. As we have seen the combination of political and journalistic activity was not unusual in Auckland or elsewhere in New Zealand. There was, however, a major difference between the combination of political representation and journalistic activity as practised by such as Creighton and Luckie and as it was practised in earlier years by such men as, for example, William Brown when he was in control of the *Southern Cross* or by another notable Aucklander, John Williamson, when he was in control of the *New Zealander*. Brown and Williamson ran unprofitable newspapers that had a major aim of furthering their political goals and careers. Creighton and Luckie were probably aided politically by their journalistic prominence, though Luckie's ambivalent position makes even this doubtful. But they were employed because of their usefulness to their employing newspapers, not because of the newspapers' usefulness to them. Having members of the House as senior staff members increased the political acumen of the newspapers. But the furtherance of their

---

6   It followed the *Lyttelton Times* which was the first to call itself a liberal advocate.

staff's political careers was not of importance to the proprietors of newspapers.

## Timaru Herald

The changing relationship between politicians and the press is well illustrated by the early history of the *Timaru Herald*. The paper began as a weekly on 11 June 1864 and became a bi-weekly in 1865 when the telegraph line reached Timaru. Founded and originally edited by Alfred George Horton, a major motive in establishing the paper was to obtain separation for the Timaru area from Canterbury Province. While this was not to be achieved Horton is credited with helping to promote the Bill in Parliament which established the Timaru and Gladstone Board of Works. This was an acceptable half measure. Ingram Shrimpton, the ex-proprietor of the *Lyttelton Times*, became a partner in 1864 as did Herbert Belfield in 1867. Both Belfield and Horton began a personal political involvement being members of the Canterbury Provincial Council from 1867-1868 and 1869-1870, respectively. But both quickly retired from politics. Horton, who was later, in Auckland, to become co-proprietor of the *New Zealand Herald,* accepted the established *New Zealand Herald* policy that proprietors should not have personal political careers.

In 1871 Horton sold out to Belfield and left for the North Island. Belfield then became editor until 1875 when he appointed as editor Edward Wakefield, who in the same year was elected to Parliament for the Geraldine seat. Until 1884 Wakefield was both M.H.R. and newspaper editor. He was not a co-proprietor but was a salaried employee. Wakefield's political advocacy for the district was thus carried on both in the newspaper he edited and in the House of Representatives. His political views were compatible with those of Belfield, the proprietor, and of course with the editorial policy of the *Timaru Herald*. His editorship did his political career no harm. But the paper was not a personal political advocate for Wakefield. He was acceptable to his employer only as long as he could be an effective editor. Political advancement would rule this out. When, in 1884 he was appointed Colonial Secretary in the Atkinson Ministry he resigned as editor and his association with the *Timaru Herald* ended.

## Newspaper Readership

As the circulation of newspapers moved from the hundreds into the thousands so was the readership enlarged. And with this enlargement came a change in the nature of the readership. It lost a class bias it had possessed since 1840. This class bias was the same as that which described the minority who ruled the country after the gaining of self-government. Speaking of this minority who ruled from 1853 to Ballance's Ministry in 1891, Reeves described them as "possessing better education and on the whole more knowledge and ability possessing too, land, money and the control of commerce and the professions.... As they often belonged by origin to the classes which in those days controlled English politics they regarded it as natural, as soon as self-government was granted, that they and their friends should direct it."[7] While there were major additions, with Vogel and Atkinson being perhaps the most important, this minority was largely drawn, in Sinclair's words from "the gentry from the original Wakefield settlements".[8] This does perhaps overstate the importance of the Wakefield settlements. Auckland politicians, with no Wakefield settlement background, were also influential in national government. But it does indicate the nineteenth century settlers' acceptance of the importance of social class. The ruling minority were drawn from those settlers who, in the original Wakefield classification, were "colonists". Not only the ruling minority but also, pertinent to this discussion, the newspaper readership was largely restricted to this class. Class-biased literacy rates, high subscription costs and an identification of newspapers with the interests of an upper class, combined to restrict newspaper readership.

The growth of newspaper circulations in the 1860s and 1870s meant not only that the newspaper readership was enlarged but that it was no longer restricted to an upper class. This enlargement of readership came with two changes in newspaper publication; the increase in frequency to daily publication and the decrease in price to 1d. With some newspapers, the *Evening Post* and the *Nelson Evening Mail* being examples, these changes come together. But for most newspapers the penny press came some years after the introduction of daily publication. Both of these changes were marked by increases in circulation, with the new readership being drawn from a population less restricted by class

---

7   Reeves (1898) p. 271.
8   Sinclair (1959) p. 108.

than before. The first change, that to daily publication, was not necessarily causal of an increased readership. More often an increase to daily publication was undertaken to take advantage of an already increasing circulation. The second change, the drop in price to 1d, was, however, often accompanied by a rapid increase in circulation and was designed to promote such an increase.

The pattern of migration in the 1860s and 1870s brought a predominantly working class population to New Zealand. But they were a working class who, unlike their emigrant predecessors in the Wakefield settlements, were increasingly literate. It was the newly literate working class who were not only the bulk of immigrants to New Zealand but also began to form the bulk of the newspaper readership.

The new patterns of newspaper readership were made possible by the combined technologies of the steam engine and cylindrical printing press. Only with this technology was it possible to print enough copies of daily newspapers to reach and maintain the higher circulations. Many argued that the new technology was causal of the increased readership. "The steam press has made the present a reading age", wrote Wakelin.[9] More modestly and correctly the steam press was the technology that allowed the daily newspaper to become part of the reading material of the large numbers of the newly literate.

**Political Emancipation and the Presss**

An important feature of the change was that it did not accompany any political emancipation. The advent of the daily press in New Zealand with its increased readership differed from that of many other countries by the fact that it preceded rather than accompanied a political emancipation. For instance referring to the United States experience Schudson argues that "Modern journalism, which is customarily and appropriately traced to the penny papers, had its origins in the emergence of a democratic market society". By "democratic" he refers to "the replacement of a political culture of gentry rule by the ideal and the institutional fact of mass democracy".[10] The extension of the franchise to all males in New Zealand was a feature of the 1880s with its effects being first felt in the 1890 election. The change of newspapers from a class-based subscription press to a mass penny press predated this and was a feature of the 1860s and 1870s.

---

9 Wakelin (1877) p.77.
10 Schudson (1978) p.57.

Nor was it in New Zealand, as in England and the United States, a case of penny papers beginning in competition with the established sixpenny papers and gradually supplanting them. There were new penny newspapers but in New Zealand the process was more one of conversion. The six-penny newspapers themselves were embarked on the same road; that of a lower unit price in quest of a high circulation with the whole concern financially supported by advertising revenue. From a six-penny political discussion forum for gentlemen the newspapers became penny journals designed to attract a mass readership which could then be sold to advertisers. But during this transition the political franchise remained unchanged and the political discussion and advocacy of the newspapers remained directed at the level of the electorate. It was an inconsistent orientation but one which was not peculiar to New Zealand. It was in keeping with the then recently enunciated English doctrine of the press as the Fourth Estate.[11] The press vented and dissipated discontent and "if by accident journalism were to become suddenly extinct, such a Parliamentary Reform as the wildest of us have never dreamed of, would become an instant and paramount necessity".[12] This tradition saw public opinion as the expression of a relatively small, elitist group with the time and the education to reach a considered judgement on political affairs.

## Newspapers and Political Advocacy

The political orientation of newspapers in the 1860s and 1870s was not of the order of the two previous decades. New perspectives arose and there were significant differences between newspapers and between types of newspapers. The rising business orientation led to change. The commercial demands often become imperatives and they bought a new perspective and definition of purpose to the New Zealand newspapers. But it was not a matter of commercial goals replacing political goals. Political goals were neither replaced nor substantially diminished. Political figures continued attempts, both successful and unsuccessful, to control different newspapers. While the propriety of such attempts was challenged, the active and partisan role of the newspaper in political life was not questioned.

---

11 Henry Reeve's classic statement of the Fourth Estate theory was first published in October 1855 in the *Edinburgh Review*.

12 "The Newspaper Press". *Edinburgh Review* Cii, October 1855. quoted in Boyce (1978) p. 23.

Some newspapers continued the older pattern of the 1850s of backing a personal, political career for the proprietor. This occured mainly among those smaller newspapers which were of the type present prior to the 1860s. With such newspapers the older situation, of a small circulation with losses small enough to be absorbed and offset against political gains, remained. But Julius Vogel is the major example in the 1860s and 1870s of a politician using his newspapers to support his political career, and his actions indicate that this behaviour had not entirely faded from the main centers. The opposite view, that newspapers should be unconcerned with political matters, was voiced by some would-be proprietors but never received public support. No newspapers with such an orientation were successfully established. More common was the view that newspaper ownership should not be linked with a personal political career. As we have noted the *Evening Post* and *New Zealand Herald* were foremost among newspapers espousing such a view. This was not, however, considered to be incompatible with political partisan advocacy. Both the *Evening Post* and *New Zealand Herald* were able to abhor the notion of personal political advocacy for a proprietor while consistently supporting particular politicians and particular policies.

There was not in New Zealand a simple movement from a political press to a business press. While business demands become significant and even became imperatives they were amalgamated with a tradition of political allegiance. Even the new commercial newspapers that considered themselves to be free of political allegiance, in the sense of party allegiance, were ready to advocate measures that were at the heart of the political divisions of the time. This is most notable in regard to attitudes towards provincialism. An illustration is the following statement from the *Morning Advertiser* which both eschews party allegiance and advocates an extreme position on the provincialism/centralism debate.

> Politics, of course, are by a large number of newspaper readers looked upon as the real measure by which their support or opposition is to be determined. It would be difficult indeed to recognize much difference in real politics in this Province. There may arise at times certain differences of opinion between leading men as to minor points of Government, or as to the merits of particular individuals, but beyond this there is but

little distinction in the views of all our representative men. The maintenance of the proper position of Auckland as the leading Province of New Zealand, and strong efforts to obtain insular separation, so that the North Island governing itself, may not be hampered and trammelled in its prosperity by the prejudices and unfair antipathies of the South, are the standpoints around which all our politicians rally. In politics then it will be simply sufficient to say that *The Advertiser* shall be completely independent of the many, and in some cases powerful local or partisan influences which check all independence in journalism, and prevent a free expression of public opinion otherwise than by the platform or the Hustings. For all that can maintain the interests of Auckland, for all that can prevent them from being injured, *The Morning Advertiser* will be a consistent and earnest advocate, but with politics, as meaning the rivalry of local cliques, or the combination of a few to do in justice to the many, *The Morning Advertiser* will have nothing to do.

(*Morning Advertiser* 4 January 1870)

The repudiation of party allegiance and the denial of the importance of party distinctions were part and parcel of the change in newspapers to a mass press attempting to attract readers of all classes and political persuasions. The fervent espousal of provincial allegiances, even though this was a topic of considerable political debate, was not inconsistent with this change. For newspapers, though trying to attract a general readership, were not geographically general. They were firmly based within a particular region and, therefore felt obliged, as well as safe, to pursue extravagently the claims of that region. Thus, the *Auckland Free Press,* starting three years after the removal of the site of Government to Wellington, had as a major part of its political platform Auckland's reinstatement as the capital.

Touching general politics, it is sufficient to say, that the aim of the *Free Press* will be to reserve the integrity of the Province until the political balance has been readjusted, and Auckland resumes its legitimate position as the Seat of Government.
(*Auckland Free Press,* 11 May 1868)

The repudiation of party allegiance made by many of the new commercial newspapers was not a retreat from political involvement. On the contrary it was an attempt to forge for the mass press a political identity and political involvement as wide as its growing readership. Its concern, it was argued, was not for a party but for the public at large and for the general welfare of the entire community. The concept of "public opinion" was used. As in the above quotation from the *Morning Advertiser,* part of a newspaper's political duty was to allow the "free expression of public opinion". As initially argued in England by Jeremy Bentham and James Mill, and later adopted by the New Zealand press, the newspaper press was the link between public opinion and the government. For Bentham the newspaper press was "not only an appropriate organ of the public opinion tribunal, but the only regularly and constantly acting one."[13] Mill extended the argument to maintain that the freedom of the press must be "regarded as an indispensable security, and the greatest safeguard of the interests of mankind".[14] It was from this body of thought that Reeves developed his 1855 statement of the press as the Fourth Estate. New Zealand newspapers in the 1860s and 1870s were to use this intellectual tradition to argue that they were concerned with general rather than particular welfare. Creighton, in his opening editorial for the Free Press, phrased it as follows.

> The *Auckland Free Press* will not be bound to a Party, nor will it be subject to undue influence or pressure of any kind. Depending entirely upon the people for its support, its aim will be to advocate measures calculated to promote the public good. (*Auckland Free Press,* 11 May 1868)

It was argued, as in the following statement from the Dunedin weekly, the *Southern Mercury,* that this independence and generality was of more worth to the society.

> Subservient to no Party, and untrammelled by personal influences, it will be our aim to promote the general welfare, ever remembering that nothing can be really beneficial which

---

13  Quoted in Boyce, (1978) p.21.
14  James Mill's article on the "Liberty of the Press" was first published in the supplement to the *Encyclopaedia Britannica* between 1816 and 1823. Quoted in Ibid. p.22.

tends unduly to advance the interests of a class at the expense of a community, and to the detriment of the Commonwealth...
(*Southern Mercury*, 3 January 1874)

In this argument, the newspaper press was seen as somehow above a Government. It was the instrument by which a Government could be kept honest. The thought was well expressed in the opening statement of the *Waikato Times*.

..it is not our intention to give unqualified support to any political coterie, being of the opinion that it is the duty of the people, and consequently that of the Press, to support those who hold the reins of power only so long as they administer the affairs of the colony in a manner that will tend to promote its well being. It will, of course, be our special duty to jealously watch over the interests of the Waikato settlers, and to point out the public works or legislation required either to develop the resources of the district, or to remove any obstructions on the road to prosperity along which it is travelling with such rapid strides. We shall reserve a column for the promulgation of public opinion on all questions of importance. Space in this column will never be refused to any writer who expresses his opinions in courteous language. The facility a newspaper affords for the interchange of ideas is its most useful, and should be its principal feature. By the concentration of thought upon any subject, and the consequent unanimity of action and opinion, all great social and political reforms have been brought about. To this fact is owing the great power the Press exercises throughout the world. A well-conducted journal cannot fail to confer great benefit upon the people of its district in which it circulates. It exposes all social and political abuses; by the former it improves the tone of society, and by the latter acts as a wholesome check on those who undertake the government of the country.
(*Waikato Times*, 2 May 1872)

In England, the view of the press as an expositor of public opinion and a check on Government was a successful attempt to find for newspapers a middle ground political role, between revolution on the one hand and subservience on the other. In New Zealand the rhetoric was adopted and the argument that the press had a wider concern than party politics also used. This argument had, as in England, a particular cogency in the years during which the franchise was restricted and the electorate was not as wide as the newspaper readership. But in New Zealand the press, even during the pre-1853 agitation for self-government, had never been revolutionary. New Zealand had no equivalent to the English working class press. Nor had the New Zealand newspapers been subservient. Newspaper managements, as we have seen, far from being lackeys of politicians, were drawn from the same social groupings as were politicians. Often the newspaper management and the politicians were the same figures. The links between politicians and newspapers since self-government had been of mutual benefit and newspapers had become integral, rather than subservient, aspects of the New Zealand political life.

The political doctrine that newspapers were guardians of the general welfare was a new ideology of non-partisan leadership that gave the press a political role distinct from that of political parties. The new ideology, however, made little difference to the actual practice of political allegiance. While the majority of newspaper managements made much of their independence, the practice of partisan political allegiance remained. New Zealand newspapers did continue as recognized supporters or opponents of the successive Ministries. Newspapers remained powerful political advocates. Politicians continued to consider newspaper support necessary both for their own electoral success and for the public and parliamentary acceptance of their policies.

The New Zealand newspapers were in an ambivalent position. They were partisan political advocates involved on one or other side of the political debates of the day. But they were also developing practices and an ideology distinct from those of politicians. These were, no matter what a newspaper's political advocacy, often to set them at odds with the Government of the day. The change is most noticeable in the use both newspapers and Governments made of the telegraph and to a study of this we now turn.

PART THREE

# THE STATE, THE TELEGRAPH AND THE NEW ZEALAND PRESS

# 9. Press, Government and the Telegraph to 1870.

The telegraph was an invention eagerly accepted in New Zealand where it was seen as an instrument of cohesion for the small and widely scattered settlements. Reader Wood, the acting Postmaster General, phrased the general view in his 1863 Annual Report:

> It is a matter of the utmost importance, politically and commercially, to the Colony, possibly even involving its integrity, that steps be taken without delay to connect the settlements of the two islands with each other by wires on land in the Middle Island and by cables in the North.[1]

Most of the prominent newspaper proprietors, editorially and as political representatives, accepted the colony's urgent need for the telegraph. This view coincided neatly with their desire to receive a regular and current supply of news and thereby to solve a problem which had bedevilled the New Zealand press since its inception.

The telegraph first gained public prominence on 24 May 1844 when Morse sent a four word question, "What hath God wrought?" between Washington D.C. and Baltimore, Maryland. This first telegraph message, the herald of the electronic age, announced a new communication device which was rapidly taken up throughout the world. The telegraph is one of those technological systems traceable to various discoveries rather than to one individual invention, though 1837 was perhaps the major year in its development. In that year Samuel Morse produced his first system of telegraph and Cooke and Wheatstone patented their five needle system with five line wires, whereby pointers were deflected to indicate various letters of the alphabet. Both systems were to be introduced to New Zealand, though, as elsewhere, Morse's less complicated one was finally to prevail.

The telegraph was to be of enormous significance to New Zealand as it allowed the unification of the country in a manner previously impossible. In a country noted for the isolation of its settlements, the

---

1 Fourth Report of the Postal Service of New Zealand. A.J.H.R. 1863. The reference to cables in the North is in line with Wood's suggestion that Auckland be connected with the southern settlements via a sea cable from the Manukau to D'Urville Island.

telegraph made possible matters as diverse as the standardizaton of time, the commencement of the weather reporting system, the standardization of merchandise pricing, and the apprehension of criminals at a distance. Politically the new amenities were an important factor in the growing ascendency of centralism over provincialism.

## New Zealand Telegraph Construction

Telegraphic links were made among the South Island settlements in the mid-1860s and a cable was laid across Cook Strait in 1866.[2] Links further north were to be delayed by the New Zealand Wars until the early 1870s, and that decade was also to see, in 1876, a cable laid across the Tasman, thus connecting New Zealand with Australia and the rest of the world.

The first references to New Zealand telegraphic use are to be found in the columns of the *Lyttelton Times,* the proprietors of which were ardent advocates for the invention. By 1858 they were writing in favour of the telegraph,[3] and they published the first schema for telegraph development. This was a reprint of a report by the General Telegraph Superintendent for Victoria and proposed the connection of Australia and New Zealand by cable.[4] This grand notion, appearing in the same year telegraph communication was established between Sydney, Melbourne and Adelaide, had to await a corresponding development within New Zealand. This development began in Canterbury. Support for the use of the telegraph by Crosbie Ward and William Reeves, the *Lyttelton Times* proprietors, was joined by the other major Canterbury newspaper figure of the period, J.E. FitzGerald, who had been in the United Kingdom since 1857 as Canterbury Agent. In 1859 he had sent out sufficient material to erect a line between Lyttelton and Christchurch. The line was completed on 18 June 1862. Otago followed closely behind Canterbury with a line from Port Chalmers to Dunedin being opened two months later on 18 August 1862. A Bill to allow for the erection of the line had twice in 1860 been unsuccessfully placed before the Otago Provincial Council. The proposal was supported by Macandrew of the *Colonist,* and the opposition led by Cutten of the *Witness* who initially saw the Bill as allowing excessive interference with private property

---

2 Details are given in Helm's admirable thesis.
3 The first reference is the editorial of 11 August 1858.
4 *Lyttelton Times,* 25 September 1858.

and, with a Port Chalmers population of only 127, also saw it as unnecessary. He was converted only after the Tuapeka gold strike. At the third attempt, the Provincial Executive decided to go ahead with the proposal. Christchurch and Dunedin are both cities situated some distance from their harbours. Their early adoption of the telegraph is understandable in contrast to its later development in the then richer Company settlements at Nelson and Wellington. The Christchurch and Dunedin newspapers, trading in information, were among the major beneficiaries of a telegraph system. This was particularly true for the *Lyttelton Times*. Its office was not moved to Christchurch until 1863 and it gained much of its news as well as most of its circulation over the Port Hills on the plains.

The next telegraph line to be erected in New Zealand was the first in the North Island. It was the line south from Auckland to the Waikato and was erected by British army engineers. The line which was "commenced during the war of 1863"[5] was to aid communication for the imperial troops. By October 1864 the line had reached its southern extremities, Cambridge and Te Awamutu. Due to hostilities, however, this line was to remain separate. Not until 1872 was Auckland connected with the rest of New Zealand and, again due to the hostilities in the Waikato, it was then to be via a line through Thames, Tauranga and Napier.

While the British army engineers were working in the north, telegraph construction was gaining pace in the south. Bluff and Invercargill, again a town at a distance from its harbour, were connected in February 1864 and work was underway on a line along the length of the South Island. The telegraph was the first device to allow sustained and regular communication among settlements. On completion of the line, newspapers of the settlements involved began a process of cooperation. Eventually this process was to lead to the uniting of most New Zealand newspapers within the United Press Association (U.P.A.). The new technology of the telegraph was felt first, however, not by the press but in the political arena. The construction of the South Island line was an early manifestation both of state development in New Zealand and of the General Government's growing ascendency over the various Provincial Governments. In constructing the South Island telegraph line the General Government was, by that

---

5   Green, (1934), p.11.

action, also developing one of the early government departments, the Department of Telegraph. It was also performing a task which was beyond the level of cooperation of which the Provincial Governments were capable.

The South Island line began in the provinces of Otago and Canterbury but was taken over and completed under the authority of the General Government. By September 1862 both the Canterbury and Otago Provincial Governments had decided to proceed with a Dunedin-Christchurch line, but first awaited a General Government response to this proposal. The senior political figure involved was Crosbie Ward, *Lyttelton Times* editor and co-proprietor, as well as General Government Postmaster General. He had already determined the practicality of erecting an Invercargill-Christchurch line. The initial General Government response, which was accepted by the Provincial Governments of Southland, Otago and Canterbury was essentially:

1) The Provinces having the means and machinery at their disposal should each within its own border provide for and superintend the erection of the line.

2) The General Government should take the control of the line when erected working it in conjunction with the Post Office.

A further section of the agreement alludes to the General Government's relative financial inability to fund the project: "The General Government, when in possession of funds, shall on the completion of the through line from border to border, or any part of such through line, repay to the Province one half of the cost constructed or estimated for as above stated".[6]

The General Government, however, was soon to take both financial and administrative responsibility for construction of the telegraph line. It was also to opt for a larger scheme, nothing less than a line connecting all the New Zealand settlements. The Canterbury and Otago Provincial Governments were able to agree on the route for the telegraph. But the Otago and Southland Provincial Governments were unable to do so. Eventually the route was determined by Alfred Sheath, the General

---

6   Quoted in Helm (1951) pp.103-4.

Government appointee to superintend the telegraph.[7] On 31 January 1864 the Colonial Secretary announced that at its last session the General Assembly had resolved that the main trunk telegraph through the Colony should be constructed by the General Government, and funds had been voted for that purpose. This change of plan implied that the General Government was prepared, and able, to take full financial responsibility for the project. It was also an expression of a desire to construct a line the length of the South Island in spite of indifference from the Provincial Governments of Marlborough and Nelson. There had been criticism of their lack of action. Helm holds "It is doubtful whether the two northern provinces would have taken any action to advance the proposal for a main trunk line".[8]

From early 1864 the General Government gradually began to take over the existing telegraph lines and, with two notable exceptions, also assumed responsibility for subsequent telegraph erection. The Invercargill-Bluff line was taken over in November 1864. The Christchurch-Lyttelton line was taken over in May 1865. The Dunedin-Port Chalmers line, erected and run by a private company, under permission from the Otago Provincial Government, became public under General Government control in 1867. In a prodigious burst of activity in the mid-1860s the telegraph was to reach most of the South Island settlements and cross Cook Strait to Wellington. Work was underway on the Invercargill to Dunedin line at the same time as the Dunedin to Christchurch line. The two were opened within days of each other in May 1865. The Provincial Governments of Otago and Canterbury did not accept the General Government's priorities which were to concentrate on connecting the two islands and then to go north to Auckland. While the General Government was implementing the General Assembly's resolution and voting of funds they went ahead with their own priorities. The Provincial Governments of Otago and Canterbury erected lines, respectively, to Queenstown and the West

---

7   The dispute between Otago and Southland was over the matter of communication with the gold diggings. The Otago view of the disagreement was given by the *Otago Daily Times*."Southland, it appears has been throwing dust in the eyes of the Otago authorities. It has refused to cooperate with any other line than that carried along the sea coast. If the proposal were adopted by Otago it wants no prophet to forsee that Southland would very soon and at very small expense carry a line to the Lake Goldfields, and enjoy the advantage of direct communication." (2 April 1863)

8   Helm (1951), p.112.

Coast, so as to link their capital towns with the gold fields. These two lines were the exceptions to the General Government's domination of telegraph construction but they were soon to be controlled by the General Government. The West Coast line was taken over in 1868, the Queenstown line in 1870. The General Government erected line, north from Christchurch, reached Picton in December 1865 and Nelson in March 1866. In August 1866 the Cook Strait cable was laid and Wellington was linked with the South Island settlements. The telegraph was ready for extension over the North Island but was now to be delayed by the hostilities of the New Zealand Wars. The line north from Wellington reached Napier by 1869, while in the west the line stretched from Wellington to Patea in 1870 and to Opunake in 1872. Due to Maori opposition this line reached New Plymouth only in 1880. New Plymouth, however, did join the telegraph network in 1876 via a line around the inland side of Mt. Egmont to Hawera. In July 1870 the Auckland-Thames line was opened, while the Wellington-Napier line was extended to Tauranga in December. These two lines were extended and met on 12 April 1872, on which date Auckland was linked with Wellington and the South Island.

### The New Zealand General Telegraph Agency

The completion in May 1865 of the telegraph line from Bluff to Christchurch also saw the start of New Zealand's first press agency. This was the New Zealand General Telegraph Agency. Its first messages appeared in *The Press* on 21 May 1865. This shortlived agency prefaced the nature of the press cooperation that was later to emerge.

The New Zealand General Telegraph Agency was controlled by Gerald FitzGerald and was situated at Campbelltown, as Bluff was then known. It was begun under the impetus of Gerald's brother, J. E. FitzGerald, proprietor of the Christchurch newspaper, *The Press*. He saw the establishment of a press agency as a method of preventing a circulation loss he suffered to the more southern papers. The mail steamers from Australia and Europe generally arrived first at Bluff, working north from there. By the time they set out for Lyttelton the newspapers in Southland and Otago had printed accounts of the news and their bundles of papers, travelling on the same steamers, gave the information a day before the local papers could print it. A telegraphed message from Bluff to Christchurch, however, was a minimum of three

## The Making of the New Zealand Press

days in advance of the steamers, giving ample time for *The Press* to beat its approaching southern competition. Such a system, of course, also gave *The Press* an advantage of several days over its local competition.

*The Press*'s first use of the telegraph was a summary of news from a mail ship, the steamer *Hero*, which arrived in port on the day the Bluff-Christchurch line opened. It is a good example of a change the new device brought to journalism.

Telegraphed news was costly and from the start a staccato presentation, concentrating on what was perceived as factual information, was adopted. The newspaper page became a mosaic of snippets of information connected by the coincidence of their occurrence in the immediate past.

LATEST NEWS PER ANGLO-INDIAN TELEGRAPH
GALLE, April 22
LONDON, April 5.

President Davis' message to Congress declares that Richmond was never in greater peril.

Sheridan continues his destructive raid with the greatest activity in the face of Lee's great army.

An attack on Mobile is imminent.

Greater efforts are being made at Richmond to organise a Negro force.

The Confederate Congress have passed this measure recommended by President Davis. He proposes if necessary to fire Richmond and to retreat.

Federal Government have withdrawn their notices of the abrogation of the Lake Treaty of 1817.

The Seward passport system ceases immediately.

Sherman was advancing on Goldsborough and Hardee had reached Whitehouse. He was continuing his destruction of railways with great activity.

It is reported that all cotton taken will be immediately shipped to England.

The Canadian Parliament has adjourned the Confederation.

New York papers of the 17th March state that the Federal General Scholfield had occupied Kingstown, Bragg retreating to Woodsford.

Sherman was within 21 miles of Richmond.

Gold has declined to 166.

Monte Video has given way in the struggle with Brazil, and peace has been restored.

A London telegram of April 3rd announces the death of Richard Cobden.

The plague is depopulating whole towns in Russia, and is travelling rapidly towards Prussia.

Mrs Theresa Yelverton has failed in her final appeal to the law.

The Fort of Ferrol fired upon the Federal steamers Niagara and Sacramento for attempting to leave that fort, in pursuit of the Confederate Ram Stonewall, within 24 hours after the latter had been ordered to sea by the authorities of Lisbon.

An engagement between the Federal vessels and the Ram off the Portugese coast was expected.

LONDON, April 6.

Business bad.

The Confederates under Johnston have been victorious over Sherman.

(*The Press*, 21 May, 1865)

The following day's telegraphed news is a further typical example; this time of a day with no mail ship arrivals.

Invercargill, Monday 2 PM. The Airedaile will leave the Bluff in an hour.Wind west, with rain.No news.

(*The Press*, 22 May 1865)

This type of presentation was to become common to all newspapers which received telegraphed news. There were publications which opted out of use of the telegraph but they were few and, by that decision, ceased to be newspapers, instead joining the growing variety of periodicals.

The New Zealand General Telegraph Agency was begun with no cooperative motivation at all. Its aim in fact was competitive and was to enable one paper, *The Press,* to have an edge over its rivals, both local and southern. But J.E. FitzGerald only partly succeeded in achieving this goal. The competition from the southern papers was beaten but at the cost of forcing local cooperation among the Canterbury papers. The problem for FitzGerald was financial and was later to be faced by the other newspaper proprietors when they used the telegraph. The economic advantages offered by the speed of telegraphed news had to be weighed against the high cost of telegrams. FitzGerald soon found that *The Press* "could not support the whole cost of the telegraph service without serious risk to its own hopes of further development."⁹ In order to retain his advantage over his southern rivals, he was forced to share this advantage with the other Christchurch papers. Pressed by Harman and Stevens, his major creditors, he successfully invited the *Lyttelton Times* and the *Canterbury Standard* to join in a partnership with the *The Press* to obtain telegraphed news reports. Thus the first New Zealand press agency, largely due to the impetus of J.E. FitzGerald, was a cooperative effort by the Canterbury newspaper proprietors. The Canterbury proprietors were not, however, the only ones to appreciate the new technology of the telegraph. Further south in Dunedin an equally significant figure was to be found in Julius Vogel.

**Vogel and Government Sponsored Press Agencies**

When the South Island telegraph line was first constructed, Julius Vogel was still co-proprietor and editor of the *Otago Daily Times,* the largest circulation newspaper in the country. Vogel, equally astute a journalist as J.E. FitzGerald, was also aware of the potential of the telegraph and began to use it as soon as the Bluff-Dunedin line was open. Vogel's strategy was to have summaries of foreign news prepared in Melbourne by a member of the staff of the *Argus,* put on the mail steamers and dispatched by telegram from Bluff immediately upon the steamer reaching that port. Hokitika was also a frequent first port of call for the steamers and, on the telegraph line reaching Hokitika, Vogel had a similar arrangement in respect of that port. Vogel's arrangements were initially only for the use of the *Otago Daily Times.* But when the Cook Strait cable was laid and, in August 1866, Wellington linked to the South Island telegraph line, Vogel's telegrams were available for sale to Wellington and, later, other North Island newspapers.

Vogel's own business arrangements were contemporary with FitzGerald's agency. Unlike FitzGerald, Vogel did not include his local competition, but, once the telegraph reached Wellington and it was thereby possible to include other non-local newspapers, he took the opportunity to widen his service and, in effect, to make it a press agency.

At this point, either in late 1866 or early 1867, a decision was taken which made news collection and dissemination a task of the General

---

9   O'Neill, (1963), p.66.

## Press, Government and the Telegraph to 1870

Government and which put out of business both Vogel's press agency and the FitzGerald brothers' agency. Three newspaper proprietors, Vogel of the *Otago Daily Times*, FitzGerald of *The Press* and Crosbie Ward of the *Lyttelton Times*, asked the Postmaster General to have the Department of Telegraph prepare and despatch telegraphed summaries of the overseas news. The Postmaster General "consented to furnish the telegrams"[10] and Vogel's arrangements were taken over by the General Government. An official of the Department of Telegraph prepared, in Melbourne, summaries of Australian news and of news brought by the English mail ships. These were sent to New Zealand by ship and telegraphed to newspapers from the initial port of call. Individual New Zealand newspapers gained access to the service on payment of an annual subscription, the amount of which was never made public.

This was a somewhat cosy arrangement. Ward, FitzGerald and Vogel were well placed to make such a request of the Postmaster General. Ward had served as Postmaster General himself from 1861 to 1863 in the Fox and Domett Ministries. Depending on the exact date the request was made, he was, perhaps, still a Member of the House of Representatives. He resigned his seat for Lyttelton on 28 January 1867. FitzGerald was in a similar position, resigning his seat for the City of Christchurch on 3 January 1867. Vogel was also in the House, representing the Goldfields, at this period.

The Postmaster General was John Hall, who held office from June 1866 to February 1869. He was appointed Electric Telegraph Commissioner, the first appearance of such a portfolio, in October 1866. Hall, one of the original promoters of *The Press* and regarded by Canterbury journalists as the doyen of their craft, was well disposed towards a favourable Government treatment of newspapers.

Vogel was later to offer two reasons for the General Government providing telegraphed news summaries. Firstly there was a need for "a common source of telegraphic news" for the "New Zealand papers could not afford...costly competition as to which should first gain the wires." Secondly he referred to a specific incident which he argued indicated a need for the General Government to take over the activity of a press agency.

---

10  The phrase is Vogels. See his letter in the *Otago Daily Times* of 24 October 1868. Also see the editorials in the *Otago Daily Times* of 23 and 24 October 1868. This was the first time the arrangements were made public.

.. a very serious complaint arose. Information as to the suspension of the Commercial Bank at Home was not furnished to the newspapers, whilst private telegrams gave the intelligence. For a whole day the Bank was kept open, a run occurred from which a few benefitted, whilst the body of creditors suffered. It then became evident... that, to allow a monopoly of the wires on the arrival of the mail might prove highly injurious, and that the best course, from a public point of view, was for the Government to furnish without delay a telegram of the leading public news.[11]

Vogel and his fellow newspaper proprietors had come up with a method of obtaining news telegrams which comfortably served both their views as M.H.R.'s and their interests as newspaper proprietors. The entry by the Government into the day-to-day business of the press, the compilation and provision of its telegraphed news, was done according to Vogel's letter above, to provide proper use of a technology that, in regard to the collapse of the Commercial Bank, had enabled a few to benefit "whilst the body of creditors suffered". While this is a proper role for a Government to play in a private enterprise system, the actions of the Government were also open to the charge that they indicated a noticeable and improper lack of distinction between public and private spheres. The *Otago Daily Times* editorial which had prompted Vogel's letter of explanation had included the following complaint.

> The General Government virtually compels the leading newspapers of the colony to accept such telegrams as it may please to send them, in return for a certain annual subscription. In doing so, it inflicts a wrong upon the public as well as upon the journalists. It undertakes a duty which it is not competent to perform, which it is not asked to perform, and which it has no moral right to perform.
> (*Otago Daily Times*, 23 October 1868)

Vogel's letter had indicated that the *Otago Daily Times* was incorrect in asserting the General Government was performing a task "it is not asked to perform". But the rest of that newspaper's complaint remained. The actions of Vogel, Ward and FitzGerald, all private entrepreneurs likely to benefit from a Government provided news service and also all

---
11 Letter from Julius Vogel in *Otago Daily Times*, 24 October 1868.

members of the Parliament that moved to provide the service, were open to questions of propriety. Although, as is evident from the *Otago Daily Times* editorial, there was a public level of discourse that saw such arrangements between press and government as improper, Vogel Ward and FitzGerald saw little distinction between their business roles as newspaper proprietors and their political roles as elected representatives. In regard to the telegraph it is evident that from the opening of the Bluff-Christchurch line there was a lack of appreciation of a problem in regard to the private use of what were public facilities. As O'Neill has pointed out, from the opening of this line FitzGerald with the New Zealand General Telegraphic Agency had competed with the Department of Telegraph for public telegrams.

> Nobody, apparently, saw any objection to the agency being allowed to compete with the similar Government service on the same state-owned and state-operated wire.[12]

The New Zealanders' general readiness to use the administrative ability of the state for activity considered private elsewhere was often to be commented on. Siegfried, for one, was to cite "this perfect mania for appealing to the state" as "one of the characteristics of their public life".[13] But this early and notable example of the characteristic, the government's collection and provision of news telegrams, is also an indication of a unanimity of opinion among press and government that was not to last. The *Otago Daily Times* was the first newspaper to complain of the arrangements. But that newspaper's complaints, first made in October 1868, although they are couched in principled phrases, only appear after the ousting of Vogel from that newspaper. There was an initial coincidence of interest of press and Government and the complaints are made only after the *Otago Daily Times* was placed outside the coincidence of interests. Charges of confusion between public and private spheres and of conflict of interests for Vogel, Ward and FitzGerald were made within a political system where the validity of such complaints was not recognized. The experience of administration of the telegraph was to be one of the factors leading to a public awareness of the need for a new method of administration.

---

12 O'Neill (1963) p.66.
13 Siegfried (1914) p.52.

## The Making of the New Zealand Press

Complaints were soon made by newspapers over the Government's control of the telegraph with regard to national news as well as to the overseas news telegrams. It was argued that an improper favouritism was shown to political supporters and conversely that difficulties were placed in the way of opponent newspapers.

An instance of the tricks which might be played by any Government having complete control over the telegraph wires, is afforded by a late Wellington Independent: It appears that a gentleman connected with the leading Auckland journal was anxious to telegraph the Ministerial statement to his paper (via Napier, to catch the S.S. Phoebe) and proceeded to the telegraph office for the purpose of sending his message. When he presented his form to the young gentleman in charge of the office he was asked, "Is this a Press telegram?" The reply was in the affirmative. "Then," was the rejoinder, "I cannot take it here; this office is for the use of members". There was, of course, no answering this; but it happened that the members of the House to whom the gentleman mentioned the circumstances informed him that they had seen the correspondents of two newspapers in the interest of the Government only that day telegraphing from that office. The New Zealand Herald, the journal referred to by the Independent, states that at the same time telegrams conveying the Government view of the matter were allowed to be despatched to the Nelson papers.
(*Otago Daily Times,* 24 October 1868)

The incident is perhaps trivial. But the fact that the *Otago Daily Times* is here echoing a *Wellington Independent* story is of some moment. That the two politically opposed newspapers are in agreement here indicates that both newspapers recognized not only that newspapers had common interests but that these common interests were, at least in this case, at odds with the political interests of the Government.

John Hall was replaced as Postmaster General and Electric Telegraph Commissioner in February 1869. Edward Stafford, the Premier, combined both portfolios under that of Postmaster General and himself took over the task. Stafford began moves to dismantle the Government-run press agency but in June 1869 his Ministry fell, William Fox became Premier and Julius Vogel became Postmaster General and Electric Telegraph Commissioner as well as Colonial Treasurer. Vogel was to be the Minister in control of the telegraph throughout the years he held Government office.

Vogel stopped Stafford's closing of the Government's provision of telegram news summaries but the respite for the service was only temporary and Vogel, from 31 July 1870, was to end the service. No official explanation for the ending of the Government service was published. The situation was that Vogel had no desire to end the Government's role in news collection and dissemination. The managements of at least most newspapers, however, were to refuse to continue their purchase of the news summaries. Vogel was left with no choice but to close down the operation.

The news summaries were frequently criticized by Vogel's opponent journals after the first complaints appeared in the *Otago Daily Times*. But by 1870 dissatisfaction with the Government service had become general among newspapers. Many complaints were in regard to the quality of journalism evident in the telegraphic reporting. Even Vogel's supporters complained, the following being an example:

> We had hoped that the repeated complaints made by almost all the papers in the colony would have led to some improvement in the compilation of the telegrams of English news which the Government practically compels the newspapers to take and pay for. We have, however, been disappointed, for the telegrams received on Sunday last, and published in our last issue are even worse than usual.
> (*Wellington Independent*, 31 March 1870)

Dr C. Lemon, the General Manager under Vogel of the New Zealand Telegraph Department, wrote to the various newspaper proprietors offering to continue the telegraph summaries at a cost to each newspaper of £36 per year for both the English and Australian mail summaries. The £36 per year charge offered by Lemon is, as is clear in his letters, a reduction on the previous charges, though the exact level of the previous charges is not given.[14]

The *Otago Daily Times* in its 3 October 1870 editorial argued that the Government service ceased when Vogel came "to the conclusion that

---

14 This reduction was offered as part of a 1 April 1870 overall reduction in prices. General telegraph charges were also substantially reduced: From 1/6 per first ten words and 6d per each extra ten words to 6d per first ten words and 6d per extra fifteen words.

even such small pickings as the receipts from 'Press telegrams' were not to be despised".[15] But the *Otago Daily Times* statement is merely an aspersion on Vogel made by his major opponent newspaper.

Whether Lemon received any newspaper acceptances for a continuation of the service is unknown. But at least a majority of newspapers were against continuation. Vogel received the political support of many newspapers but their allegiance did not extend to allowing him to continue a news service they had found wanting. It was their denial of the service that led to its demise. It was to be replaced by two press agencies.

**Competitive Press Agencies**

The *Otago Daily Times* had in 1866 under Vogel's stewardship established its own news service. In 1870 the *Otago Daily Times* management reestablished and expanded this service. The paper's own version of events after 31 July 1870 is as follows:

> We made arrangements for supplying the foreign mail and interprovincial telegrams to the *Daily Times*, and to the principal newspapers in the other provinces. Agents were appointed in Melbourne and San Francisco to compile telegraphic summaries of the mail news; and agents were also appointed in every town and port of importance in New Zealand. The leading newspapers in the other provinces cordially approved of this system, and agreed to take their telegrams from our agents. The agreement was, in every instance but one, accompanied with a condition that we should not supply telegrams to any rival newspaper in the same town. These arrangements were purely a matter of business. Political considerations had nothing whatever to do with them. Ministerial as well as Opposition newspapers agreed to join. The Lyttelton Times, the Press, the Evening Post, the Hawke's Bay Herald, the Nelson Colonist and Examiner, the Wanganui Chronicle, the Wairarapa Mercury, the Grey River Argus, the Marlborough Express, the Westport Times, the Timaru Herald and the Oamaru Times are supplied with our telegrams.
> (*Otago Daily Times*, 3 October 1870)

---

15 This *Otago Daily Times* version of events has been accepted uncritically by most commentators. It was repeated by Fenwick in his history (1929, p.4) and then echoed by Scholefield (1958, p.11), O'Neill (1963, p.70), and Sanders, (1979, p.2).

## Press, Government and the Telegraph to 1870

Whether *The Press* does correctly appear in this listing is open to doubt. The statement that "The agreement was, in every instance but one, accompanied with a condition that we should not supply telegrams to any rival newsaper in the same town" runs at odds with the fact that two Nelson papers as well as the *Lyttelton Times* and *The Press*, two Christchurch papers, are in the listing. If *The Press* was in the *Otago Daily Times* group it was only for a short period for it soon became part of a competing agency.

The *Otago Daily Times* agency was a restricted one usually not open to rival newspapers in the same town. The telegraph credit line of the *Otago Daily Times* service appeared in newspapers in the weeks after the closing of the Government news service. Concurrently with the start of the *Otago Daily Times* service, the telegraph credit line "Greville's Telegram Company, Reuters Agents" began appearing in newspapers that were not receiving the *Otago Daily Times* summaries.

Greville's Telegram Company began as part of Reuter's developing international news carrier service. Reuter, who had moved to London weeks before the opening in 1851 of the first international submarine cable, linking Dover and Calais, had followed a policy of establishing agents in "his"[16] parts of the world as the telegraph network expanded. Sometimes, as in the New Zealand case, for the Australia-New Zealand cable was not laid until 1876, he anticipated the network. Greville obtained the agency for Reuters and also obtained his international news via that source. Greville was an Australian journalist and his was primarily an Australian press agency serving newspapers in that country.[17] His New Zealand agency was a branch of a larger press agency based in Australia. Greville appointed C.O. Montrose as the manager of his New Zealand central office which was in Wellington. His was the agency for those newspapers not members of the *Otago Daily Times* service. The dominant trio were the *Dunedin Star*, *The Press*, and the *Wellington Independent*.

---

16  Under a cartel agreement with Havas of France and Wolff of Germany, the two other leading agencies of the time, Reuter was given Britain and all of its Empire, Holland and its dependencies, the East Indies and most of the Far East. The agencies agreed not to poach on one another's territories, and to exchange their respective news services. (Boyd-Barrett, 1978, pp. 196-197.)

17  In Australia the agency was known as Greville and Bird. It was based in Sydney and was probably the first press agency there. Reuters cabled news summaries to Alexandria. The summaries travelled by ship to Albany where Greville and Bird's agent boarded the vessel and prepared a summary to be telegraphed from Glenelg (Walker, 1976, p.202.).

*The Making of the New Zealand Press*

No Auckland papers appear on the listings for either of the agencies. This omission is on account of the telegraph, at that time, not having reached Auckland. Auckland newspapers, however, did have an affiliation with the agencies. While the Auckland newspapers could continue to gain their non-local news in the time-honoured manner of reprinting it from other papers, the agencies did need access to Auckland news and did need Auckland agents to hasten southwards the despatches from those mail ships that first called at Auckland. Thus the *Auckland Star*'s proprietor Henry Brett became the Greville's agent, while W.J. Wilson, proprietor of the *New Zealand Herald* filled the corresponding position with the *Otago Daily Times* grouping. Once Wellington and Auckland were connected by telegraph in 1872 the Auckland newspapers, of course, were in the same position as their southern counterparts.

The two press associations ran as opposing agencies for two years. The *Otago Daily Times* remained a strong opponent to the Fox-Vogel Ministry and the revival of its press agency was, at least partly, an attempt to escape from what it saw as Vogel's political control of the compilation and dissemination of news summaries. However both associations were primarily business rather than political organizations. Newspapers with opposing political outlooks were present in both agencies. The two Nelson papers in the *Otago Daily Times* group were in political opposition to one another. The *Evening Post* was an opposition paper while the *Hawke's Bay Herald* supported the Government. Most notably the *Lyttelton Times* was a staunch supporter of Vogel while the *Otago Daily Times* was his most fervent opponent. The *Wellington Independent* was with the Greville group, and, while it was a Vogel supporter and thus at odds with the *Otago Daily Times*, both it and the *Otago Daily Times* held that their presence in opposing press agencies was on account, not of political differences, but of an inability to agree on a price for the supply of telegrams.

**Press Cooperation**

The new telegraphic presentation was quickly adapted to New Zealand political news and was accompanied by a change in the style of political reporting. The following extract from the *Nelson Evening Mail* on the occasion of the debate leading to the fall of the Stafford Ministry is an illustration. While perhaps verbose to modern ears it is taciturn in comparison to earlier practice. More importantly, rather than a discussion of the substantive issues of the debate and advocacy for one side in it, there is a reporting of the holding of the debate and an estimate of its future course. It is a story as opposed to a discussion and is one that supporters of either side of the debate could use. Significantly it was shared by the *Nelson Colonist* and the *Nelson Evening Mail*.

(From the *Colonist*)
Telegraph Intelligence. Wellington. Thursday 7.22PM.
Mr Fox opened the debate on the motion of want of confidence on Tuesday evening. His speech lasted two hours and was very spirited and effectively given.Mr Stafford followed at once and defended his government dexterously and brilliantly. The debate continued last night in a rather desultory manner. It is expected to drag on for five or six nights. The Opposition confidently expect a majority of at least six. Mr Stafford has intimated that if the no confidence motion is carried he will not resign but will dissolve Parliament".
(*Nelson Evening Mail*, 18 June 1869)

The means given by the telegraph to send news rapidly was a major factor in changing the nature of the newspaper. The preeminence of local political discussion was gradually displaced as the priority task of a newspaper. It was the provision of news which newspapers increasingly perceived as their major service for the public.

The desire for what was regarded as an adequate news service was to force cooperation between newspapers and to place them at odds with the General Government. Until the complaints in the *Otago Daily Times* no dissatisfaction had been expressed with the Government service. By 1870, when dissatisfaction was widespread, the singleness of purpose between Government and press, evident when men such as Vogel, FitzGerald and Ward occupied dominant positions in both spheres, was ending. This is attested to by the above quote from the *Wellington Independent*[18] where even that stalwart Fox-Vogel supporter is prepared to criticize the Government. Notably, the criticism is on a journalistic matter, the quality of its overseas news telegrams, and it indicates that in such areas the newspaper's professional needs have priority over its political loyalties. Newspapers, which previously had given priority to political goals, began to view journalistic needs as paramount.

---

18 See p.197 above.

## The Making of the New Zealand Press

Press use of the telegraph and the commercial growth of newspapers at times gave newspaper concerns professional needs that were in conflict with their political loyalties. A notable instance of this conflict between political loyalty and professional business demands is to be found in an extract from a letter from A.W. Follet-Halcombe, editor of the *Wellington Independent*, and also related by marriage to the Premier, William Fox, to G.B. Barton, editor of the *Otago Daily Times*. The letter is dated 1 December 1869, though it came to public attention only during the 1871 trial for criminal libel of Barton, and concerns an attempt to extend a within-New Zealand telegraphic news network.

> We have special advantages in undertaking the communication with Auckland via Napier, which renders it desirable that that part of the work should be done by us, as by a private arrangement with the General Government we are enabled to send and receive messages for Auckland via Napier without charge for telegraph, the Government requiring in return a copy of our summary of Auckland news. This proposed arrangement is, however, quite private, and I should be obliged by your not mentioning it outside the circle of those interested in these arrangements.[19]

Follet-Halcombe's desire for secrecy is understandable for his letter is evidence of what opponents to the Fox-Vogel Ministry would have regarded as an improper collusion between the Government and the management of the *Wellington Independent*. It also indicates that the interests of the press could no longer be subsumed under any Government-press linkage. Follet-Halcombe's desire for secrecy was not only a concern to keep the information from the public in general and the Fox-Vogel Ministry's opponent newspapers in particular. He also would have had no desire for Fox and Vogel to learn that he was proposing to use the private arrangement between the Government and the *Wellington Independent* as part of a wider telegraph news network involving the *Otago Daily Times*, the Government's main opponent newspaper.

Follet-Halcombe's letter is evidence that as early as 1869 New Zealand newspapers, or at least the *Wellington Independent* and the *Otago Daily Times*, were making arrangements for the sharing of New

---

19 *The Telegraph Libel Case*, p.42.

Zealand news. Not only was there cooperation for the reception of telegraphed news summaries from Australia and England but there was also cooperation for news transmission within New Zealand. Newspapers were to forward news from their province and in return were to receive a similar service from other provinces. The various patterns of news networking that came with the telegraph acted as commercial imperatives often at odds with the political alliances of the day. Follet-Halcombe's letter is one example of the quest for the most inexpensive possible use of the telegraph leading to a business alliance of newspapers that publicly were implacable political opponents.

The cooperation between newspapers was such that political rivals muted their antagonism in the interest of a cooperative, and cheaper, use of the telegraph. It was this interest that was an ever-present impetus towards collaboration among the New Zealand newspapers. Political rivalry was not allowed to interfere with commercial cooperation. But commercial cooperation was not among all newspapers. It was very much a selective cooperation. Business rivalry continued. The original commercial wisdom was as stated by the *Otago Daily Times*.

> So far as the leading journals in different Provinces are concerned, there can be no objection to an association among them for procuring telegraphic or other intelligence...But journalists who understand their business would hesitate before they entered into any association with their local competition.
> (24 October 1868)

It was this understanding, allowing both cooperation and competition, which led to the formation in 1870 of two press agencies. The next decade, however, was to bring considerable modification to this selective cooperation and competition. The commercial wisdom as expressed by the *Otago Daily Times* had already been upset three years earlier in Christchurch during the months of FitzGerald's New Zealand General Telegraphic Agency. There FitzGerald, or more likely Harman and Stevens, had considered the cost of the telegraph such that, so as to defray expenses, *The Press* had shared its advantage with the other local newspapers. The 1870s were to bring not only considerations of cost but also political experiences that further increased press cooperation.

# 10. Press, Government and the Telegraph in the 1870s

The two press associations, the *Otago Daily Times*-administered service and the Reuter agency controlled in New Zealand by Greville, ran as opposing agencies for two years. They began in mid-1870 and continued to the second half of 1872. The *Otago Daily Times* remained a strong opponent to the Fox-Vogel Ministry and its revival of its press agency was at least partly an attempt to escape from what it saw as Vogel's political control of the compilation and dissemination of news summaries. But both the *Otago Daily Times* association and Greville's association were primarily business rather than political organizations. Newspapers with opposing political outlooks were present in both agencies. This meant that marked political bias in agency despatches would always be unsatisfactory to some member newspapers. This itself led the agencies to attempt a political neutrality in their telegrams. Press agency interest became distinct from the involved interest of politicians. An appreciation of press interests as being distinct from the political interests of a Government or its opposition was aided by the normal working patterns of the two press associations. But apart from this there were two major reasons for a perceived separation of Government and press interests at this time. One centered around the heavy usage of the telegraph system.

**Press Associations Use of the Telegraph Service**

There was a strong practical reason for a growing appreciation of press and Government interests being distinct. It had to do with the everyday use of the telegraph, then still very much a limited facility. The Government, as custodian of the resource, found telegraph use by the two competing press agencies made difficult the commercial and public use of the system. Complaints from the commercial and public sectors placed the Government at odds with the press. The problem was well stated by Vogel in his 1873 report as Commissioner of Telegraphs:

> ...the arrangements made by two competing Press Associations for supplying intelligence to newspapers were among the chief causes of public dissatisfaction. On the arrival of a steamer from Australia, the Associations endeavoured to excell each other in supplying to their customers English and Australian

news; consequently there was a substantial repetition of a very long message to each of the principal stations; and it was precisely when the Department was temporarily overweighted by those long repetitions, that the commercial public sent in most messages and was most sensitive if the delivery of any of them was at all delayed. Again, for reasons inseparable from the Telegraph system in New Zealand, long press telegrams transmitted from the Bluff have a greater tendency to monopolize the wires than have equal messages transmitted from Hokitika or from Auckland: and it was at the Bluff that the longest messages were received for transmission during the period of constant pressure and of complaint.[1]

The submarine cable between Australia and New Zealand was laid in 1876. Until that time each mail ship brought a backlog of news that had accumulated for up to eight days. The heavy press usage of the telegraph that occurred with the arrival of each mail ship was exacerbated not only by the presence of two press associations but by the actions of each of them to gain advantage over the other. Speed to and from the mail ships was all-important and various strategies were employed by competing journalists to be first with the news. Although the competitive tactics began in the south they are best recorded in the reminiscences of the *Auckland Star* proprietor, Sir Henry Brett. As illustrations:

> Mr Brett (of the *Auckland Star*) conceived the plan of having a fast horseman on one of the points down Orakei way. As soon as he got his papers from the mail boat he pulled smartly for the point, handed his letters and files to the horseman, who succeeded in beating the waterman's boat back to town.... On one occasion, Saturday afternoon, a rowing club racing whaleboat, pulling three oars, was paddling innocently in the vicinity of the mail steamer when she dropped anchor, .. Mr Brett went down to the North Head as usual in his ordinary waterman's boat .. but as soon as he got his files from the mail boat he pulled alongside the whaleboat, jumped in, and took an oar, the crew opened their backs, and the surprised opposition was left lamenting.

---

1   9th Report, N.Z. Telegraph Department, A.J.H.R., 1873.

## The Making of the New Zealand Press

Some of the strategies employed, however, were scarcely calculated to foster harmonious relations between the press and other telegraph users. Whichever press agency was first to use the telegraph was keen to delay access to it to its competitor. Having sent their message they were often prepared to continue to monopolize the telegraph. Thus material such as extended biblical extracts was at times telegraphed. Such activity not only made the telegraph unavailable to the competing press agency but also denied it to all potential users. As ever Sir Henry Brett was an advanced player of this delaying game.

> ...Mr Brett went up to Emily Place... to see how the boats were getting along when returning from the mail steamer. He was dismayed to see his man hopelessly out of the race to the wharf... so he rushed down to the *Star* office to put into execution a plan that flashed through his mind. Unearthing the remains of the *European Mail* and *Home News,* two English publications which gave the month's news and catered for colonial readers, he wrote out the first sheet of his telegraphic message from these journals. These papers had really been gutted a month before, as they reached Auckland by the previous steamer. "I had to do something," said Mr Brett, "as the first man to get the wires in those days held them until he was through with his message.
>
> Going down to the Telegraphic Office, I made out the first sheet of my message with items of no interest, ready to hand to the operator as soon as my rival appeared. Mr W. Berry came dashing along, firmly convinced that he had beaten us this time. As soon as I saw him I handed in my message to Mr H. Hemus... who was then operator and clerk..."
>
> "Mr Brett hasn't got the wires first this time," called out Mr Berry, but as far as Mr Hemus knew the message he had just received was quite genuine, so he refused to interfere.
>
> "I will go and see Mr Wilson" (of the *Herald*) was the protest of Mr Berry, and off he went to his employer.
>
> "This was just what I wanted," said Mr Brett, and before Mr Berry could get back from the *Herald* Office, Mr Geddis had arrived with the real message.[2]

---

2   Brett (1927) pp. 5-6.

## Press, Government and the Telegraph in the 1870s

Brett reports that it was this particular incident which led to a change in the telegraph regulations whereby, whenever other messages were awaiting transmission, long telegraph messages could only have a total of 200 words transmitted before having to vacate the line for other users. This administrative checking of abuse by regulation is an indication of the separate and, in this case, opposed interests of the Government and the press associations. The regulation effectively reduced the press agencies to alternate 200-word bursts and took much of the perceived need for speed out of their competition.

### The Telegraph Libel Case

Competition for use of that scarce resource, the telegraph wire, was not the only reason for a growing separation of press and Government interests in regard to the telegraph. The other was a series of incidents whereby the Government was accused of holding back telegrams from opponent newspapers, thus favouring its supporters, and even of taking copies of telegrams from one agency, holding back the contents from the intended recipients while providing them to friendly papers of the opposing agency. These incidents cut across agency loyalties, became increasingly well publicised scandals and finally forced an acceptance as improper of such collusion between Government and newspapers. Government leaders continued to use, or attempted to use the press in the same idiom as before but the new press leaders could no longer accommodate them.

The most serious incident involving improper use of the telegraph occurred in 1870 during Vogel's control of the Telegraph Department. It was an incident which escalated eventually to become the *cause célèbre* known as The Telegraph Libel Case. It was during the Franco-Prussian War and had to do with the news of the victory of Prussia, the surrender of Napolean III at Sedan and the declaration of France as a republic. The *S.S. Gothenberg* was about to leave for Bluff when the news began arriving at Melbourne. The ship waited until a telegraphic summary for the *Otago Daily Times* group was prepared and thus sailed with the *Otago Daily Times* agency news summary aboard but not that of the rival agency. And yet this news was carried in the *Wellington Independent* before it appeared in either the *Otago Daily Times* or the *Evening Post*, the Wellington member of the *Otago Daily Times* agency.

## The Making of the New Zealand Press

The *Otago Daily Times* at first accused the Government of holding back its telegrams until opposition news summaries appeared.

> By Electric Telegraph. Wellington September 30. The English mail telegrams this morning were kept back until a message containing a summary of the news had been sent to the Government. The contents of this message were communicated by the Government to the *Independent* which thus issued an Extra before a single line of the Press telegrams was received. The *Evening Post* denounces this conduct as grossly unfair and dishonest.
> (1 October 1870)

It editorialized on the same day.

> A greater degree of excitement has never been witnessed in Dunedin on any similar occasion than that which seized all classes of the community yesterday, when the nature of the English mail news was made known. A crowd of two or three hundred literally beseiged our doors... We regret the delay which took place in the publication but the delay was not owing to any neglect on our part... We assert that the Telegraph Office, acting of course under instructions from the General Government unnecessarily delayed our telegrams in order to serve a political purpose. The object of this delay is sufficiently explained in the Wellington telegram which appears in another column.

Two days later, after comparison of its own news columns with those of its rivals, the *Otago Daily Times* made a more serious charge.

> The telegram in this morning's issue of the *Independent* differ materially from their Extra, and are simply a reproduction of ours, a few unimportant items which were in our message – but which we did not print as being unimportant or anticipated being given word for word. It is perfectly evident that the Government's first telegram was compiled from ours... The bitterest opponent of the present Government would hesitate to believe that a transaction of this nature, which cannot appear in any other light than that of an infamous breach of trust, could take place under its administration. We believe that we have legal evidence, however, to prove the astounding

## Press, Government and the Telegraph in the 1870s

fact that the Government not only suppressed the news for several hours throughout the colony, but that it appropriated to its own use the telegrams to which it had no more right than it has to the pocket handkerchiefs or the watches of private individuals.

In earlier years, beginning with the rush in New Zealand on the Commercial Bank after its collapse in England, there had developed an understanding and acceptance that a Government had a duty and a moral right to learn of overseas news as soon as possible. Prior to 31 July 1870 this had been accomplished by giving Government agents responsibility for the collation and despatch of press telegrams. After the formation of the two press associations and the cessation of the Government service, the Government's need to acquire information remained. In practise it meant Government officials regularly perused the press associations' telegrams.[3] The charges by the *Otago Daily Times*, and other newspapers, were both against the practice and against its abuse. One charge was that members of the Government, through press telegrams, had appraised themselves of the nature of the diplomatic emergency. At least in the first months of the new press associations there was not a general acceptance of a Government's continuing moral right to keep itself informed of overseas events. This was a charge the Fox-Vogel Ministry would have had little difficulty defending. But a further charge was that members of the Government had then interfered with the delivery of the press telegrams so as to give their supporting newspapers a first publication of the eagerly awaited news.

The Government had little option but to defend itself and chose to do so by trying G.B. Barton, the editor of the *Otago Daily Times*, on a charge of criminal libel. This did little to placate public opinion as G.B. Barton's solicitor was able to portray such a choice, rather than the more obvious one of libel proceedings against the proprietors of the newspaper, as indicative of Vogel's personal animosity against the man who had succeeded him as editor. The lack of any proceedings being taken against the *Evening Post*, which had been at least equally outspoken, added to such an impression. Furthermore, the charge itself came to naught, being abandoned after it reached the Supreme Court where it had foundered on the questionable constitutionality of a free

---

3   Perusal of press associations' material remains normal activity for most Governments. See Boyd-Barrett, (1980), p.22.

pardon offered to a sub-editor of the *Otago Daily Times* so as to force him to attest to G.B. Barton's authorship of the articles in question.

The abandoning of proceedings was generally regarded as a victory for the *Otago Daily Times* and a vindication of its stand. It also pointed to an increasing separation of press and Government interests. The earlier general identity of interests between press and Government began to crumble once some of the major papers ceased to enjoy high level access to the Government. The *Otago Daily Times*, then the largest paper in the country, no longer had its officials also holding high Government office. It was the first to find itself the object of Government antagonism and vigorously and successfully to defend itself by defining the Government action as improper. Previous collusion between press and Government, such as that between the proprietors of the major papers and Hall, the Electric Telegraph Commissioner, in 1866-67, had been successful when it was acceptable to all parties. Now, with the identity of interests no longer present, Government and press began to be not only publicly defined as distinct domains but also acceptable limits to their cooperative endeavours began to be acknowledged.

**The Holt and McCarthy Agency**

Beginning in July 1872 there began major changes to the New Zealand press agencies which led, by November 1872 to their amalgamation into the one agency known as the Holt and McCarthy agency. The credit for the inauguration of a single nationwide press agency open to and accepted by all newspapers is usually given to the United Press Association (U.P.A.), begun in January 1880.[4] But, while the U.P.A. did replace two competing press agencies, which existed from June 1878 to the end of 1879, it is the Holt and McCarthy agency, in operation from mid-1872 to mid-1878, which is New Zealand's first non-competitive agency accepted by all papers.

The only public acknowledgement of the amalgamation of the two agencies appears to be a passing reference by Vogel in his 1873 Report. After discussing the problems faced by the Telegraph Department from two competing press agencies, he writes: ".. the special pressure before

---

4   Sanders, (1979) Chapter One. O'Neill, (1963), Chapter 7. Scholefield,(1958), p.11. Fenwick, (1929).

mentioned has ceased because one of the Press Associations has ceased to exist."[5]

Neither of the named principals of the Holt and McCarthy agency were owners of the enterprise. They were working executives but the use of their names disguised the fact that, with the new agency, Julius Vogel had made a successful bid to regain control over the collection and dispersal of New Zealand news. Holt had previously been private secretary to James Brogden, the railway magnate who had a contract to build railways for the New Zealand Government. He had met Vogel during that time. McCarthy was the journalist of the pair. During the lifetime of the Holt and McCarthy agency, McCarthy's journalistic connections were with the *Wellington Independent*. When the agency began the *Independent* was still owned by Thomas McKenzie, but McCarthy was one of the quartet who controlled the paper. The Holt and McCarthy agency was thus run from Wellington with the locus of control and coordination being the *Wellington Independent*.

The major impetus behind the formation of the Holt and McCarthy agency, however, was Julius Vogel, a politician always supported by the *Wellington Independent*. Vogel, in 1872 at the time the Holt and McCarthy agency began, was Colonial Treasurer, Telegraph Commissioner and Postmaster General as well as proprietor of the *Southern Cross*.[6] In spite of the debate at the time of the Telegraph Libel Case, with the formation of the Holt and McCarthy agency, he was again to provoke large scale discussion on the propriety of the close connections between his press and political interests. With the telegraph finally reaching Auckland in 1872 New Zealand was only now a country administratively capable of acting as a centralized state. In this new situation Vogel moved to control news transmission. He was not only to replace the two press associations with a single organization but was to have that organization under his personal control for the next four years, until he resigned as Premier and left for London.

In April 1872 a mail steamer service between San Francisco, New Zealand and Melbourne was finalized with a subsidy from the Victorian Government of £32,500 per year and the New Zealand Government of

---

5   9th Report, N.Z. Telegraph Department, A.J.H.R., 1873.

6   Vogel lost his Ministerial portfolios on 10 September 1872 when the Stafford Ministry came to power but regained them on 11 October 1872 when the Waterhouse Ministry replaced that of Stafford.

## The Making of the New Zealand Press

£27,500 per year. From July 1872 Australia was in telegraph communication with England.[7] It was the build-up to these events that led to the changes in the New Zealand press agencies. Vogel was in Melbourne in early 1872 negotiating with the Victorian Government in regard to the mail steamer service. While there he concluded an agreement with Hugh George, manager of the Melbourne *Argus* and the Australian Associated Press, for the Reuter agency for New Zealand.[8] The agreement was open as to whether Vogel acted as a Government Minister or a newspaper proprietor.

> For the sum of five hundred pounds (£500) per annum this office is prepared to sell to your Government, to yourself, or to any agent appointed by you, for the use of the newspapers published in New Zealand, the exclusive right of treating with those newspapers for the publication of Reuters messages in New Zealand.[9]

The agreement was a final rather than initial proposal and included completed practical arrangements.

> I have today written to our London agent, instructing him to see Reuter, and to request that the price of New Zealand securities, New Zealand bank stock, New Zealand hemp, as well as any item of special New Zealand interest be included in the direct telegraphic reports from London.[10]

Montrose, the New Zealand manager of Greville's Telegram Company, saw the agreement as calculated to end his agency.

> The object of the Associated Press is to drive the (Greville Telegram) Company out of the field. ...With the same object it would, of course, be glad to contract with Mr Vogel on such

---

7  The Java to Darwin cable was opened on 20 November 1871. The Overland Telegraph from Darwin to Adelaide (with a gap of 200 miles covered by horse express) was opened on 24 June 1872. Communication was frequently disrupted, often for long periods. (Walker, 1976, p.203.)

8  The management of the *Sydney Morning Herald* and the Melbourne Argus in June 1872 formed the Australian Associated Press and for £4000 per annum gained from Reuters an agreement that Reuters would in Australia supply its news only to the A.A.P. (Walker, 1976, p.205.)

9  George to Vogel, printed in *Wellington Independent*, 18 June 1872.

10 Ibid.

terms as would drive the New Zealand branch of Greville's Telegraph Company out of the field.[11]

And so it was to prove, with the Greville telegraph credit line last appearing in New Zealand newspapers in November 1872. Montrose further argued there was a connection between the mail steamer negotiations with the Victorian Government and the press agency agreement with the Australian Associated Press.

> ... in entering into this contract Mr Vogel has been making a bid for the support of the Melbourne *Argus* and *Sydney Morning Herald* in his negotiations with the Australian Governments.[12]

The *Argus,* which had initially opposed subsidizing the mail steamer service, did change its position and came to support a Victorian subsidy for the enterprise. Subsequent debate, however, centered not on this point but on Vogel's improper use of his official position.

In signing the agreement with Hugh George, Vogel had acted on his own initiative without a mandate from his political colleagues. Montrose's statement that "...(Vogel) acted on his own personal responsibility without in any way consulting his colleagues who were ignorant of what he had done until I myself actually informed them"[13] was not challenged.

As eventually stated by Vogel's ally, the *Wellington Independent,* Vogel's aim was to return to a Governmental provision of a news service.

> Mr Vogel's idea was that it would be a good thing for the colony if the Government were to purchase these telegrams, with the view of supplying them to the papers in New Zealand free of cost except wire charges, the Government trusting to more extended use of the wires to recoup it for the outlay; but in the arrangements with Mr George he did not in the slightest degree commit the Government and ultimately the sale was made to Mr Vogel himself, or any association to which he might transfer it.
>
> (*Wellington Independent,* 15 June 1872)

---

11 Letter from Montrose to editor of *Wellington Independent* printed per favour of editor of *Evening Post,* 10 April 1872.
12 From a circular by Montrose quoted by *Wellington Independent,* 10 April 1872.
13 Letter from Montrose, *Wellington Independent,* 20 April 1872.

The implication is that Vogel did not receive sufficient support from his Ministerial colleagues for a return to a Governmental provision of news telegrams. As a result Vogel began a private agency managed by Holt and McCarthy but under his own control.[14] The question of the propriety of Vogel's actions was intriguingly acted on. It was not accepted that Vogel could act for the Government and force it to become the news controller. But it was acceptable for Vogel as a private individual to assume this control. That Vogel was also a newspaper proprietor and the dominant elected politician of the day was not regarded as disqualifying him from the control of the press agency.

The events, however, were viewed harshly by Vogel's opponents.

> Mr Vogel's agreement with the Australian Associated Press, in regard to the English telegrams, was of the double blooded character we predicted. He made it in his capacity as a member of the Government, and used his influence as such to induce Mr George to come to terms with him, but, knowing he had no authority to enter into such a contract officially, he added a proviso, that in the event of the Government refusing to ratify it, he would in his other capacity, as proprietor of the Southern Cross, carry it out himself.

(*Evening Post*, 29 April 1872)

The opposition was heated with continued reference to such matters as

> the unscrupulous use Mr Vogel has made of his official position as Treasurer of New Zealand to further his own individual interests in the matter of Press telegraphy.

(*Evening Post*, 13 June 1872)

The Holt and McCarthy agency was to have a commanding position in the collection of news. Reuters cartel agreements had been concluded by 1872 and Reuters was the only international news agency to collect and distribute news in, among other places, Australia and New Zealand. The managements of various Australian newspapers at times organized their own news supplies. Various New Zealand newspaper managements

---

14 The Managing Committee of the Holt and McCarthy agency was Vogel, of the *Southern Cross*, Reeves, of the *Lyttelton Times*, and Harrison of the *Wellington Independent*. (*Evening Post*, 19 and 20 June 1872.) Vogel and Reeves were proprietors. Harrison was an employee of the *Independent*. He had been a foundation staff member of Vogel's *Otago Daily Times*.

*Press, Government and the Telegraph in the 1870s*

did the same via Australia with Henry Brett of the *Auckland Star* being the most persistent. But his exclusive purchase of the Reuters agency was to give Vogel domination in New Zealand over overseas news despatches.

Initially, however, the Holt and McCarthy agency was not conceived of as monopolistic. The original intention was to restrict membership to morning newspapers. In spite of the political nature of the debate concerning the foundation of the agency, its membership was considered on commercial grounds. Morning newspapers included both allies and foes of Vogel. The rationale for this arrangement was presented by the *Lyttelton Times*.

> There is an exceedingly good reason why evening papers should be excluded (from Mr Vogel's proposed new Press Telegraphic Association). If they were admitted the morning papers would simply be contributing a considerable sum annually to assist in the extremely delightful process of cutting their own throats. Thus, when the Anglo-Australian telegraph is completed, which it will be presently, the most important telegraphic messages will come from Australia by the weekly, or thereabouts, steamers. In a majority of instances these arrive either at Hokitika or the Bluff at such an hour as would allow the summaries to be transmitted in time for publication in the evening papers. It follows, therefore, that ordinary prudence compels the proprietors of morning papers to exclude evening journals from the Association.
> (*Lyttelton Times*, 8 June 1872)

This rationale was somewhat exaggerated by the *Lyttelton Times*. While arriving mail boats naturally chose to enter harbour if possible during daylight hours, their arrivals were conditioned by the tides and did, of course, occur during all daylight hours. Morning arrivals were to the advantage of the evening papers but from early afternoon any arrivals were too late for the evening papers to be able to print the news that day. It is possible that the restriction to morning papers was an application in New Zealand of an Australian Associated Press requirement. In Australia the services of that association were at first available only to the morning papers. Entry there to evening newspapers was offered only after New South Wales morning papers failed to get a legal monopoly for their cable service.

However, the restriction, in New Zealand, to morning papers was short-lived. The rationale for restricting the agency to morning papers, as outlined by the *Lyttelton Times,* became irrelevant from 1876 when the Australia-New Zealand sea cable was completed. But well before this, by the end of 1872, the Greville credit line had disappeared from the New Zealand press and Holt and McCarthy was the only press agency operating.

Not only was the Holt and McCarthy agency to become the only one in New Zealand handling overseas news. It was to be the only New Zealand agency. It gained a monopoly control over internal news dissemination within New Zealand. The Holt and McCarthy agency rules of association do not survive. It is not known if it followed the common pattern of not allowing subscriber newspapers to also receive competitive services. However the *Otago Daily Times* service ceased. It need not have been forced out of existence by the Holt and McCarthy agency. Expense was an everpresent impetus towards amalgamation. The logic of sending costly, and usually similar, long press telegrams to separate press associations had often been questioned.

The Holt and McCarthy agency not only acted as the coordinator for the reception and dissemination of overseas telegraph news, thus doing away with the duplication that had previously existed, it also established "a service of interprovincial news... available for all New Zealand newspapers that cared to subscribe to it".[15] It is doubtful if this was the first agency handling New Zealand news. As we have seen, in 1869 the *Otago Daily Times* and *Wellington Independent* had been involved in negotiations for such a service. But for the first time the communication difficulties for newspapers within New Zealand were met by establishing a system of cooperative mutual exchange of news among all newspapers.

The Holt and McCarthy agency was soon to be accused of political bias. Vogel was the dominant New Zealand politician of the time and the Holt and McCarthy agency was at times accused of being more interested in supporting him and the Waterhouse Ministry than in its ostensible role of news reporting.

It is important to notice that the telegrams of the New Zealand Press Association omit to mention the destruction by the natives of the Wanganui Bridge.[16] We have noticed other

---

15 Fenwick, (1929) p.7.
16 The Holt and McCarthy Agency was also known as the New Zealand Press Association. Both titles were used in telegraph credit lines.

omissions. The defeats of the Ministry during the last few days of session were passed over in silence. ...The frequency and character of these omissions show that the telegrams are supervised with paternal care in high quarters, nothing coming out through their instrumentality which could impair the trust and filial piety of a loving party.
(*Nelson Examiner,* 13 November 1872)

Similar accusations were made throughout the six years the Holt and McCarthy agency was the sole New Zealand press agency. Vogel was, furthermore, to exacerbate the concern felt by his opponents by the successful moves he made to control the *Wellington Independent*.

## The New Zealand Times

Vogel had purchased the *Southern Cross* in Auckland after being ousted from Otago journalism. But this purchase came immediately prior to his move to Wellington, when he took national political office, and proved to be too distant from his seat of operations. Although the *Southern Cross* was not sold until 1876, Vogel on becoming Premier in 1873 disposed of his interest in it, and found a Wellington base for his journalism. McKenzie's *Independent* was the obvious paper for him to look toward. It was a prestigious paper, being the only morning daily and the oldest paper in the city as well as the administrative centre of the Holt and McCarthy agency. Moreover, it was his political supporter. Vogel formed the New Zealand Times Co. in 1873 with a capital of £10,000. Vogel had, from the sale of his interest in the *Southern Cross,* made a profit of £4000. His personal investment in the New Zealand Times Company gave him a controlling interest in the concern. The *New Zealand Mail* was taken over in 1873 and, at the end of January, 1874 the *Independent* was also purchased. The *Independent* continued until the end of May when it was renamed the *New Zealand Times,* though it continued the serial numbers of the *Independent.*

McKenzie, who, with the *Independent,* the *Mail* and his printing business, was by now head of a large and successful concern, was under no financial need to join with Vogel. Nor, although he had been running the *Independent* since 1845, was he an old man. To quote Scholefield, "McKenzie was only 46 years of age, vigorous in mind and body and under no necessity to think of retirement, but he succumbed to the blandishments of Vogel and merely retained a sizeable interest in the new company".[17] McKenzie may have fallen to Vogel's eloquence, but, equally, he may have shared much of Vogel's vision for New Zealand and joined with him in that cause. His public reason for the change was published in a letter to the *Independent*.

> I have disposed of the sole proprietorship ... but shall retain a considerable interest in the concern ... A general desire was expressed that a colonial paper should be established, one that could embrace the interests of the Colony as a whole; and Wellington, from its central position, was considered the most fitting place for its publication. With this view a company was formed, including a majority of leading citizens of Wellington. Being equally anxious to advance the interests of the Colony, there was no difference of opinion in this respect between the projectors and myself.
> (*Independent*, 30 January 1874)

Vogel aimed to make the *New Zealand Times* a national, rather than merely a Wellington newspaper. This is clear from both his manifesto for the paper and McKenzie's letter. This highly impracticable dream was one shared by McKenzie. He had, for example, started his *New Zealand Mail* with a similar intention.

> We shall be well content, at starting, to make the *Mail* the best patronised journal in the province; but we hope to secure for it eventually a colonial circulation; and to obtain this object we shall spare neither trouble nor expense. The publication of several editions of the paper, each specially adopted for the districts in which it will circulate, will rather facilitate than retard this object; it will combine the advantages of a metropolitan with those of a local newspaper; and there is no place in the colony which offers such facilities for these purposes as Wellington.
> (*New Zealand Mail*, 25 February 1871)

It may have been that both Vogel and McKenzie wished to try to start a national paper and both considered that only together could they attempt such a task. This, from the available material, is a possible explanation and the only likely one for McKenzie voluntarily relinquishing control.

---

17  (1958), p.33.

Vogel's motives were considered to be political as well as commercial. He "aimed at consolidating his political position through the medium of a national newspaper."[18] However the *New Zealand Times* did not become a national newspaper. In the 1870s a variety of difficulties prevented any serious pursuit of the matter. With the 1872 arrival of the telegraph in Auckland, the four main centers were finally linked and it may have been possible to attempt separate regional printings of four, or more, daily editions of a *New Zealand Times.* However, the large scale financial gamble involved in any attempt to, in effect, start four large daily papers, each in its own competitive market, all with records of failure for late-comers, was apparently too much, even for Vogel. The *New Zealand Times* remained a Wellington newspaper.

With his dominance of the *New Zealand Times* and the Holt and McCarthy agency, Vogel was in a position to exercise considerable control over the collection and dissemination of news in New Zealand. But his political duties (he was Premier at the time he purchased the *Wellington Independent*) precluded him from assuming day-to-day control. More importantly, his long absences from New Zealand during this period kept him from exercising effective command of the paper or the agency. Vogel left New Zealand in September 1874 on political duties. The addition of health problems delayed his return until February 1876. He was back in New Zealand for a period of mere months. Resigning the Premiership in September 1876 after appointing himself Agent-General in London, he moved to London taking up residence there early in 1877.

However, at least until September 1874, Vogel was able to exercise control. In spite of the later constraints on his personal usage of his newspapers and the Holt and McCarthy agency, his position gave concern to other newspaper proprietors.

His actions also indicated a return to the earlier situation whereby prominent politicians were also prominent newspaper proprietors. Vogel, in his ousting from the *Otago Daily Times,* had been a victim of the new commercial ideology. His return to newspaper prominence in Wellington represents a resurgence of the orientation by which newspapers were used as political supports by prominent politicians. It also indicates that this orientation was compatible and capable of parity with the commercial ideology.

---

18 Scholefield, (1958), p.33.

*The Making of the New Zealand Press*

The control of the *New Zealand Times* by Vogel was to signal a return to direct political control of newspapers, which was to be a feature of the capital city until well into the twentieth century. Vogel's example was soon to be followed during Grey's Ministry.

**The New Zealander**

Grey became Premier in October 1877 and his Ministry endured for two years, until October 1879. With the *New Zealand Times* now being an opposition journal, members of Grey's Ministry looked for a supporting newspaper in the capital and established the *New Zealander*. The newspaper made its politics clear from the start.

> No apology is needed to account for our appearance as a candidate for public support. Wellington has long been at a disadvantage as compared with the other chief towns of the Colony in the matter of a morning journal ... In politics we shall give no uncertain sound. To the advocacy of a Liberal policy we shall devote our earnest attention. The principles which have been placed before the country by the present Administration are broad and progressive. They are calculated to promote the prosperity of the country and the happiness of its inhabitants. While the members of the present Government continue to act on these principles we will accord them our warmest support.
> (*New Zealander*, 29 April 1878)

The allusion to the defects of the other morning paper, the *New Zealand Times*, was made clearer in subsequent issues, nowhere more so than in the final issue of that year.

> Our morning contemporary ... is not a people's journal and it has no sympathy with the people's interests. Its aims and objects are to perpetuate the political anachronisms we have inherited. It objects in a new land, to concede to the people the constitutional rights they have obtained by entail.
> (*New Zealander*, 30 December 1878)

The *New Zealander* was a political organ, following in the path laid by the *New Zealand Times*, in that it was a daily paper owned by and offering support for the members of the Government. The ownership of the *New Zealander* was discussed by William Fox. Fox, speaking in the

House, held that among the proprietors of the *New Zealander* were the following:

> First of all was the Hon. the Native Minister, who was not called so on the register, but Mr Sheehan. Then there was the Hon. Colonel Whitmore. Each of them held 50 shares. Mr Larnach, who was lately a member of the Government and who is now an officer of the Government, and the Attorney-General, each held 50 shares. The Postmaster-General— he did not know why they had put the honorable gentleman off with so small an interest in a profitable concern—had 20. The Minister for Public Works had not got any, and that seemed hardly fair. Then there was the honorable gentleman who interrupted him just now whose name was on the list of shareholders: Mr Seymour Thorne George was down for 150 shares.[19]

Edited for most of its two years by E.T. Gillon, the *New Zealander* kept up a fulsome praise for its political owners. The election of Grey's nephew was greeted with the following:

> We rejoice in... the return of Mr Seymour Thorne George as a member for Hokitika. It is a great triumph for the liberal cause. (*New Zealander*, 28 June 1878)

There was no hint given in the article that Mr George was also Chairman and Managing Director of the paper.

### The Return to Competitive Press Agencies

Grey's Ministry is also notable for the formation of a further press agency, the New Zealand Press Association. This agency, like that of Holt and McCarthy, was formed "for the mutual exchange among its members of telegraphic intelligence, and the procuring of cable news from overseas". But, unlike Holt and McCarthy, it was an exclusive agency and "should include only one morning and one evening newspaper in each of the towns or cities of the colony".[20] While Sanders holds that the *Otago Daily Times* management was the major force behind the formation of the new association, arguing that it "was not prepared to sit back and let Holt and McCarthy rule the roost" and "had already set the wheels turning by making arrangements with the Government for

---

19 N.Z.P.D. Vol.28, 14 August 1878.
20 From the articles of association, quoted in Fenwick, (1929) p.8.

the leasing of a special wire for the dispatch of press telegraphic news",[21] it is not immediately understandable why one member of the cooperative should so wish to challenge the existing arrangements.

The return of competitive agencies was not a manifestation of any *Otago Daily Times* desire to assert its pre-eminence. It was rather a concomitant of the resurgence of political favouritism offered to some of the New Zealand newspapers. It was not until Grey's Ministry was in its second year that the New Zealand Press Association was formed. It was some months in the planning. A resolution to enter into discussions with other newspapers for the establishment of an association appears in the minute book of the Otago Daily Times and Witness Company dated 18 June 1878 but this is clearly not the first mention of the matter. The Government, in October 1878, gave the Association use of a special wire for transmission of its telegrams. The first General Meeting of the Association was held on 17 December 1878, though the draft basis of association had been submitted and adopted at a preliminary meeting a month earlier. There were 30 foundation member newspapers in the Association. The dominant ones were four, the *Otago Daily Times*, the *Lyttelton Times*, the *New Zealand Herald* and the *New Zealander*. The common bond among the papers, apart from the Association, was their support of Grey. The manager of the Association was E.T. Gillon, the editor of the *New Zealander*, the new Wellington daily begun to support Grey.

Grey's Ministry was widely accused of political favouritism to friendly newspapers. This had first occurred in the matter of the placement of Government advertisements. These appeared mainly in the columns of those newspapers that were members of the New Zealand Press Association. In the main centers they were placed exclusively in the columns of the *New Zealand Herald*, the *New Zealander*, the *Lyttelton Times* and the *Otago Daily Times*, all supporters of Grey. It was argued that the *New Zealander* would not have been able to survive without the financial support given by copious Government advertisements, many of which were regarded as irrelevant to the Wellington region.[22]

In Christchurch the directors of *The Press* reprinted the Government advertisements, accompanying them with an attack on Grey's Ministry.

---

21 (1979) p.4.
22 *Evening Post*, 17 February 1880.

## Press, Government and the Telegraph in the 1870s

... The Directors of the Press Company, perceiving that the absence of the Government notices in *The Press* will place the subscribers to that journal at a disadvantage, have determined to publish without charge all Government notices appearing in the *Lyttelton Times*, but withheld from *The Press*... In making this pecuniary sacrifice the Directors of the Press Company feel that they will have public sympathy, and that public opinion will justify their present action in resisting any attempt on the part of the Government to use Government advertising as a means of securing political support.[23]

Charges of political favouritism were also made throughout the country in regard to the New Zealand Press Association. These charges were applied particularly to the special wire arrangement. The *New Zealand Times*, among others, pointed out the financial subsidy inherent in the special wire arrangement.

The actual cost to the Colony of a special wire was shown by the General Manager of Telegraphs to be over £4000 a year, and it was shown that its earnings at ordinary rates would be over £5000 a year. Nevertheless the Premier (Sir George Grey) agreed, privately always, to grant the use of a special wire to these three papers, (the reference is to the *New Zealand Herald*, the *Lyttelton Times* and the *Otago Daily Times*) all out-and-out supporters of his Government, for the sum of £2000, that is for £2000 a year less than the estimated actual cost of the service to the people, and for £3000 a year less than the earnings of the wire in the ordinary work of the department. (22 February 1879)[24]

Charge and counter charge echoed through the country's newspapers. The debate also figured prominently in the House of Representatives during the final months of 1878, the Government being accused of

---

23 In, for example, *The Press* of 18 December 1878. The statement appeared regularly during late 1878 and in 1879. The *Lyttelton Times* argued that it received the Government advertising purely because of its higher circulation. See the *Lyttelton Times* of 13 March and 15 March 1879.

24 The General Manager of the Telegraph Department priced it differently. While it does not remove the fact of financial subsidy he calculated "the price for the special wire at £3160 per annum". From a memorandum to the Minister, quoted in the House of Representatives by W. Rolleston. N.Z.P.D., Vol.30, p. 1046.

attempting to start a press monopoly while its defence was that, on the contrary, it was attempting to break down the existing Holt and McCarthy monopoly. That the favouritism to the New Zealand Press Association was a means of coping with the political opposition coming from the Holt and McCarthy agency was, of course, not conceded by Grey's opponents.

The Grey Ministry's eventual answer to the charge of political favouritism was to grant the lease of a second telegraph wire to the other group of newspapers, those which had remained with Holt and McCarthy. From 1 January 1879 the two agencies were leased, during certain hours,[25] the use of two special wires, each for a cost of £2000 per year.

This was a fair and proper arrangement, given that there were to be two press agencies. The principle of public morality embodied in such a decision was, however, not one willingly embraced by Grey. It was forced on him by the intense and prolonged debate on the propriety of his political favouritism.

**Pressures Towards Amalgamation**

Thus the New Zealand newspapers returned to competitive press agencies. The system was to last for less than a year before again, and this time finally, amalgamation took place. Fenwick argues that cost was the reason for amalgamation. "The efforts of each group to provide a service superior to that of its opponents were conducted with lavish expenditure in many directions ... It was, however, soon felt on all sides that the cost of two rival services was far too wasteful, and that combination was imperative."[26]

While cost was clearly a major reason for amalgamation it was equally clearly not the only reason. The provision of two special wires placed considerable pressure on the Telegraph Department's resources. While no public statement was made by Dr Lemon, the General Manager of the Department, he had expressed himself clearly on the point at the time the Grey Ministry sought the special wire arrangement: " .. it must be perfectly understood that the wire resources of the department would not admit of two special wires at one time, nor would the department be justified in erecting a special wire to meet this

---

25 ...."from 8 p.m. to 1 a.m. for five days in the week, from 7 p.m. to 10 p.m. on Saturdays; and from 6 p.m. to 7 p.m. on Sundays". N.Z. Telegraph Department Annual Report, A.J.H.R., 1879.

26 Fenwick (1929) pp.10-11.

particular class of business ..."[27] While Grey had overruled his Departmental Head there must have been Departmental pressure, and, after the fall of the Grey Ministry, perhaps Governmental pressure, to amalgamate the special wire services.

A further reason for amalgamation of the two services was concern at the quality of journalism resulting from the competitive system. The two agency arrangement was, inevitably, a more expensive method of news gathering and newspapers at times moved to the outer reaches of verisimilitude in attempts to reduce their costs. Some of these attempts had an amusing aspect, as in the following reprint.

> "Special" Telegraphic News—we hear a good deal nowadays about "special" wires, and so forth, opened for the exclusive benefit of this and that newspaper. But seeing that every newspaper in the Colony, if it so chooses, can sport a "special wire" heading, there does not seem to be very much exclusiveness in the matter. It is amusing sometimes to learn the tricks resorted to by enterprising journals to outwit their fellows and the *Free Lance*, an Auckland paper, gives an expose of how the *Auckland Star*, a leading evening paper, was able to publish six columns of a "special" telegraphic report of the opening of the Sydney Exhibition. According to the *Lance*, the report was sent by mail, held over to the opening day, when a short and inexpensive telegram regarding the opening was sent from Sydney. The telegram announced the opening, and the mailed report was made to duty, with its detailed descriptions and a telegraphic despatch. Unfortunately, the *Lance* says, a procession of military and naval men that never took place was dilated upon, and distinguished individuals were spoken of as being present, who had not then reached Sydney. The letter was remarkably well got up, but the knowledge that it was written beforehand, somewhat took the gilt off the gingerbread.
>
> (*Nelson Colonist,* 30 September 1879)

Attempts to defray expenses were not the only reason for inaccurate reporting during 1879. There were more serious attempts deliberately to plant false information within rival agencies. The following is an

---

27 From a memorandum by Lemon to his Minister, quoted in the House of Representatives by W. Rolleston. N.Z.P.D., Vol.30, p.1046.

to plant false information within rival agencies. The following is an example of this.

> (Special) London. April 19. It is understood that Sir J. Vogel returns from the Agency for the purpose of joining a commercial firm. Mr G.M. Reed, who has recently arrived as Irish Immigration Agent, will administer the affairs of the London Office until a permanent appointment is made by the New Zealand Government.
> (*Lyttelton Times*, 23 April 1879)

As is clear from the editorial of the same day, newspaper proprietors had learned to become suspicious of the accuracy of their telegraphed news.

> The announcement of the probable retirement of Sir Julius Vogel from the Agent-Generalship ought to take no one by surprise. Whether the report is correct or not and the Government we observe by our Wellington telegram knows nothing of the matter retirement is undoubtedly an alternative which Sir Julius Vogel ought to face. ... There is one reason why the rumours respecting the Agent-Generalship in its present shape must be regarded as untrue. It is, we imagine, most unlikely that anyone would place Mr Reed in the position left vacant by the retirement of Sir Julius Vogel.
> (*Lyttelton Times*, 23 April 1879)

The *New Zealand Herald* was to place this incident in the context of a history of similar frauds.

> It will be remembered that the celebrated "fall of Plerna" telegram, and the more recent one by which Lord Napier of Magdala was appointed to the command of the forces at the Cape, were from the same source—almost enough, indeed, to justify the impression that more than the Julius Vogel telegrams own as their birthplace a certain sanctum sanctorum on this side of the line.[28]
> (*New Zealand Herald*, 24 April 1879)

As a final point in regard to this incident we can note, as was discussed by the *New Zealand Herald*, that such frauds tended to take in more than the intended victims.

---

28 Henry Brett, of the *Auckland Star* was alleged to be responsible.

We may point out that the trick was a failure. Its prime object was to show the superior morality of the Press Agency to the new Press Association, but no sooner was the cablegram published in Wellington as an extra by the *Chronicle,* one of the subscribers to the Association, than the rival Agency took possession of it and transmitted it to its subscribers throughout the Colony, thus doing what was stated to be the very object of the telegram–to detect and expose the morning papers.
(*New Zealand Herald,* 30 April 1879)

There were thus various reasons for dissatisfaction with the system of dual press agencies. After the fall of the Grey Ministry it was not surprising to see a change in the existing arrangements.

### The Closing of the New Zealander

The New Zealand Press Association was managed by E.T. Gillon who was also editor of the *New Zealander.* As well as sharing political ties with the Grey Ministry, the newspaper and the agency were linked administratively. The fall of the Grey Ministry, as well as leading to changes in the press agencies also signalled the demise of the *New Zealander.* The paper slipped in popular support as support for Grey ebbed away. Even at its height, there was doubt about the paper's financial viability without the extensive advertising support given it by the Government. The *New Zealander* survived the fall of Grey's Ministry by four months before the copyright was purchased by the *New Zealand Times* and the paper closed down. The proprietors acknowledged that they had "had the conviction forced upon them that on the support of a political principle they have expended quite enough".[29]

Opposing papers left no doubt as to their view of the fate of the *New Zealander.* The strongest statement came from the *Evening Post.* In an expression of a new awareness of the role of the press, it saw as improper what had been, after the gaining of self-government, normal journalism. The political connections of the *New Zealander,* although in a similar mould to that of the *New Zealand Times,* were, however, a reversal of a general change that had been occurring among the New Zealand newspapers since the 1860s. The *Evening Post* no longer saw the old order as acceptable.

---

29 The statement was by R.C. Reid M.H.R. Quoted by Scholefield, (1958), pp.35-36.

> ... Sooner or later Nemesis must overtake the journal which is content to debase the Press into a servile organ of the political party in power. Such a state of things is essentially rotten and corrupt ... We cannot deplore the death of a hireling organ which in its very existence represented a principle of journalism which cannot be too stenuously condemned, one which must strike at the root of a journal's highest function–that of promoting, leading and even forming a healthy public opinion upon political matters.
> (*Evening Post*, 17 February 1880)

In contrast to this is the *New Zealander*'s own view of its demise. Using the simile of the mercenary, the editor appears to assume support for a political party is inevitable and that the main ethical question for a journalist is consistency.

> ... and so the end has come. It would have been a breach of the canons of honest journalism to have shown a sudden change of front, to have veered round in weather cock fashion with the first symptoms of wavering public opinion. A journalist, if he be true to his work, no matter what his private opinions, fights for the flag he is under. Like a soldier of fortune he may be impelled by turns to range on either side but he must in honour end one campaign on the side he enters ere he enrolls himself under another leader. So also with the journal itself. It would have tarnished its fair fame and character for consistency had the *New Zealander* gone over unreservedly to the side holding present political power.[30]
> (*New Zealander*, 17 February 1880)

The *Evening Post*'s criticism represents an important variation in understanding of the role of the press. In the 1860s it had been found that it was commercially irresponsible for a newspaper to offer open and unwavering support for any one politician or Ministry. If such loyalty

---

30 Richard Sherrin, who succeeded Gillon as editor, when Gillon refused to accept the dictation of the directors that the paper was "no longer an unmeasured supporter of the Grey Government", (Scholefield, 1958, p.36) and who presumably wrote this editorial, seems himself to be as much an example of a developing political awareness as of a mercenary. Employed in 1878 by the liberal Richard Wakelin on the *Wairarapa Standard*, after Wakelin's son-in-law partner had left, Sherrin, after editing the *New Zealander*, is next recorded in Auckland in 1884 editing a weekly called *Labour*, the earliest labour publication with surviving copies.

was given a newspaper was likely to decline as its political champion declined. The experience of the *New Zealander* indicated that such was still the case. Since the 1860s most newspapers had given consistent support to one or other of the political groupings in New Zealand. But they had also been prepared and able to transfer their allegiance when public support for that political grouping dimmed irretrievably. Thus Reeves, and his *Lyttelton Times,* was able to support Vogel during his years in office and then to offer a similar advocacy for Grey. The *Evening Post,* however, is doing more than shifting allegiance. The *Lyttelton Times* accepted that political leaders were political leaders. The duty of a newspaper was either to oppose, or to follow, their lead. The *Evening Post's* above editorial, however, represents a full flowering of the press as a Fourth Estate. The function of a newspaper is "that of promoting, leading and even forming a healthy public opinion upon political matters". In this view there is a separation of the press from politicians. The press sits above and separate from politicians and leads the public in its judgement of the actions of politicians.

## The United Press Association

The amalgamation of the Press Agency and the New Zealand Press Association, when it did come, took place rapidly. At a committee meeting of the New Zealand Press Association on 3 December 1879, at which the dominant trio were George Fenwick of the *Otago Daily Times,* William Reeves of the *Lyttelton Times* and A.G. Horton of the *New Zealand Herald,* a resolution was passed that it was desirable that all members of the New Zealand press be admitted to the New Zealand Press Association. This was probably not the first mention of the topic for *The Press* quickly became the first newspaper from the other agency to join and, on 19 December 1879, there was a conference in Timaru at which the two agencies were combined. Those attending included the above trio as well as Henry Brett of the *Star,* Auckland, W. Jago of the *Star,* Dunedin, and H. Blundell of the *Evening Post,* Wellington. Both existing agency titles were discarded and United Press Association was adopted as the new name.[31] The new association began operations on 1 January 1880 with E.T. Gillon, the New Zealand Press Association manager and ex editor of the now defunct *New Zealander,* being first manager.

---

31 The title remained until 1942 when the association was renamed the New Zealand Press Association so as to distinguish it from the American United Press Association.

One of the first actions of the new association was to apply for the lease of a special wire as had been granted to the two previous press agencies. A.G. Horton, on behalf of the United Press Association, applied for a lease and, surprisingly, in view of the experience of the previous two years, was told the Government had no power to grant such a request.[32] John Hall, the new Premier and Commissioner of Telegraphs moved to correct the position. He introduced the Electric Telegraph bill, passed by the House in 1880, the object of which was to give the Government the legal authority to grant use of a special wire.

The granting of a special wire was accompanied by a condition that was a partial recognition of a monopolistic pattern inherent in the composition of the United Press Association. As Hall, the Premier, stated the matter, "The association, by the concession of a special wire, was placed at so great an advantage that no morning newspaper could be started except under serious disadvantages, if it was refused admission to the benefits of the association and of the special wire."[33] The condition on which the special wire was granted was that any new morning newspaper should also be admitted to the United Press Association. As the special wire provisions applied particularly to morning papers it was felt that such a condition could not be extended to include evening papers.

Such a condition had little point for it was the United Press Association itself, rather than the special wire, that gave member newspapers protection from competition. By joining the Association, newspaper proprietors saw themselves as having common business interests which could best be treated by cooperative endeavour. Under the umbrella of the United Press Association each newspaper's local news was made available to the United Press Association, thus forming a pool of national news from which the other New Zealand newspapers could draw. International news, along with the pool of national news, was supplied by the United Press Association. The New Zealand press did not join in a full cooperative for, at the local level, newspapers retained their separate staffs, reporting and commenting on local affairs in their own fashions. It was, however, a much muted competition with each newspaper's national and international news being taken from the

---

32 See the letter of 16 March 1880 from A.T. Maginnity, Secretary to the Commissioner of Telegraphs. A.J.H.R., 1880. The implication was that the Grey Ministry had acted beyond its legal power.

33 N.Z.P.D., Vol.37. 1880, p.545.

single supplier, the United Press Association. At this point the New Zealand newspapers had common interests which bound them as a cohesive entity, as the New Zealand press.

The outcome was that the Association became, as long as the major dailies stood firm, the only possible press agency in the country. In practice all newspapers desiring press agency services had to join it. Nor could there be a strong enough alternative grouping of newspapers to begin another agency. Already the United Press Association had passed a resolution effectively denying competition: "... no member of the Associaton should join any other agency for procuring Telegraphic news or in any way compete with the Press Association in procuring news from outside the colony".[34] While this did not stop non-United Press Association members from forming another press agency, in practise all competition was removed. For, as long as the major metropolitan dailies remained with the United Press Association, no group of non-United Press Association members would have a high enough circulation base to support another agency.

As the New Zealand newspapers combined eventually to form the United Press Association, members of the Government saw the press as a cohesive entity and began to worry about the power available to such a group. Concern was particularly felt about the major dailies. Gillon, the United Press Associaton manager, commented on this in his letters to his Chairman during the 1880 hearing by the Press Telegrams Committee of the House of Representatives to allocate a special wire to the United Press Association.

> The Committee seem to fear that the larger morning papers want to obtain a monopoly to prevent any other papers starting and to give them entire control over the supply of telegraph news and the Press generally."[35]

A further protection for members of the United Press Association was obtained by actions following an April 1882 meeting of the Association. A resolution was passed to seek the passage of a Copyright Bill giving

---

34 Minutes of Conference of Representatives of the New Zealand Press held for the purpose of forming a United Association for the conducting of the Telegraphic business of the Press of the Colony, 17 December 1879. United Press Association Manuscripts.

35 Gillon to Reeves, 8 July 1880. Outward correspondence, United Press Association Manuscripts.

## The Making of the New Zealand Press

a 36 hour copyright to Association telegrams. E.T. Gillon the manager, was instructed to draft such a bill,[36] and it was introduced into the House. The eventual form of the bill was the Protection of Telegrams Act, which received its final assent in September 1882. Although less than the original request of the United Press Association, it copyrighted overseas telegrams for 18 hours from first publication and effectively stopped non-United Press Association members from reprinting the overseas news published in association members' newspapers. From this point on, and especially after the first conviction under the Act (of the Wellington *Evening News* in the following year) newspapers had little choice but to join the United Press Association.

The concern over monopoly continued and featured again during the 1882 hearing on the Press Telegrams Bill. The large entrance fee of £500 proposed for any future newspapers wishing to join the United Press Association was often queried, though not changed.

> The entrance fee is the great bugbear and the £500 was a powerful weapon against us. ...Altogether this Bill has been the most strongly opposed one before the House this session.[37]

Gillon exaggerates the opposition to the measure. The Bill was shepherded through the House easily enough. On the contrary more pertinent is the remark, made during the debate on the Protection of Telegrams Bill, that the House was "showing an affectionate regard for the proprietors of newspapers and Baron Reuter".[38] However, the inauguration of the United Press Association and the passage of the legislation connected with it does represent a stage in the growth of the New Zealand press in which it could no longer be subsumed under political allegiances. It was a distinct organization with its own interests.

The organizational expression of the commercial cooperation that become a feature of the New Zealand press was the United Press Association and it was this association that gave the newspapers commercial security. The major features of the association, that it was open to all newspapers, that news was available to all members and

---

36 Gillon drafted the Bill after perusing the South Australian and Victorian Acts on the subject. Gillon to Reeves, 25 April 1882. United Press Association manuscripts. For this and his lobbying in support of the bill he was to receive a bonus of £50. Sanders (1979).

37 Gillon to Reeves, 5 July 1882. United Press Association manuscripts.

38 N.Z.P.D., Vol.41, p.453.

that member newspapers were not permitted to take other sources of news, long remained substantially unchanged. Not until 1926 with the first appearance of the special correspondent, supplying news and articles slanted specifically towards the needs of the hiring newspaper, was there a dent in the U.P.A. monopoly and only in the 1960s, with the appearance of television and its own news service, was the association's monopoly challenged. While the U.P.A. service was also available to any intending newspapers, in practice the association served to protect the existing members from competition. Financially unable to begin a new press agency and thus obliged to join the U.P.A., intending newspapers both had to share their news and had to report U.P.A. news in the same words as other members. The adherance to the dominant pattern thus forced on newcomers meant none could offer any novelty of approach to offset the disadvantage of appearing against established competition. Those newspapers which had become dominant in the 1860s and 1870s had, by the formation in 1880 of the U.P.A., ensured their dominance in the coming century.

# 11. Conclusion

Changes in the New Zealand newspapers between 1840 and 1880 are consequences of the organizational and political concerns of newspaper controllers. These concerns vary in importance during the period and are in an ambivalent relationship to each other. Until the 1860s, financial profit was seldom possible for newspapers and they were oriented principally in terms of the political ambitions of their controllers. The role of the press as a form of *de facto* political representation during the Crown Colony Government period led, from 1853, to opportunities for political office being available to press personnel. Newspapers acted as political advocates for individual politicians. Operated either by politicians, or in the service of politicians, the newspapers became not observers on matters political but a part of the political system and advocates for political positions within it.

Within the various provinces the political linkages of the newspapers were open and accepted as proper. The linkages were often direct as in the many instances where the same man was a newspaper proprietor and a prominent Provincial politician. Where this was not the case, the linkages were supportive, in that each newspaper was a recognized mouthpiece for a politician even when not directly owned or operated by that politician. Newspaper growth in the various provinces followed political lines with a Government and an Opposition paper being the normal situation.

This arrangement was challenged in the 1860s. Starting with the *Otago Daily Times*, the New Zealand newspapers began a circulation growth which offered a financial return hitherto unexperienced. The increase in population made it possible for the first time for newspapers to be profitable commercial concerns. This had various consequences. The New Zealand situation was a specific version of a general pattern of change in newspapers that was occurring, or had already occurred, in many countries. The price of newspapers fell. Eventually the penny paper became common. This accelerated a trend which, with a larger and more literate population had begun to take place, than of a extension of newspaper readership beyond the confines of an upper class. The frequency of newspaper appearance increased and daily newspapers became dominant. This enabled newspapers to become chroniclers of the events of a day and, coupled with the increased news flow, which the improving methods of transportation and, in particular,

## Conclusion

the telegraph allowed, the newspapers shifted their emphasis from that of political forum to that of newspaper. Advertising increased in importance to become the financial mainstay of a newspaper. Although its proportion, as a percentage of newspaper space, did not significantly increase, its absolute volume, because of increased newspaper size and frequency, did increase. And, because of the decrease in newspaper purchase price, the importance of advertising to a newspaper's finances became paramount.

Economic growth brought attendant organizational concerns for newspaper controllers that conflicted with their personal political choices. While it had previously been possible for a wealthy proprietor to carry the financial losses of his newspaper and offset them against his personal political gains, the costs in maintaining a high circulation daily newspaper became prohibitive. For a daily newspaper to continue it had to remain a profitable business enterprise. This requirement led to modification to the political role of the New Zealand newspapers. Specifically, newspaper controllers' preferred political use of their newspapers—that being a personal political advocate for a particular politician—jeopardized their newspapers continued public acceptance and economic profitability. The challenge was such as to modify rather than remove the political role of the press. Individual newspaper advocacy for individual politicians became a revocable allegiance given by a number of newspapers to a more general political grouping.

At the same time the economic and organizational concerns of newspaper controllers were modified by their continuing political involvement. Profitability became and remained a *sine qua non* for newspaper concerns. While this stipulation conflicted with an unswerving loyalty to any single politician it still allowed considerable political involvement. There is no newspaper conducted purely in terms of an economically defined rationality. The major counter to it in New Zealand was the continued use of newspapers for political purposes.

The difference in the values of the early newspapers and their later commercial counterparts was that profit, rather than personal political advancement, became the dominant motive for the later newspapers. Unlike the earlier newspapers the commercial dailies were concerns too large to be able to continue at a loss. But although political involvement was challenged as the major value, it did not disappear. Nor was it possible for newspapers to be apolitical. The nature of press activity, which includes reporting and commenting on political matters, is such that political involvement is inevitable. Added to this was the accepted journalistic practice in New Zealand, namely, for newspapers to advocate particular political stances. This applied to the new "promoter" newspapers as much as to their elder counterparts and the new newspapers were quickly to establish definite positions on a variety of political matters. While political involvement was no longer the *raison d'être* for newspapers it remained an everyday working context.

In consequence there was an important change in the nature of newspaper political involvement. The process of change was not to remove the fact of political allegiance but to transfer it from being a support for an individual to a more general political grouping. This represented a resurgence of newspaper control for political purposes but is a resurgence which understood and had come to terms with the commercial realities. The political advocacy presented was not irrevocably committed to any individual but was for a more general orientation which the newspaper owners felt should receive a continuing support in New Zealand public life.

It is in an analysis of the advocacy given by newspaper controllers to a more general political grouping rather than to an individual politician that their long-term influence on the course of New Zealand politics is most apparent. The pattern of general political advocacy began in the early years of the continuous ministry—the conservative coalition which governed New Zealand until the Liberal ministry took office in January 1891. The continuous ministry is regarded as holding power from 1869-1891 but it was not a group that suddenly seized power in 1869. With the notable exception of Julius Vogel the men involved had generally been politically prominent since self-government. What was new about the continuous ministry was not its personnel but that it was a national ministry as opposed to a coalition of politicians each with paramount loyalties to their home provinces. The provincial system was not formally ended until 1876. But from 1869 there began a stable series of national ministries with a wider allegiance than the provincial origins of the individual ministers who formed them.

The continuous ministry resembled, at the national level, the political order of the group that had ruled since the gaining of self-government. This group has been termed oligarchical.[1] While it is an instance of government by the few, this group should be seen rather as representatives of a New Zealand ruling class. European settlers came

---

1   Reeves (1898), pp. 270-280.

## Conclusion

to New Zealand with a privileged group already present among them. This group became the major land and business owners in the new colony. There was not only an identity of interests but often an identity of personnel between these land and business owners, the political figures who emerged after self-government, and the controllers of the various early newspapers. This identity continued until the 1860s when newspaper control and management became a full-time specialty. A similar change took place in regard to political office. The holding of political office also became a full-time specialized occupation. The continuing connections between newspaper personnel and political figures is evident. The connections between land and business ownership and press and political prominence also remained. Land and business ownership, political office holding and newspaper control are to be seen, not as to preserves of distinct groups but as different and developing specialities within a ruling class.

Newspaper controllers interpreted the behaviour of politicians as being in support of, or in opposition to, the Government of the day. There were political divisions within the ruling class and newspaper advocacy was offered in terms of these divisions. Newspapers were similarly divided. While the political divisions were real, they were the internal divisions of a ruling class. They were presented by the press as the main political divisions of the New Zealand colony in general. The New Zealand newspapers are to be seen as expressing the perspective of a New Zealand ruling class. The support offered by newspaper controllers was such as to allow a ruling class view to be the first of any class perspective to receive a cohesive presentation on a national basis. The cooperation of newspaper controllers that led to the formation of the United Press Association was of major significance to the development of this cohesive presentation.

With the United Press Association the newspapers became a cohesive grouping that could appropriately be called the New Zealand press. The United Press Association became the administrative expression of the New Zealand press. Within this association each newspaper's individual reporting responsibilities were restricted to local events and their communication to the association. The rest of a newspaper's material was press releases from the United Press Association. While each newspaper retained its editorial power to select or reject copy, the fact that United Press Association members were not allowed to belong to any other news organization and, thus, their individual choices had to be made from the single supply of United Press Association copy, ensured a profound similarity among all the newspapers of New Zealand.

Not only did this arrangement give the individual newspapers the most inexpensive news supply possible, it also offered a protection from competition which made more likely any individual newspapers' long term survival. The existing newspapers operated from an established position that gave them an ability to withstand the competition from any subsequently attempted newspapers. This ability to withstand competition was entrenched by the United Press Association. Any would-be new newspaper, comparable to the established newspapers, would have to become a member of the United Press Association, it being the only press agency available. But by becoming a member of the United Press Association and being bound by its rules, a new newspaper would be unable to offer an alternative perspective or any novelty of approach that would enable it to gain a circulation against the established competition.

The New Zealand press by the early 1880s had become a cohesive national organization which offered considerable protection to member newspapers and which presented a uniform news service to all New Zealand newspaper readers. While each individual newspaper was able to direct most of its attention to its own local region, the sharing of national and international news gave them both a national focus and a distinctive national character. And yet this process of nationalisation took place well before analogous processes occurred in other aspects of New Zealand life. Sinclair argues that the beginnings of a consciousness of nationality in New Zealand are to be detected in the 1880s and 1890s.[2] Until late in the nineteenth century most settlers thought of themselves as belonging to their particular settlement, not to the colony of New Zealand. Oliver refers to "the nationalisation of regional life" being a period of transformation taking place between 1880 and 1930.[3] This dating is generally accepted and while I do not quarrel with it, the point I wish to make is that the press is in the vanguard of this process of nationalisation. Before other New Zealand organizations underwent a process of nationalisation and homogeneity the press had moved from a provincial diversity to a national uniformity.

---

2  (1959), p.226.
3  (1971) p.181.

*Conclusion*

The use made of the telegraph is basic to this process of nationalization and homogeneity for it was the telegraph which enabled the day-to-day coordination and news sharing among the various newspapers. That the bias of the telegraph is such as to favour centralization is applicable to the nature of government as much as to newspaper control. In New Zealand control of the telegraph represents an early acceptance by the General Government of a central responsibility and an early development of an administratively capable state apparatus.

A differentiation of the concerns of the state from those of the press first appears with the use of the telegraph. The initial setting up of the Governmental provision of telegraphed news, plus the ending of this system, plus Vogel's later efforts to reintroduce it were undertaken for a combination of journalistic, commercial and short-term political reasons. That these actions represented an amalgamation of state and press appears not to have been a topic for consideration. The separation of interests of press and state first appeared publicly in 1868 with the *Otago Daily Times* argument against the arrangements for the supply of telegraphed news. After ousting Vogel as editor, the *Otago Daily Times* no longer experienced the same identification between press and Government. Only then did it discuss the propriety of the telegraph arrangements. From this time the spheres of press and Government began to diverge. This divergence occurred both in terms of a growing public demand for a demarcation between the responsibilities of press and Government and in terms of a growing objective distinction, and often conflict, between the interests of press and Government.

The separation of interests of press and Government applies particularly to the use of the telegraph a device of which newspapers were major users while the state was its owner and regulator. Such a separation does not imply that press and Government were to remain with no interests in common. Nor does growing newspaper cooperation imply that newspapers were to be allies in all areas. Cooperation between newspapers was with particular regard to news sharing. At least when it was not in conflict with their interests as members of the New Zealand press, newspapers continued their political rivalry. The newspaper practise of partisan political support did not cease. They continued as allies of either the Government or its opposition. This was in accord with the role of the press as stated editorially in the early years of the Provincial system of Government. But it was at variance with the role of the press as stated in other years.

## The Making of the New Zealand Press

This role of the press is one we can entitle nonpartisan leadership. The press is presented as an autonomous force independent of both state and political groups. In New Zealand the ideological nature of this definition is apparent when the relationship between newspapers and both state and political groups is considered. The links that both Vogel and Grey had with various newspapers while they were Premier indicates that ownership and direct control of newspapers by senior state officials did occur. And this was not peculiar to the 1870s but a continuation of a pattern existing since self-government. Furthermore, the links between press and state in regard to telegraph use are examples of the interdependence of the two institutions. The continuing relationships between newspapers and political groups are also obvious. The commercial growth of the press disturbed the pattern of newspaper political control and allegiance. But this pattern was modified rather than stopped. Newspapers retained close links with political groups and retained their partisan political interests.

The notion of the press providing a nonpartisan leadership in the interests of the community as a whole is ideological. It disguises the links newspapers had with the state and political groups and in particular with the class represented by the state and these political groups. Newspapers began as class journals. The development of political linkages was a continuation of this bias. In the 1840s this class bias was justified ideologically in terms of the high moral value of journalism, in particular its ability to promote "civilization" in the new colony. From the 1860s this view was augmented by the ideology of nonpartisan leadership. But throughout the period the press continued as a partisan advocate within New Zealand society.

In New Zealand, at least, the concepts press and state denote the results of distinct processes of institutionalization. Both are early instances of a growing centralist focus in New Zealand. Yet both developed virtually exclusively within the context of a developing ruling class.

A distinction between press and state is implicit in the understanding of the role of the press advanced in the commercial newspapers that rose to dominance in the 1860s. The earlier newspapers—epitomized by the opening statement of the *Nelson Examiner*—saw themselves as having not only wide-ranging civilizing and nation-building duties, but also the ability to carry out these duties. The later commercial newspapers offered a more prosaic understanding of their role. Their orientation

## Conclusion

was primarily towards their commercial profitability and survival. To achieve this end they concentrated less on moral leadership than on news, commercial information and the means of advertising. As did the earlier newspapers, they saw themselves as providing a service. Concurrently they saw themselves as able to comment upon but stand apart from the debates of their country. Some, particularly the evening newspapers, aimed to neglect these weightier arenas, substituting instead a light, family entertainment. Most, however, chose to see themselves as disinterested rather than uninterested. The argument of the *Nelson Evening Mail* is typical. It was "attached to no party, devoted to no faction, seeking only to advance the interests of this Province and the Property of the entire Colony".

At first sight this indicates a considerable change in press values, from an espousal of partisan advocacy to an acceptance of the role of disinterested but concerned reporter. Yet the role of a neutral supplier of information was not foreign to the first New Zealand newspaper proprietors; even though, for at least the first two decades, the newspapers were unable to offer a regular or comprehensive news coverage. But the newspaper proprietors of these years saw this as one of their tasks and valued it highly. They published news they received as rapidly as they could. Likewise they were generally open in regard to the authenticity of their news, developing eventually a many layered gradation in regard to the reliability of their sources. They, like the later newspapers, were keen to obtain and publish news. The major distinction between them and the later newspapers was one of technology rather than values. The later newspapers had both the telegraph and more reliable mail services which enabled them to publish the news on a regular schedule quite denied the earlier newspapers.

Similarly the early newspapers failed to achieve any significant commercial success, not because they did not value such success, but because it was simply unavailable for newspapers at that time.

Conversely, the later newspapers did not undervalue their role as their readers guides and leaders. This is most apparent in regard to the area of political discussion. Political discussion was among the major values shared by the newspapers of the 1860s and 1870s with those of the earlier decades. And this discussion was seen as a leadership of the newspaper's readers. The *Evening Post,* for instance, called "a journal's highest function that of promoting, leading and even forming a healthy public opinion upon political matters". It is difficult to distinguish this from a positive valuation for a political advocacy by newspapers, yet the quotation is from an editorial critical of the *New Zealander,* the newspaper established by members and allies of the Grey Ministry for the support of that Ministry. This, the *Evening Post* sees as "a servile organ of the political party in power....(and) essentially rotten and corrupt". It brands the *New Zealander* as a "hireling journal". Such a hireling journal was the normal type of newspaper in New Zealand prior to the appearance of the commercial press. It is a nice distinction whereby a newspaper can both value the role of political leadership and also deride those newspapers explicitly formed for a particular political advocacy and leadership.

The distinction obfuscates the fact that newspapers were still active as supporters or opponents of the Government in power. They maintained and, on occasions, exercised the right to independent expression. The clearest instances of their independence concerned the defence of journalism itself. When newspaper controllers considered the efficient conducting of their newspapers was obstructed by political considerations they spoke out in disagreement.[4] But, generally, newspaper controllers were content to follow the lead given by their political allies. Neutrality was not practiced. The ideology of nonpartisan leadership did not describe their actual political behaviour. As normal practice newspapers remained partisan political advocates.

Epilogue

As a final point mention must be made of the significance of the events discussed to the later New Zealand political parties. Their press support was set predominantly in the years up to 1880.

The various newspapers that formed the Liberal Government's press backing during and beyond the 1890s were already present in the 1870s. And, at that time, some of them, such as the *Lyttelton Times* and the *Nelson Colonist,* had been in existence and calling themselves liberal for more than a decade. These newspapers advocated and helped define a liberal position. Prior to the rise of the Liberal party and its domination of New Zealand political life, a substantial number of the New Zealand newspapers prefigured the appearance of the party by advocating a liberal political philosophy. It was never possible to have more than a small number of high circulation newspapers and, by

---

4   That such remains the case can be seen from the discussion in Cleveland (1972).

## Conclusion

holding so many of the existing newspaper positions, they were able to present the eventual party with a ready phalanx of press supporters.

It has been argued that during the decades covered by this study political advocacy was possible only as long as it did not impinge on the economic prerequisites the newspapers had as business organizations. This situation allowed advocacy for both the conservative ministry and the nascent Liberal party. Both were compatible with this business orientation. Both served the class interests of their joint origins. The next body of political thought; that of the labour movement was quite a different matter. This political movement, which eventually achieved a period of political dominance, did so in the face of concerted opposition from the New Zealand press. Support for the labour movement was not considered compatible with the business orientation of the press. With all the major newspapers united in opposition to labour the cooperation evident in the United Press Association was to be extended to include areas of editorial conduct.[5]

The labour philosophy was inimical to the values of the existing newspapers and the labour movement was to be denied newspaper backing.[6] New newspapers were unable to rise against the entrenched press.[7] Even when, in the early twentieth century, the Liberal party declined, support was still denied the labour position. The liberal newspapers rallied around the, for them, only viable alternative and the conservative voice was the only political expression to receive newspaper advocacy.

---

5   In 1919, for instance, "with a general election not far distant, (UPA) agents were to be warned of political leaders who might spread the creeds of Bolshevism and the International Workers of the World movement,. They were to be strictly enjoined on no account to report anarchist utterances." Sanders, p.55.

6   A notable exception is the Greymouth newspaper, the *Grey River Argus*.

7   The most notable attempted labour newspaper was the Wellington based *Southern Cross*. Its failure is recorded in Blake.

# Appendix

**Barton, George Burnett (1836-1901)** was born in Sydney and called to the bar in 1860. He was engaged in journalism in Australia when, in the 1860s, he moved to Dunedin where he began legal practise. In 1868 he succeeded Vogel as editor of the *Otago Daily Times*. He retired from this position in 1871 so as to prepare, successfully, for his defence on a charge of criminal libel in the Telegraph Libel case. After this he returned to New South Wales.

**Bathgate, John (1809-1886)** was born in Edinburgh where he became a lawyer, agent of the Union Bank of Scotland as well as being involved in journalism. He moved to Dunedin in 1863 to become manager of the Bank of Otago. He was involved in the formation of the Otago Daily Times and Witness Co. Ltd. in 1866. In 1868 he resigned from his banking position and became the company Managing Director. For a period after the ousting of Vogel he edited the *Otago Daily Times*. He entered political life in 1870 and on his second attempt joined the Otago Provincial Council in 1871. He was there until 1874. In 1871 he also became M.H.R. for Dunedin City and from October 1872 to February 1874 was Minister of Justice in the successive Waterhouse, Fox and Vogel ministries. He resigned from his political offices to become district judge and resident magistrate in Dunedin, a position he held until 1880. He continued his journalistic interests being business manager of Thomas Bracken's *Saturday Advertiser*, founded in 1875. In 1881 he returned to Parliament as M.H.R. for Roslyn. After defeat in 1884 he was in 1885 made a Legislative Councillor.

**Bell, Francis Dillon (1821-1898)** was a kinsman of E.G. Wakefield and from 1838 worked for the New Zealand Company. He arrived in New Zealand in 1843 and in the 1840s occupied various positions for the Company as well as being prominent in land purchase negotiations. He was a regular contributor to settlement newspapers, especially the *Nelson Examiner,* in the 1840s and 1850s. In a long political and administrative career he was in Parliament in 1855 and 1856 and from 1859 to 1875. He was a member of four Ministries. He was Agent-General in London from 1881 to 1891.

**Bell, George (1809-1899)** was from Yorkshire. In 1863 he emigrated to Dunedin after spending some years in Australia. He was a member of the *Otago Daily Times* staff, and for a period, editor of the *Witness* before becoming a newspaper proprietor in 1869 by co-founding the

*Appendix*

*Independent*. He soon amalgamated the *Independent* in a new purchase, the *Evening Star* and was its sole proprietor until his retirement in 1894.

**Bennett, John Boyle (1808-1880)** was from County Cork. He graduated M.D. but combined medicine with journalism. He edited the *New Zealander* from 1849 to 1855 when he was appointed Registrar of Births, Deaths and Marriages for Auckland Province. In 1866 he became the national Registrar-General.

**Bluett, Thomas (      )** was an early Wellington settler who in September 1841 edited and printed the single issue newspaper, the *Victoria Times*.

**Blundell, Henry (1814-1878)** was the principal figure in the early years of the *Evening Post*. Born in Dublin where he worked for many years on the *Evening Mail* he arrived in Dunedin, by way of Victoria, in 1861. He worked for the *Otago Daily Times* and *Lyttelton Times* before, with David Curle, founding the *Havelock Mail*. In 1865 Blundell and Curle moved to Wellington and started the *Evening Post*. Curle soon withdrew because of the papers precarious financial position. Blundell, with the assistance of his three sons, remained with the *Evening Post* until his retirement in 1874. As a matter of policy he never stood for political office for fear of compromising his newspaper's independence.

**Bowen, Charles (1830-1917)** sailed with his family to Canterbury in the *Charlotte Jane* in 1850. An early and regular contributor to the *Lyttelton Times*, he was its co-proprietor from 1856 to 1859. Bowen was an associate of William Moorhouse (in 1857 elected Superintendent of Canterbury), especially in regard to the Lyttelton tunnel scheme and he supplied much of the data for the scheme. Bowen was private secretary to John Robert Godley for two years in the early 1850s. In 1852 he was appointed Inspector of Police in Canterbury. In 1854 he became Provincial Treasurer. In 1858-59 he was an Executive member of the Provincial Council. He left Canterbury for England, via North and South America, in 1860 and returned to New Zealand in 1862. He was resident Magistrate in Christchurch 1864-74. He was elected M.H.R. for Kaiapoi in 1875 and held his seat to 1881. He was Minister of Justice and Commissioner of Stamps 1875-77. He was appointed to the Legislative Council in 1891.

**Brett, Henry (1842-1927)** migrated to New Zealand in 1862 and settled in Auckland. He came from Sussex where he had been employed as a printer. He found employment as a reporter with the *Southern Cross* and then as a printer with the *New Zealand Herald*. In 1870 he became co-proprietor of the *Evening Star* (later renamed the *Auckland Star*). He was sole proprietor from 1876 to 1889 when Thomas Leys, the editor, became Brett's co-proprietor. Brett was an innovative newspaper proprietor who was influential in developing faster news gathering methods from the early use of carrier pigeons to the eventual formation of the United Press Association. While not personally involved in elected political life, he was a longtime supporter of liberalism. He was knighted in 1926.

**Brittan, Joseph (1805-1867)** was from Gloucester. He came to New Zealand in 1852. He was founder, proprietor and editor of the *Canterbury Standard* (1854-66). Brittan was in the Canterbury Provincial Council for Christchurch City, 1855-57 and 1861-62. He was the leader of the executive in 1855 and was Provincial Secretary under Tancred, 1855-57.

**Brittan, William Guise (1809-1876)** was a brother of Joseph Brittan. He studied medicine and surgery and was employed as a surgeon on voyages on the *General Palmer*. In 1841 he became part proprietor and editor of the *Sherborne Mercury*, a conservative paper. A prominent member of the Canterbury Association, he arrived in Lyttelton in 1850. He was a regular contributor to the *Lyttelton Times* in its early years and later to *The Press*. Defeated in the first elections in 1853, Brittan took no further part in elected political life.

**Brown, William (1809-1898)** was a native of Dundee who arrived in New Zealand in 1840. Brown took part in Auckland affairs from the founding of the town. He founded and owned the *Southern Cross* from 1843 to 1869 when he sold it to a company controlled by Julius Vogel. He was a member of the Legislative Council 1844-45 and again 1847-48. He unsuccessfully contested the first Auckland superintendency election in 1853 but did gain the post in 1855. In August 1854 he was elected M.H.R for the City of Auckland. Resigning his political offices he left New Zealand permanently in 1855. His longtime business partner, from their meeting in 1840, was John Logan Campbell.

**Brown, Charles (1820-1901)** a founder and co-proprietor of the *Taranaki News*, was born in Eire. He migrated to New Zealand in 1841. In 1853 he was elected the first Superintendent for Taranaki, holding

*Appendix*

the office until 1857. He was again Superintendent from 1861 to 1865. He was a M.H.R. from 1855-56, 1858-60, 1864-65 and 1868-70, and was Colonial Treasurer in the Fox Ministry of 1856.

**Campbell, John Logan (1817-1912)** was a native of Edinburgh who arrived in New Zealand in 1840. He and William Brown set up a business in December 1840 and were soon leading merchants in the north. He was associated with, and at times in control of, Brown's newspaper, the *Southern Cross*. Campbell named the newspaper, taking the title from a hotel he had stayed at in Adelaide in 1842. In 1844 Campbell declined a seat in the Legislative Council. In 1852 he was elected, by Auckland Suburbs, to the New Ulster Legislative Council. When Brown left New Zealand, Campbell won both elections to find his successor and became M.H.R. and Superintendent. He was a member of Stafford's Cabinet in 1856 but then resigned all his offices and went to England. He was again M.H.R. in 1860.

**Carleton, Hugh Francis (1810-1890)** was educated at Eton and Cambridge and came to Auckland in 1845. He contributed to the *New Zealander* and for a time was its editor. In 1848 he established the *Anglo-Maori Warden*. This paper's opposition to Governor Grey and his Administration cost Carleton his association with the *New Zealander*. He then contributed regularly to the *Southern Cross* and edited that newspaper for a time from 1856. He was M.H.R. for the Bay of Islands from 1853-1870, and was a member of the Auckland Provincial Council from 1855-57 and 1859-75.

**Creighton, Robert James (1835-1893)** was a journalist in Belfast and Londonderry before moving to Auckland in 1861. His first New Zealand employment was with the *Southern Cross*. He edited the paper until 1868 when he became proprietor and editor of the short-lived *Auckland Free Press*. In Dunedin he later became manager and editor of the *Otago Guardian*. In 1874 he became manager of the *New Zealand Times*, Vogel's Wellington daily, and followed this with a period as editor of the *New Zealand Herald*. Creighton was in the Auckland Provincial Council from 1865 to 1873 and was a M.H.R. from 1865 to 1866 and 1869 to 1875. He settled in San Francisco in 1876.

**Curle, David (1837-1917)** was the partner of Henry Blundell in 1864 in the *Havelock Mail*, and in 1865 in the (Wellington) *Evening Post*. He was, in 1868, founder of the *Havelock Daily News*, in the 1870s proprietor of the *Ross Guardian*, in 1878 co-founder of the *Fielding Guardian* and the (Wellington) *Evening Chronicle*, in 1880 manager of the (Hokitika) *Evening Star*, and from 1893 proprietor of the *Dannevirke Bush Advocate*.

**Cutten, William Henry (1822-1883)** was born in London where he had studied law. He became a merchant and auctioneer in Dunedin, having arrived there in 1848. He was son-in-law to William Cargill, the Otago settlement leader. One of a group of settlers who started the *Otago Witness*, he was appointed its inaugural editor and from 1853 became sole proprietor. Cutten entered a partnership in 1861 with Julius Vogel and they started the *Otago Daily Times*. Cutten left the partnership and his newspapers in 1864. Cutten was a member of the Otago Provincial Council (1853-63) and also served on its Executive and as Provincial Treasurer. He was M.H.R. for Dunedin County (1853-55) and for Taieri (1878-79). He was an unsuccessful parliamentary candidate in 1863 and 1881.

**Domett, Alfred (1811-1887)** a Nelson settler who was a regular contributor to the *Nelson Examiner*. He edited the paper in 1844 and 1845 and during the provincial election campaign of 1857. He had an extensive political career being a member of the Nelson Provincial Council and that Council's Executive from 1857 to 1863, M.H.R. from 1855 to 1866, Premier of New Zealand from August 1862 to October 1863 and a member of the Legislative Council from 1866 to 1874.

**Elliott, Charles (1811-1876)** co-proprietor, with his brother James, of the *Nelson Examiner*. In Nelson Charles and James were known, respectively, as the political Elliott and the printing Elliott. Charles Elliott owned a London printing business before he migrated to Nelson. At various times he also edited the *Examiner*. He was a run holder in the Wairau. Elliott was a member of the Nelson Provincial Council representing Wairau (1853-59), Amuri (1860-61) and Nelson (1863-64). He represented Awatere in the Marlborough Provincial Council (1860-61). He was M.H.R. for Waimea (1855-58).

**Falwasser, Henry ( -1846)** an Englishman who migrated to Auckland after living for a time in Sydney. He founded and edited the *Auckland Times* in 1842. The last number was issued a week before his death.

**Farjeon, Benjamin Leopold (1838-1903)** was born in London. In 1854 he sailed for Victoria where he was engaged in various activities as a journalist. In 1861 he moved to Otago and joined the staff of the *Otago Daily Times*. He was the paper's co-proprietor from 1864 to 1867 when he returned to London.

**Featherston, Isaac Carl (1813-1876)** was born at Newcastle-on-Tyre and graduated in medicine at Edinburgh. He came to Wellington in 1840-41 as surgeon on the *Olympus* and started a practice in that city. In 1845 he became the first editor of the *Wellington Independent* and was its controlling figure throughout the Crown Colony Government years. The *Independent* supported him throughout his political career. He took a major part in the Settlers' Constitutional Association and in 1853 became Wellington's first Superintendent. Four times elected to that position he held it to 1871. He was M.H.R. for Wanganui and Rangitikei (1853-55) and for Wellington City (1855-70). He would not accept a cabinet position apart from joining Fox in July and August 1861 to meet an emergency and again in the Executive, without portfolio, in Fox's last ministry (1869-71). He concluded the mail steamer agreements by which Wellington and Melbourne became linked in 1857 and by which, in 1866, New Zealand and Australia were linked with England via Panama. He was Agent-General in London from 1871 to his death.

**Fenwick, George (1847-1929)** began an apprenticeship in 1859 with the *Otago Witness*. His six-year apprenticeship coincided with the foundation of the *Otago Daily Times* and covered the years of most rapid change in New Zealand journalism. In 1867-68 he was co-proprietor of the *Tuapeka Press and Goldfields Gazette*. In 1869 he founded the *Cromwell Argus* and was its proprietor until 1875 when he returned to Dunedin and became manager of the *Otago Guardian*. He was for a time in 1876 proprietor of the *Evening News* but became co-proprietor of the *Otago Guardian* and in 1877 co-proprietor of the *Otago Daily Times*. He remained with that newspaper for the rest of his life and was its editor from 1890 to 1909.

**FitzGerald, Gerald George (1834-1904)** was a younger brother of James FitzGerald. He was a co-founder in 1862 of the *Southland Times*. In 1865 he founded, under his brother's impetus the New Zealand General Telegraphic Agency, New Zealand's first press agency. In 1865 he became a goldfields warden on the West Coast and resident magistrate in Hokitika. In later years he edited the *Wanganui Chronicle*, the *New Zealand Times* and the *Timaru Herald*.

## The Making of the New Zealand Press

**FitzGerald, James Edward (1818-96)** arrived in Lyttelton on the *Charlotte Jane* in December 1850. He edited and managed the *Lyttelton Times* until 1852. At the same time he was Immigration Agent and Inspector of Police. He was first Superintendent of Canterbury, 1853-57, and M.H.R. for Lyttelton, 1853-57. From 1858 to 1860 he was in England. In 1861 he founded *The Press* and was its sole proprietor from 1862 to 1867. He was in the Canterbury Provincial Council 1861-62. He was M.H.R. for Ellesmere 1862-66 and for the City of Christchurch 1866-67. He lived in Wellington from 1867 to 1896.

**Forsaith, Thomas Spencer (1814-1898)** was from London. He arrived in Northland in 1838 and settled in Auckland when the Crown Colony government was established there. He held the position of sub-protector and then protector of the aborigines until the office was abolished during Grey's governorship. He was associated with the *New Zealander* and was its editor for a year. Forsaith was M.H.R. from 1853 to 1860. He was New Zealand's most rapidly forsaken Premier, holding the office for three days in 1854. His political career ended in 1860 when his pro-Maori beliefs ensured his electoral defeat. He moved to Dunedin in 1862 where he was associated with the *Colonist*. In 1865 Forsaith was ordained in the Congregational church and from 1867 he was engaged in church work in New South Wales.

**Fox, William (1812-1893)** a son of the deputy lieutenant of the County of Durham, was an Oxford graduate who arrived in Wellington in November 1842. He edited the *New Zealand Gazette and Wellington Spectator* for three months in 1843 before succeeding Arthur Wakefield as resident agent for the New Zealand Company in Nelson in September 1843. In September 1848 he succeeded Colonel Wakefield as principal agent in Wellington. Later in 1848 he declined both a seat in the Legislative Council and the vacant Attorney-Generalship. From 1850 he took an active part in the Settlers' Constitutional Association, travelling to London as its political agent. On his return in 1854 he became a City representative in the Wellington Provincial Council (1854-57) and then a Wanganui and Rangitikei representative (1857-62). He was M.H.R. for Wanganui (1855-60, 1876-79) and for Rangitikei (1860-65, 1868-75, 1880). He was Premier of the short-lived Ministry in 1856, again Premier from July 1861 to August 1862 and from June 1869 to September 1872. He formed the 1863-64 Ministry but himself took Native Affairs and the Colonial Secretaryship, not the Premiership.

*Appendix*

Originally a strong philo-maori he was, by 1863, an advocate for vigorous prosecution of the war and for land confiscation. He was constantly engaged in journalism, the *New Zealand Gazette and Wellington Spectator,* the *Nelson Examiner,* and the *Wellington Independent* being his main vehicles of publication.

**George, Seymour Thorne (1851-1922)** came to New Zealand in 1869 on the advice of Sir George Grey, a friend of his father. He married Grey's niece in 1872. He was a M.H.R. 1878-1884, and in 1903 became a Legislative Councillor. He was managing-director of the Wellington daily, the *New Zealander,* during its two year life, 1878-1880.

**Gillon, Edward Thomas (1842-1896)** was born on the Isle of Man and came to New Zealand with his parents in 1851. He joined the staff of the *Otago Witness* and then became inaugural chief reporter of the *Otago Daily Times.* In Otago he was involved in the founding of both the *Bruce Herald* and the *Bruce Standard.* He moved to Wellington in 1867 and joined the Hansard staff but soon left that to return to journalism, this time with the *Evening Post.* He was managing the *Otago Daily Times* news agency in 1872 when the two press agencies were amalgamated into the Holt and McCarthy agency. At this point he became editor of the *Evening Post.* He resigned this position to contest, unsuccessfully, a parliamentary seat and then became editor and co-proprietor of the *Argus.* In 1878 he became editor of the *New Zealander* and manager of the New Zealand Press Association. In 1880 he became the inaugural manager of the United Press Association, a position he left in 1884 to return to the *Evening Post,* again as editor. In Gillon's eventful career he was also a strong founding supporter of the Journalists Association.

**Graham, Henry ( -1851)** was proprietor, printer and editor of the first Otago newspaper, the *Otago News.*

**Halcombe, Arthur William Follett (1834-1900)** came to New Zealand early in the 1860s. He was in the Wellington Provincial Council from 1865 to 1872 and on the Executive on four occasions. He edited the *Wellington Independent* from 1869 to 1871.

**Hall, John (1824-1907)** was born in Hull and migrated to Canterbury in 1852. He was a contributor to the *Lyttelton Times* and one of the original promoters of *The Press.* He was a M.H.R. from 1855 to 1860, from 1866 to 1872 and from 1879 to 1893. He was Premier from 1879 to 1882 and a member of five other Ministries. During the Stafford

Ministry, Hall, as Minister of Telegraphs, began the government run news service for New Zealand newspapers.

**Hanson, Richard Davies (1805-1876)** was an English barrister who was associated with E.G. Wakefield in the South Australia scheme. One of fifty settlers who combined to start the *New Zealand Colonist and Port Nicholson Advertiser,* he was its editor throughout its year of existence. He had been appointed Crown Prosecutor in Wellington in 1841 and combined this with the position of editor in 1842 and 1843. Hanson later became Chief Justice of South Australia.

**Harman, Richard James Strachan (1826-1902)** with his partner, E.C.J. Stevens, controlled *The Press* from the mid-1860s to the early 1870s. Harman started a business in 1851 as a land and estate agent. From 1853 to the end of the 1870s he is recorded as having several thousand acres freehold. From 1857-1860 he was the Provincial council representative for Heathcote and was a member of the Executive, 1856-1858. In 1859 he led the Executive. From 1860-1862 he was the Provincial Council Representative for Akaroa and in 1871 he was elected Deputy Superintendent.

**Harrison, William Henry (1831-1879)** was from Yorkshire. He migrated to Auckland in 1860 and moved the following year to Dunedin where he joined the staff of the *Otago Daily Times*. In 1865 he became the inaugural editor of the *Grey River Argus*. In 1871 he became editor of the *Wellington Independent* but in 1872 returned to the *Argus* again as editor. He was M.H.R. for Westland Boroughs and then Grey Valley from 1868 to 1875.

**Horton, Alfred George (1842-1903)** was from Yorkshire where he had been a journalist. He came to New Zealand in 1861 and began working for *The Press*. He founded the *Timaru Herald* in 1864 and was its proprietor and editor for eight years. After two years as co-proprietor of the *Thames Advertiser* he purchased the *Southern Cross* in Auckland. At the end of 1876 this paper was merged with the *New Zealand Herald* and Horton became that paper's co-proprietor. Horton spent four months on the Canterbury Provincial Council but later followed a policy whereby as a newspaper proprietor he should not stand for political office.

**Hutchinson, William (1820-1905)** was born in Banffshire, became a journalist and, in 1866, came to Auckland to work on the *Southern*

*Appendix*

*Cross*. He soon left to become editor of the *Wanganui Chronicle*, a position he held for seven years. He founded the Wellington paper, the *Tribune*, in 1874 selling it the following year. He later edited the *Nelson Colonist*. From 1884 his journalistic career was in Dunedin where he was also much involved in trade unionism. He was in the Wellington Provincial Council from 1867-74, Mayor of Wanganui 1873-74, Mayor of Wellington 1876-77 and 1879-81. He was a M.H.R. from 1879 to 1884 as a Wellington representative and from 1890 to 1896 as a labour representative for Dunedin City.

**Jollie, Francis** (1815-1870) arrived in Nelson in 1842 where he was a regular contributor to and second editor of the *Examiner*. He acted for a time as New Zealand Company resident agent. He stood unsuccessfully for the Nelson Superintendency in 1853. He then moved to Canterbury. He was in England from 1855 to 1858. He returned to Timaru and was a leader writer for the *Timaru Herald*. He was M.H.R. for Timaru 1861-66 and Gladstone 1866-70.

**Lance, Henry Porcher** (1830-1886) was a member of the syndicate which began, and originally owned, *The Press*. Lance and his brother had interests in several Canterbury properties. Lance represented Sefton in the Canterbury Provincial Council, 1862-65, but his main preoccupations appear to have been horse breeding and racing.

**Leys, Thomson Wilson** (1850-1924) was born in Nottingham. He came to Auckland with his father in 1863 and served an apprenticeship as a compositor on the *Southern Cross*. He was a sub-editor with that paper for a period. In 1872 he joined the *Auckland Star* and became its editor in 1876 and held the position for 45 years. He became the paper's co-proprietor in 1889.

**Lucas, Robert** (1817-1876) was an English printer who migrated to Nelson in 1860. He began a printing business there and in 1866 founded the *Nelson Evening Mail*.

**Luckie, David Mitchell** (1828-1909) was a Scottish journalist who migrated to Nelson in 1863. He edited successively the *Nelson Colonist*, the *New Zealand Herald* and the *Evening Post*. He was a M.H.R. from 1872 to 1875. In 1879 he became Commissioner of the Government Insurance Department.

*The Making of the New Zealand Press*

**Macandrew, James** (1820-1887) was a merchant from Aberdeen who arrived in Dunedin in 1851 aboard his schooner, the *Titan*. He was immediately commercially and politically prominent. He had considerable journalistic involvement being co-founder, co-proprietor and the major personality of the *Otago Colonist* and the *Daily Telegraph*. He was M.H.R. from 1853 to 1860 and 1865 to his death. He was a member of the Forsaith, the Grey and the Stout-Vogel Ministries. He was Superintendent of Otago in 1860 until his dismissal in 1861 and from 1867 until the 1876 abolition of Provincialism.

**Main, George Martin** (1835-1902) was born in Scotland but came to Auckland as a child. He did an apprenticeship as a compositor with the *New Zealander* and in 1863 joined the *New Zealand Herald*. In 1880 he joined that paper's literary staff. He is the author of a history of the Auckland press.

**Martin, John** (1822-1892) was a clergyman's son from County Down. He migrated to Wellington in 1840 where his early employment was with pick and shovel and as a carter. Starting a business as a merchant, he prospered and eventually branched into shipping and farming. In 1878 he was called to the Legislative Council by the Grey Government. In 1879 he purchased the Waihenga property of 34,000 acres for £85,000, later subdividing a portion of it for the town of Martinborough. His one newspaper venture was his purchase in 1867 of the soon defunct *New Zealand Times*.

**Martin, Samuel McDonald** ( -1848) Born on the Isle of Skye, he migrated to New South Wales. He first visited New Zealand in 1839. Appointed editor of the *New Zealand Herald and Auckland Gazette* in January 1842 he was dismissed and the paper closed three months later. He was inaugural editor of the *Southern Cross* in 1843-44. In 1844 he was appointed a member of the Legislative Council. He returned to England in 1845. He died in Berbice, British Guinea, where he was a stipendary magistrate.

**McCarthy, Florence Romuald** (1834-1914) was a Canadian who had become a compositor in New York. He arrived in Otago in 1861 as part of the great influx of gold seekers. He later obtained work in Otago as a printer. He was an employee of the *Wellington Independent* in the 1870s and one of the principals in the Holt and McCarthy press agency.

*Appendix*

The final thirty-five years of his life were spent as editor of the *Grey River Argus*.

**McKenzie, Thomas Wilmor (1827-1911)** Born in London, he emigrated with his mother to Wellington arriving in 1840. Apprenticed to Samuel Revans he helped produce the first issues of the *New Zealand Gazette*. At the age of eighteen he was one of the five compositors who began the *Wellington Independent* in 1845. The other partners one by one left the partnership until, from February 1865, McKenzie was sole proprietor. He controlled the paper to 1874 when he sold the majority interest to Vogel. McKenzie made no attempt to enter the Provincial Council or Parliament, but was a member of the Wellington City Council between 1881 and 1887 and contested the mayoralty unsuccessfully. McKenzie, after selling out to Vogel, remained on as secretary and manager to the New Zealand Times Company until he retired from active service.

**Moorhouse, William Sefton (1825-1881)** was from Yorkshire and landed at Lyttelton in the *Cornwall* in 1851. He was a regular contributor to the *Lyttelton Times* and edited it in 1856 and 1857. He was in the Canterbury Provincial Council from 1855 to 1857 and 1863 to 1866. He was Superintendent of Canterbury from 1857 to 1863 and 1866 to 1868. He was a M.H.R. in six of the first seven parliaments, beginning in 1853 and ending with his death.

**Moss, Frederick Joseph (1829-1904)** was born at St Helena. He migrated to New Zealand in 1859 and settled in Dunedin in 1861. He was active in Otago Provincial politics being a Council member from 1863 to 1867 and on three occasions an Executive Member. He was in Fiji from 1868 to 1873 when he settled in Auckland. He was M.H.R. for Parnell from 1876 to 1890. From 1890 to 1899 he was the British resident in the Cook Islands. He founded the *Otago Daily Mail*, an early and short-lived rival to the *Otago Daily Times*.

**Murison, William Dick (1837-1877)** was an Otago run holder, politician and journalist. He was a member of the Otago Provincial Council (1863-65) and M.H.R. for Waikouaiti (1866-68). He was a director of the Otago Daily Times and Witness Newspaper Co. Ltd, from 1867/8 to 1877 and was the third editor of the *Otago Daily Times*. His editorship was from 1871-1877.

**Quaife, Barzillai (    )** was a congregational minister who, in the 1840s, was minister and school teacher in Russell. He was the editor of

*The Making of the New Zealand Press*

both the Bay of Islands newspapers of the 1840s, the *New Zealand Advertiser and Bay of Islands Gazette* in 1840 and the *Bay of Islands Observer* in 1842.

**Reed, George McCullagh (1832-1898)** was educated in Belfast where he was ordained in the Presbyterian Church. He moved to Auckland in 1870, after twelve years in Australia. He was co-proprietor of the *Evening Star* to 1876 when he moved to Dunedin as editor of the *Evening News*. He soon became co-proprietor of the *Otago Guardian* and, through merger in 1877, editor of the *Otago Daily Times* and the *Otago Witness*. He left New Zealand in 1878 for Belfast but returned again in 1881. Continuing his nomadic life style he was subsequently to spend time in Australia and London as well as New Zealand. He continued in journalism being variously editor of the *Evening Bell,* and a leader writer for the *Sydney Morning Herald* and the *New Zealand Herald*. He died in Auckland.

**Reeves, William (1825-1891)** became co-proprietor of the *Lyttelton Times* in 1859. He was proprietor of the paper until his death. He also founded, in 1868, and owned the Christchurch *Star*. Reeves is best known as the father of William Pember Reeves but had a political career in his own right. He was M.H.R for Avon 1867-68 and for Selwyn 1871-75. From 1884 he was a member of the Legislative Council.

**Revans, Samuel (1808-1888)** did a printing apprenticeship in London. In the 1830s he lived in Canada where he began the *Montreal Daily Advertiser,* Canada's first daily. His support of the movement for self-government ended with a price being put on his head and he being forced to flee. In England he supported Chartism before aligning himself with the New Zealand Company. He is "father of the New Zealand press" by virtue of being proprietor of the first newspaper printed in the country, the *New Zealand Gazette*. He owned the paper, soon renamed the *New Zealand Gazette and Wellington Spectator,* until shortly before its close in 1844. He was also frequently the paper's editor. After the collapse of the *Gazette* he became a landowner and sheep farmer in the Wairarapa. In 1851-52 he was at the California gold diggings. He was an M.H.R and member of the Wellington Provincial Council, 1853-58.

**Reynolds, William Hunter (1822-1899)** was from Kent but spent much of his early life in Portugal. Brother-in-law to James Macandrew he migrated to Otago with Macandrew's party in 1851. Reynolds was

*Appendix*

manager and editor of the *Otago Witness* during Cutten's absences. He was a member of the Otago Provincial Council throughout its existence from 1853 to 1876. He was a M.H.R. from 1863 to 1878 and was a member of the Waterhouse, Fox, Vogel, Pollen and Stout-Vogel Ministries. Reynolds was a Legislative Councillor from 1878 to his death. He was a businessman in London prior to 1851 and subsequently in Otago. He was the negotiator who oversaw the change of ownership of the *Otago Daily Times* that accompanied its merger with the *Otago Guardian*. He then became Chairman of the newspaper's Board of Directors.

**Richardson, George Rycroft** ( -1843) was a lawyer who was among the first Nelson settlers. He was the inaugural editor of the *Nelson Examiner*. He was killed at the Wairau.

**Roe, Edward** ( ) was an associate in London of Samuel Revans where Roe published the first number, on 21 August 1839, of Revans *New Zealand Gazette*. Roe became in Wellington an original staff member for Revans. Roe published the *New Zealand Gazette and Wellington Spectator* in its final weeks of publication in 1844. He was one of the group of five printers of the *New Zealand Spectator and Cook's Strait Guardian* who, on being fired in 1845, began the *Wellington Independent*. Roe was a co-founder and, from 1859 to 1867, co-proprietor and editor of the *New Zealand Advertiser*.

**Sale, George Samuel** (1831-1922) was a fellow of Trinity College Cambridge in 1856. In 1860 he emigrated to New Zealand. On the strength of Sale's education, James FitzGerald appointed him, in 1861, inaugural editor of *The Press*. From 1865 to 1867 he was Commissioner of the West Canterbury Goldfield. He was associated in 1868 with the *Westland Observer*. Sale later became inaugural Professor of Classics and English at the University of Otago where he taught for thirty-seven years.

**Shrimpton, Ingram** (1812-1878) an Oxford printer and a member of the Canterbury Association was the absentee founder and principal financial backer of the *Lyttelton Times*. He arrived in Lyttelton in 1854 and managed the paper. After the death of his son in 1856 he sold the control of the paper. Shrimpton then began farming in North Canterbury. In 1864 he, with A G Horton, started the *Timaru Herald*.

**Simmons, Frank Churchill (1829-1876)** was an Oxford M.A. and minister who in 1864 moved to Otago to become Rector of the Otago Boys High School. He moved to Nelson College in 1868. He was a contributor to the *Otago Daily Times* and to the *Colonist*, which he also edited for a period.

**Southwell, Charles (1814-1860)** was an English journalist who migrated to Auckland in 1856. He founded the *Auckland Examiner* and edited it until his death.

**Stafford, Edward William (1819-1901)** was born in Edinburgh and educated at Trinity College, Dublin. He arrived in Nelson in 1843. He had a distinguished political career. In 1853 he was elected first superintendent of Nelson. He resigned this position in 1855 at which point he was elected M.H.R. for Nelson. He remained in Parliament until 1878 when he retired to England. Stafford was Premier from 1856 to 1861, from 1865 to 1869 and in 1872. He had less journalistic involvement than most of his contemporary political office-holders but was a frequent contributor to the *Nelson Examiner* in the 1840s and 1850s.

**Stevens, Edward Cephas John (1837-1915)** with his partner, R.J.S. Harman, controlled *The Press* from the mid 1860s to the early 1870s. Stevens joined with Harman as a land and estate agent. The two were New Zealand agents for a number of absentee landowners. From 1863-1866 Stevens was a member of the Provincial Executive. From 1866-1870 he was M.H.R. for Selwyn. From 1875-1882 he was M.H.R. for Christchurch City. From 1822-1915 he was a member of the Legislative Council and from 1887-1891 he was a member of Atkinson's cabinet.

**Stokes, Robert (1810-1880)** was born in England where he was trained as a surveyor. He also practised as an architect. He came to New Zealand in 1839-40 as a member of the survey staff for the New Zealand Company. He left the employ of the Company in 1842 and began a printing business in Wellington later in the decade, probably the business purchased surreptitiously from the *Wellington Independent*. He was editor of the *New Zealand Spectator and Cook's Strait Guardian* from 1845 and its proprietor from 1846. His latter movements are open to doubt. Scholefield states he moved to and settled at Hawke's Bay in 1858, but he is recorded as being Government Printer in Wellington in 1862. Stokes was one of the City representatives on the Wellington

*Appendix*

Provincial Council (1857-65) and, after losing at the 1865 election, became a representative for Wairarapa (1865-67). He was a member of the Legislative Council (1862-79).

**Swainson, William (1809-1884)** was born at Lancaster. He was called to the bar in 1838 and sailed for New Zealand in 1841 after being nominated for the Attorney-Generalship. On the introduction of the 1852 constitution he was the first member appointed to the Legislative Council. He remained a member until 1867. Swainson was the author of three books on New Zealand matters. His involvement in journalism was as editor of the *Auckland Standard* in 1842.

**Tancred, Henry John (1816-1884)** was a member of the syndicate which began, and originally owned, *The Press*. Tancred was the youngest son of Sir Thomas Tancred, sixth Baronet. He was a candidate for the Canterbury Superintendency in 1853. From 1853-57 he was a member of the Provincial Council for Christchurch County, from 1853-54 he led the Provincial Executive and was again on the Executive from 1855-57 and 1857-58. From 1858-61 he was a member of the Stafford Ministry and, in 1862-63, of the Domett Ministry. From 1863-69 he was M.H.R for Ashley. From 1864-74 he was in the Provincial Council, first for Wainui and then for Lincoln. From 1871 until his death he was the first Chancellor of the University of New Zealand.

**Terry, Charles ( -1859)** was an Englishman. In London in 1833, he was elected a Fellow of the Royal Society. He emigrated to Melbourne and then to New Zealand where he became the first resident of Auckland. A noted scientist he was also the pioneer of New Zealand's flax-milling industry. In 1841 he was the inaugural editor of the *New Zealand Herald and Auckland Gazette* before leaving later that year for England. In 1845 he was the inaugural editor of the *New Zealander* and also at one stage edited the *Southern Cross*.

**Vogel, Julius (1835-1899)** came to New Zealand in 1861. He was co-founder of the *Otago Daily Times*. He was co-proprietor and editor of the *Otago Daily Times* and the *Otago Witness* (1861-1868). He then, in Dunedin, founded and edited the *New Zealand Sun* (1868-69). In Auckland he was proprietor of the *Southern Cross* and the *Weekly News* (1869-73). In Wellington in 1873 he became proprietor of the *New Zealand Mail* and in 1874 the *Wellington Independent*, renamed the *New Zealand Times*. He was influential in the development of press agencies in New Zealand and founded the Holt and McCarthy agency (1872-78). He was on the Otago Provincial Council (1863-70) and was the head of the Government there (1867-69). His national political career began in 1863 when he was first elected an M.H.R. He was an M.H.R. 1863-77 and 1884-89. He was twice Premier, from 1873-75 and again in 1876. Apart from the Stafford Ministry which held power for one month in 1872, Vogel was a member of all the Ministries from 1869 to the fall of the Vogel Ministry in September 1876. He again held power in the Stout-Vogel Ministry of 1884-87. While a Minister, Vogel generally controlled the portfolios of Colonial Treasurer and the communication portfolios of Postmaster-General and Commissioner of Telegraphs.

**Wakelin, Richard (1816-1881)** was from Warwickshire. He was a journalist in England, editing both Temperance and Chartist publications. He came to New Zealand in 1850. In 1851 he began reporting for the *Wellington Independent* and from May 1852 was its editor. He was at different times editor of the *New Zealand Advertiser* and the *New Zealand Mail*. With the *Wairarapa Journal* and *Wellington Journal* he attempted, in 1868, to found his own newspaper. He was successful in 1872 when he purchased the *Wairarapa Mercury* which he renamed the *Wairarapa Standard*. He edited this paper until his death.

**Ward, Crosbie (1832-1867)** was co-proprietor of the *Lyttelton Times* from 1856-1867. He edited the paper from 1857-1867. He was the Akaroa member of the Provincial Council 1855-57. He was M.H.R for Lyttelton from 1858 to 1866 when he was elected M.H.R for Avon. He was Postmaster-General and Secretary for Lands 1861-63.

**Wicksteed, John Tylston (1806-1860)** In London he had been associated with the literary staff of the *Spectator*. He arrived in New Zealand in 1840. He was editor of the *New Zealand Gazette and Wellington Spectator* before, in May 1842, becoming the New Zealand Company resident agent in New Plymouth, a post he held to 1847. He was in 1852 elected to the Legislative Council of New Ulster. He was in 1852-3 the inaugural editor of the *Taranaki Herald* and in 1853 an unsuccessful candidate for the Taranaki Superintendency. In 1853 he moved to Wanganui where he was editor of the *Wanganui Chronicle*.

**Wilkie, William (1814-1891)** was from Scotland. He arrived in Nelson, via New South Wales, in 1842. He became a storekeeper and was the co-founder and principal financial backer of the *Colonist*.

*Appendix*

**Williamson, John (1815-1875)** learnt his trade as a printer in Northern Ireland. He emigrated to Sydney and went to Auckland in 1841 where he had been engaged to work on the *New Zealand Herald and Auckland Gazette*. He began the *New Zealander* in 1845 being proprietor and then co-proprietor, with W.C. Wilson. He had a long political career beginning with his election to the Auckland Provincial Council in 1853. He remained a member to 1856 when he was elected Superintendent. He served as Superintendent 1856-62, 1867-69 and 1870-75. He was M.H.R for Pensioner Settlements 1855-60 and for City of Auckland West 1861-75.

**Wilson, William Chisholm (1810-1876)** was a printer who learnt his trade in Edinburgh before emigrating in 1833 to Tasmania. He came to New Zealand in 1841. He was employed by the Auckland Printing Company and thus worked on various Auckland newspapers in the early 1840s. He was publisher of the 1842 newspaper, the *Bay of Islands Observer*. He was John Williamson's partner from 1848 to 1863 in the company which included in its publications the *New Zealander*. In 1863 Wilson founded the *New Zealand Herald* and controlled that paper until his death.

**Wilson, William Scott (1835-1902)** was the son of W.C. Wilson. He was apprenticed in 1846 to the *New Zealander*. He was in charge of the printing department of the *New Zealand Herald* before becoming, on his father's death, that paper's co-proprietor.

**Woon, Garland William (1831-1895)** was born in Tonga. In 1846 he was apprenticed to Williamson and Wilson, publishers of the *New Zealander*. He set up as a printer in New Plymouth on completing his apprenticeship and in 1852 became co-founder and co-proprietor of the *Taranaki Herald*. He sold the paper and left journalism in 1867.

# Bibliography

Abrams, Philip, (1982), *Historical Sociology*, Open Books, Somerset.

Allan, Ruth M., (1965), *Nelson: A History of Early Settlement*, A.H. &A.W. Reed, Wellington.

Arnold, Rollo, (1981), *The Farthest Promised Land*, Victoria University Press, Wellington.

Asquith, Ivon, (1978), "The Structure, Ownership and Control of the Press: 1780-1855", in *Newspaper History from the Seventeenth Century to the Present Day*, edited by George Boyce, James Curran and Pauline Wingate, Constable, London.

Blake, Robert, (1950), "The Southern Cross: A Hostage to the Capitalist Press", *Landfall*, Vol.4, No.2. pp.105-116.

Boyce, George, (1978), "The Fourth Estate: the Reappraisal of a Concept", in *Newspaper History from the Seventeenth Century to the Present Day*, edited by George Boyce, James Curran and Pauline Wingate, Constable, London.

Boyd-Barrett, Oliver, (1978), "Market Control and Wholesale 'News': The Case of Reuter", in *Newspaper History from the Seventeenth Century to the Present Day*, edited by George Boyce, James Curran and Pauline Wingate, Constable, London.

Boyd-Barrett, Oliver, (1980), *The International News Agencies*, Sage Constable, London.

Brett, A.R., (1927), *The Race for the Wires: Old Time Journalism: Some Reminiscences of the late Sir Henry Brett*, Auckland Star.

Broad, Lowther, (1892), *The Jubilee History of Nelson from 1492 to 1892*, Broad, Finney & Co., Colonist Office. [Capper Press Reprint 1976]

Burdon, R.M., (1948), *The Life and Times of Sir Julius Vogel*, Caxton Press, Christchurch.

Burns, Patricia, (1957), *The Foundation of the New Zealand Press, 1839-1850*, Ph.D.thesis, Victoria University of Wellington.

Campbell, Michael David Neville, (1972), *The Evolution of Hawke's Bay Landed Society, 1850-1914*, Ph.D. thesis, Victoria University of Wellington.

# Bibliography

Chapman, H.S., (1843-1851), Letters from New Zealand. 3 Vols of typescript, in possession of the Alexander Turnbull Library.

Cleveland, Les, (1972), "Pressure Groups and the Press", in *The Anatomy of Influence*, Hicks, Smith and Sons, pp.113-128.

Dalziel, Raewyn (1975), *The Origins of New Zealand Diplomacy: the Agent-General in London, 1870-1905*, Victoria University Press, Wellington.

Dalziel, Raewyn (1986) *Julius Vogel: Business Politician*, Auckland University Press: Oxford University Press.

Eldred-Grigg, Stevan, (1980), *A Southern Gentry*, A.H. & A.W. Reed, Wellington.

Fairweather, John R., (1985), "White-Settler Colonial Development: Early New Zealand Pastoralism and the Formation of Estates", *Australian and New Zealand Journal of Sociology*, Vol.21. N.o2. pp. 237-257.

Fenwick, George, (1929), *The United Press Association: Foundation and Early History*, Otago Daily Times and Witness Co. Ltd., Dunedin.

FitzGerald, J.E., Letters to H.S. Selfe, in Hunter, William John, M.S. Papers 1777; Alexander Turnbull Library.

Fox, William, (1851), *The Six Colonies of New Zealand*, J.W. Parker, London. (Hocken Library, Dunedin, 1971).

Fox, William, (1890), *How New Zealand Got It's Constitution*, Auckland.

General Report, (1925), *New Zealand Census 1921*, Government Printer, Wellington.

Green, J.E., (1934-38), "Early Telegraph History of New Zealand" *Extracts from The New Zealand Post and Telegraph Journal*.

Grimstone, S.E., (1847), *The Southern Settlements of New Zealand*, R. Stokes, Spectator Office, Wellington.

Harvey, D.R., (1987), *Union List of Newspapers*, National Library of New Zealand, Wellington.

Helm, A.S., (1951), *The Early History of South Island Telegraphs, 1862-1867*, M.A. Thesis in History, Victoria University of Wellington.

Herron, David, (1959), *The Structure and Course of New Zealand Politics 1853-1858, Ph D.* thesis, University of Otago.

Herron, David, (1959a), "Alsatia or Utopia? New Zealand Society and Politics in the Eighteen-Fifties", *Landfall,* Vol.13, No.4, pp.324-341.

Herron, David, (1963), "Provincialism and Centralism, 1853-1858" in *Studies of a Small Democracy,* edited by Robert Chapman and Keith Sinclair, University of Auckland.

Hight, J., and Bamford, H.D., (1914), *The Constitutional History and Law of New Zealand,* Whitcombe and Tombs, Christchurch.

Hocken, T.M., (1901), "The Beginnings of Literature in New Zealand: Part II, the English Section Newspapers",*Transactions and Proceedings of the New Zealand Institute,* Vol.34, pp.99-114.

Innis, Harold A., (1951), *The Bias of Communication,* University of Toronto Press.

Lafrentz, T.C.A., (1938), "Pioneering the Telegraph Service in New Zealand", *The Katipo,* August-December.

Lee, Alan J., (1976), *The Origin of the Popular Press in England: 1855-1914,* Croom Helm, London.

Maginnity, T.A., (1880), *Telegraphy in New Zealand,* A paper read before the Society of Telegraph Engineers, London. Hocken Library Dunedin.

Main, G.M., (1891), *The Newspaper Press of Auckland,* N.Z. Herald.

Martin, S.M.D., (1845), *New Zealand in a Series of Letters: Containing an Account of the Country, both Before and Since Its Occupation by the British Government,* Simmonds & Ward, London.

Marx, Karl, (1954), *Capital,* Progress Publishers, Moscow.

Mayer, Henry, (1964), *The Press in Australia,* Lansdowne Press, Melbourne.

McLintock, A.H., (1949), T*he History of Otago,* Whitcombe and Tombs Ltd., Dunedin.

McLintock, A.H., (1958), *Crown Colony Government in New Zealand,* Government Printer, Wellington.

*Bibliography*

McLintock, A.H., (1966), (editor) *An Encyclopaedia of New Zealand*, Government Printer, Wellington.

Meiklejohn, G.M., (1953), *Early Conflicts of Press and Government*, Wilson and Horton, Auckland.

Mineka, Francis E. ed., (1963), The Early Letters of John Stuart Mill, *Collected Works of J.S. Mill*, Vol. XIX. University of Toronto Press.

Morrell, W.P., (1964), *The Provincial System in New Zealand 1852-1876*, Whitcombe and Tombs, Wellington.

Mulgan, Alan, (1939), *The City of the Strait: Wellington and Its Province*, Whitcombe & Tombs Ltd, Wellington.

Newsam, R.A., (1979), *The Changing Role of the Press in Otago 1848-1861*, Unpublished Ms., University of Otago.

O'Boyle, Lenore, (1968), "The Image of the Journalist in France, Germany, and England, 1815-1848", *Comparative Studies in Society and History*, Vol.X, No.3, pp.290-317.

Oliver, W.H., (1971), *Challenge and Response* E.C.D.R.A. Gisborne.

O'Neill, R.B., (1963), *The Press 1861-1961: The Story of a Newspaper*, Christchurch Press Co. Ltd.

O'Neill, R.B., Manuscripts, Canterbury Museum, Christchurch.

*Otago Daily Times*, (1924), reprint of the Diamond Jubilee Issue, 15 November 1921, Otago Daily Times and Witness Newspaper Company Ltd, Dunedin.

Palmer, Michael, (1978), "The British Press and International News, 1851-1899: of Agencies and Newspapers", in *Newspaper History from the Seventeenth Century to the Present Day*, edited by George Boyce, James Curran and Pauline Wingate, Constable, London.

Paul, J.T., (1924), *The Press of Otago and Southland*, Otago Daily Times and Witness Newspapers Company Ltd., Dunedin.

Puseley, D., (1858), *The Rise and Progress of Australia, Tasmania and New Zealand*, Warren Hall & Co., London.

Reeves, William Pember, (1898), *The Long White Cloud*, George Allen & Urwin, London, (Fourth edition, 1950).

Robinson, Howard, (1964), *A History of the Post Office in New Zealand*, Government Printer, Wellington.

Sanders, James, (1979), *Dateline-NZPA. The New Zealand Press Association 1880-1980*, Wilson and Horton Ltd. Auckland.

Saunders, Alfred, (1896), *History of New Zealand 1642-1861*, Whitcombe and Tombs.

Scholefield, Guy H., (1958), *Newspapers in New Zealand*, A.H. & A.W. Reed, Wellington.

Scholefield, Guy H., (ed), (1950), *New Zealand Parliamentary Record 1840-1949*, Government Printer, Wellington.

Schudson, Michael, (1978), *Discovering the News: A Social History of American Newspapers*, Basic Books, New York.

Siegfried, André, (1914), *Democracy in New Zealand*, London, (Victoria University Press Edition 1982).

Sinclair, Keith, (1959), *A History of New Zealand*, Penguin, London.

Smith, Anthony, (1978), "The Long Road to Objectivity and back again: the kind of truth we get in journalism", in *Newspaper History from the Seventeenth Century to the Present Day*, edited by George Boyce, James Curran and Pauline Wingate, Constable, London.

Stone, Russell, (1973), *Makers of Fortune: A Colonial Business Community and its Fall*, Auckland University Press.

Stone, Russell, (1980), "Auckland's Political Opposition in the Crown Colony Period 1841-53", in *Provincial Perspectives*, edited by Len Richardson and W. David McIntyre, University of Canterbury Press, Christchurch.

Stone, Russell, (1980a), "Auckland Party Politics in the Early Years of the Provincial System, 1853-58", *The New Zealand Journal of History*, V.14, N.2, October, pp.153-178.

Sutch, W.B., (1966), *The Quest for Security in New Zealand*, Oxford University Press, Wellington.

"The Telegraph Libel Case: (1871), Report of Proceedings in the Resident Magistrates Court, Dunedin, on the hearing of the charges of libel brought by the General Government of New Zealand against Mr George

*Bibliography*

Burnett Barton, in the case of Regina V Barton". Printed at the Daily Times Office, Dunedin.

Turnbull, Michael, (1959), *The New Zealand Bubble; The Wakefield Theory in Practice,* Price Milburn, Wellington.

United Press Association Manuscripts. ACC 75-213. Alexander Turnbull Library.

Wakefield, E.G., (1914), *Art of Colonization,* Clarendon Press, Oxford.

Wakefield, E.J., (1845), *Adventure in New Zealand,* John Murray, London. Undated facsimile edition published by Wilson and Horton Ltd.

Wakelin, Richard, (1877), *History and Politics: Containing the Political Recollections and Leaves from the Writings of a New Zealand Journalist, 1851-1861-1862-1877,* Lyon and Blair, George N. Dutton, Wellington. Reprinted by Hocken Library, 1973.

Walker, R.B., (1976), *The Newspaper Press in New South Wales 1803-1920,* Sydney University Press.

Ward, Louis E., (1928), *Early Wellington,* Whitcombe & Tombs Ltd., Wellington.

Weber, Max, (1947), *The Theory of Social and Economic Organization.* Free Press, New York.

**Abbreviations**

Appendices to the Journals of the House of Representatives. (A.J.H.R.)
New Zealand Parliamentary Despatches. (N.Z.P.D.)